A New History o
in Chi

THE GLOBAL CHRISTIANITY SERIES

The Global Christianity Series charts the history, development and current state of Christianity in key geographical areas around the world. In many cases, these are areas where Christianity has had a controversial past and where the future of Christianity may yet be decided. Each book in the series will look at both the history of Christianity in an important region and consider the issues and themes which are prevalent in the lives of contemporary Christians and the Church. Accessibly written by area experts, the books will appeal to students and scholars of World Christianity and others who are interested in the history, culture and religion of Christianity around the world.

Published

Christianities in Asia edited by Peter C. Phan

A New History of Christianity in China Daniel H. Bays

Forthcoming

Christianity in Africa Robert Kaggwa

A New History of Christianity in China

Daniel H. Bays

A John Wiley & Sons, Ltd., Publication

This edition first published 2012
© 2012 Daniel H. Bays

Blackwell Publishing was acquired by John Wiley & Sons in February 2007. Blackwell's publishing program has been merged with Wiley's global Scientific, Technical, and Medical business to form Wiley-Blackwell.

Registered Office
John Wiley & Sons Ltd, The Atrium, Southern Gate, Chichester, West Sussex, PO19 8SQ, United Kingdom

Editorial Offices
350 Main Street, Malden, MA 02148-5020, USA
9600 Garsington Road, Oxford, OX4 2DQ, UK
The Atrium, Southern Gate, Chichester, West Sussex, PO19 8SQ, UK

For details of our global editorial offices, for customer services, and for information about
how to apply for permission to reuse the copyright material in this book please see our website at www.wiley.com/wiley-blackwell.

The right of Daniel H. Bays to be identified as the author of this work has been asserted
in accordance with the UK Copyright, Designs and Patents Act 1988.

Library of Congress Cataloging-in-Publication Data

Bays, Daniel H.
  A new history of Christianity in China / Daniel H. Bays.
     p. cm. – (Blackwell guides to global Christianity)
  Includes bibliographical references and index.
  ISBN 978-1-4051-5954-8 (hardback) – ISBN 978-1-4051-5955-5 (paperback)
  1. China–Church history. I. Title.
  BR1285.B39 2012
  275.1'08–dc22
                                                          2011012209

A catalogue record for this book is available from the British Library.

This book is published in the following electronic formats: ePDFs 9781444342833; Wiley Online Library
9781444342864; ePub 9781444342840

Set in Sabon 10/12pt by Thomson Digital, Noida, India.

4   2015

To
Andrew Walls of Aberdeen
and
Thomas S. Y. Li of Tianjin
Both of whom I am humbly grateful to call
Teacher and Friend

Contents

Acknowledgments

In researching and writing this book, I have become a debtor to many. It all began in 1985, with the Henry Luce Foundation's support for my History of Christianity in China project, at the University of Kansas. Terry Lautz, the Asia Program Officer at the foundation, was consistent in his support of that project and in many other ways since; he has been a valued friend for 25 years.

Colleagues in the field of China missions and China Christianity studies have been faithful in assistance and encouragement: Gary Tiedemann, Chan Kim-kwong, Kathleen Lodwick, Murray Rubenstein, Bob Entenmann, Ryan Dunch, Lian Xi, Jessie Lutz, Carol Hamrin, Dick Madsen, David Mungello, Phil West, Silas Wu, among others.

Some senior China scholars not in the Christian studies field have nevertheless found time to be helpful in their support of my endeavors. Al Feuerweker and Ernie Young were wonderful mentors in my years in Ann Arbor in the 1960s, and always ready since then to write one more letter of recommendation. My thanks as well to the late John King Fairbank, the late K. C. Liu, to Paul Cohen, and to Jonathan Spence for assistance in many ways. I gained a much wider horizon of views on Christian history from my exposure to scholars of American religion: Grant Wacker, Mark Noll, Joel Carpenter, Nathan Hatch, Edith Blumhofer, among others. I am grateful to Jerry Anderson for including me in a group based during most of the 1990s at the Overseas Ministries Studies Center in New Haven. There I was exposed to stimulating new ideas and modes of analysis by Andrew Walls, Lamin Sanneh, Bob Frykenberg, and Dana Robert.

Very early in my odyssey, James Cha (Cha Shih-chieh), of National Taiwan University and China Evangelical Theological Seminary, played a key role by providing full access to his rich collection of Christian materials at the seminary during my stay in Taiwan in 1984–85. And the late Jonathan T'ien-en Chao did the same with his collection of rare historical materials at the Chinese Church Research Center, Hong Kong, all through the 1980s. Also in Hong Kong, Kim Chan has been a treasured colleague, collaborator, and friend for over twenty years; and I have enjoyed the friendship and hospitality on several occasions of Hong Kong colleagues Peter Ng, Philip Leung, Timothy Wong, and K. K. Lee.

In China my debts are legion. In the autumn of 1986 I travelled all over Shandong Province with Thomas S. Y. Li (Li Shiyu). We visited churches, also banged on hotel doors at 3 am, slept on concrete, rode farm wagons for taxis, and visited the original still-operating site of the Jesus Family, among other adventures. Thomas, at age 65, beat me to the top of Taishan, and drank most of the bai'ger. I owe him endless thanks, for friendship as well as for advancing my understanding of popular religion.

Other colleagues and friends in China are Tao Feiya and Liu Tianlu (both then of Shandong University; Tao is now at Shanghai University), Edward Xu of Fudan University, and Liu Jiafeng of Central China Normal University. Among senior scholars, Professor Lu Yao at Shandong University and President Zhang Kaiyuan of Central China Normal have always been hospitable and helpful. I also appreciate the assistance of Zhuo Xinping, Director of the Institute of World Religions of the Chinese Academy of Social Sciences (CASS), and of Zhao Fusan, formerly of CASS. All these, and others unnamed, made my research in China over the years thoroughly enjoyable in addition to being challenging intellectually.

Special thanks to Mark Noll and Joel Carpenter, who went the extra mile to read and give me feedback on the first draft of all the chapters. Thanks also to my editors at Blackwell (now Wiley-Blackwell), Andrew Humphries and Isobel Bainton, for their patience when I did not meet deadlines or otherwise misbehaved. I am grateful to Calvin College for a sabbatical in 2007 and for generous travel assistance over several years, and to the Calvin Center for Christian Scholarship for providing support at key times. My colleagues in the History Department and the Asian Studies Program at Calvin College welcomed me warmly upon my arrival here a decade ago, and they have provided a congenial environment for thinking and writing.

In some ways, ideas finding expression here began well over 30 years ago. Though I have learned much from others, the remaining defects and short-comings of this book are mine alone.

I have dedicated this volume to Andrew Walls, always gracious and polite as he drops blockbusters which challenge our assumptions about Christian history outside the West, and to Thomas S. Y. Li, who, like Andrew, has taught me much about life as well as scholarship.

Finally, very special appreciation to my wife Janny, who for all these years has shared my love for China and has kept me on task. Without her there would be no book. Thank you, Sweetheart.

Daniel H. Bays
Grand Rapids, Michigan
October 2010

Introduction

This book has been close to my heart for many years, and in some ways it has been implicit in all my academic endeavors for the past three decades. In the early 1980s, when Christianity, along with other religions, was being resurrected in China after the Cultural Revolution and was showing immense vitality, I became part of a new generation of scholars, Chinese as well as American and European, who saw in the history of Christianity in China an important understudied area. Some topics in this area had in fact been studied; these studies centered mainly on the foreign missionaries and the story of what they did in China. But the other, and arguably more important, piece of the picture was the rise of Chinese Christians in the joint Sino-foreign endeavor to establish and nurture the faith in Chinese soil. This process was characterized by a persistent, overriding dynamic: the Chinese Christians were first participants, then subordinate partners of the foreign missionaries, then finally the inheritors or sole "owners" of the Chinese church. It was also a "cross-cultural process," the result of which has been the creation of an immensely varied Chinese Christian world in our day.[1] I have attempted to track some of the main features of this cross-cultural process over several centuries. I have also focused on China proper, making little reference to Christian stirrings among China's minority peoples and in overseas Chinese communities. Both of those topics are worthy of in-depth attention by other scholars.

I have been told by many that there is a need for a volume such as this. I myself have felt compelled to write it, if only for the sake of my own understanding. My aim has been, in the writing process, to incorporate the considerable amount of research of the last 25 years into a coherent narrative. Previous accounts which are somewhat comparable to this effort include Kenneth Scott Latourette's *A History of Christian Missions in China* (London, 1929), a large and remarkably detailed reference-type work which is unfortunately 80 years old. A 1988 book by the Rev. Bob Whyte,

A New History of Christianity in China, First Edition. Daniel H. Bays.
© 2012 Daniel H. Bays. Published 2012 by Blackwell Publishing Ltd.

Unfinished Encounter: China and Christianity (London, 1988) was a very respectable general history by the project officer of the China Study Project, an ecumenical multi-year endeavor sponsored by several British Protestant and Catholic bodies, foremost among them the Conference for World Mission of the British Council of Churches. It has long been out of print, and at any rate cannot include the significant scholarship, much of it by Chinese scholars, of the past quarter century. Finally, Fr. Jean-Pierre Charbonnier has given us *Christians in China A.D. 600 to 2000* (in English, San Francisco, CA: Ignatius Press, 2007; original French edition, Paris, 2002),). With this volume Father Charbonnier, China Director of the Paris Foreign Mission society, has given us a very substantial and useful account, mainly of the Catholic efforts in China. Perhaps Charbonnier's stress on Catholics balances out the greater weight given to Protestants by the other works, including this one.

In writing I tried to strike a balance between the early modern (pre-1800, with two chapters), modern (1800–1950, with four chapters), and recent (1950–present, with two chapters) periods. The heart of the book is the middle four chapters, Chapters 3 to 6. Here the basic tension between (foreign) mission and (Chinese) church is played out over a century and a half. Another large theme which recurs is the always-present instinct of the Chinese state, or political regime, to monitor and control religious movements; as a result Christianity was usually not seen only, indeed not even primarily, as a "religion" or belief system, but as a behavioral phenomenon which could cause endless trouble.

The appendix provides a brief history of the Russian Orthodox Ecclesiastical Mission to China from the late seventeenth century until the mid twentieth century, when it ended. This mission was unique in several ways, and its story should be included somewhere. Rather than try to include it in pieces scattered among a few chapters, I have given a concise version of it which has been relegated to an appendix.

I have decided not to include a separate "conclusion" at the end of the book. Christianity in China is in a state of flux (as are many things in China), and I do not wish to extrapolate the present into the future any more than I have in the last few pages of Chapter 8 – especially when observers are so little agreed on the shape of the "present." But there are some larger themes which I hope the reader will derive from this effort. One is the notion that Christianity, when it is separated from its bonding with Western culture in a package we may call "Christendom," is perfectly capable of adapting to function in different cultural settings, often after a period of cross-cultural interaction which may be disruptive. The lesson: one can have Christ without Christendom. The other notion that I hope is manifest in this account is the remarkable flexibility and creativity in the Chinese relationship with Christianity (or perhaps with "Christianities"). Examples abound: the Daoist and Buddhist terms used by the Nestorians; the powerful Biblical visions of the Taiping leaders in the nineteenth century; devices of Chinese Catholics in renaming the ancestral ceremonies in order to finesse the Pope's proscription; and today's frequent occurrence of White Lotus-like Protestant millenarian sects in the Chinese countryside. One is tempted to observe, *"plus ça change, plus c'est la même chose"*.

Notes

1. Andrew Walls, "From Christendom to World Christianity," in *The Cross-Cultural Process in Christian History*, ed. Andrew Walls (Maryknoll, NY: Orbis, 2001), pp. 149–171.

1

The Nestorian Age and the Mongol Mission, 635–1368

Prologue

The new Beijing City Museum is a stunning showcase of daring recent Chinese architecture, built about 2004 or 2005, and is one of several monumental buildings that make central Beijing visually much more interesting than when the official style was "Stalinesque Victorian." The city museum had formerly been in a one-story wing of the "Confucius Temple," a peaceful but run-down structure on the northeast side of the city, with far too little viewing space to display its holdings. When the museum moved to its spacious new quarters on the main East–West artery, visitors could see an entire floor of artifacts, photos, exhibits, and other items all on the history of the city of Beijing, including history from the time before it was called Beijing. For of course it used to be called Kambaliq, or Dadu (Great capital) when the Mongols ruled China. Walking through the exhibits of that period of Beijing's history, it is hard to miss a cross carved on a large stone slab. This is a Nestorian cross, with the four spikes of equal length, a symbol of the Christian Church of the East, often just called Nestorian. Moreover, there is a photo of a pile of rubble and perhaps part of a stone wall, identified as (possibly) the remains of a Nestorian Christian monastery in the suburbs of Beijing. These items do not date back to the very beginnings of Christianity in China – another stone we will discuss

A New History of Christianity in China, First Edition. Daniel H. Bays.
© 2012 Daniel H. Bays. Published 2012 by Blackwell Publishing Ltd.

presently will do that. But it adds concrete visual evidence of the recurring Christian presence in pre-modern China, which began almost 15 centuries ago, if not earlier.

Just exactly when Christianity first entered China is a matter of some debate and even dispute among scholars, church representatives, and other interested parties. Much of this uncertainty has arisen only in recent years. It is due to the discovery, almost 30 years ago in the early 1980s, of some very interesting bas-relief sculptures on a rock face at Kongwangshan, near the city of Lianyungang, in what is now Jiangsu Province. Lianyungang was an important port city in earlier times, first port of entry into China for many who came by sea. These bas-reliefs depict three persons. The undeniable existence of these sculptures, and probable dating of them to the reign of the Mingdi emperor (r. 57–75 CE) of the Later Han Dyasty (25–220 CE), have led to the conclusion that these are from the period of the very early entrance of Buddhism into China, and depicted Buddhist figures. This conclusion would not have been seriously questioned, until recently. Within the past five to ten years, however, some have begun to think that these carved figures might not be Buddhist, rather that the evidence pointed to their being Christian; the human figures on the rock face were the Apostle Thomas and Mary the mother of Jesus, with a variety of candidates for the third figure.

This idea of Thomas in China is not new. His alleged visit to China has never been questioned by the Mar Thoma church in India, which has always claimed direct descent from the claimed church-planting of the Apostle there in the early 60s CE. Their books and church traditions clearly have Thomas in the 60s CE coming to India, then to China, and back to India, where he died. Two breviaries (concise liturgy books) of the Church in later centuries, one from Malabar, south India, and one in Syriac from the Church of the East, also seem possibly to refer to Thomas and China. Nevertheless, few people believed the Thomas-in-China theory; there simply was not enough concrete evidence to take it very seriously. In the late sixteenth and early seventeenth century, the early Portuguese explorers, chroniclers, and historians who came to India related the stories of the Indian church on the southeast coast concerning St. Thomas and China. Some favored accepting the claim, others were highly skeptical. Matteo Ricci, the first great Jesuit China missionary (in China 1583–1610), encountered there some ambiguous references to (possibly) Thomas. But no one had any concrete evidence.[1] Then in 2008, two Frenchmen wrote a book strongly advocating the Thomas-in-China thesis. They based their argument on the Kongwangshan bas-reliefs and other evidence that they adduced, and concluded that Thomas went from India to China by sea, because of an outbreak of unrest on the Old Silk Road through central Asia. They also claim that rather than Buddhism setting the bar for other religions, Christianity may have influenced Buddhism, which was just in its formative stages in China at this time. Now there is some controversy over these issues, because of their linkage to those of national self-image and questions such as which of the world religions got to a given place first.[2] For example, Professor Perrier found a group of scholars of religion at Nanjing University, the school with some expertise in this period, quite resistant to his suggestions about the content of the bas-reliefs.[3] I, for one, cannot see where this argument will end, or if it will end. The key evidence seems not at all clear-cut, so a more cautious stance would seem in order until more mainstream scholars become involved.

Regardless of the above controversy, when we turn to later times it is accurate to say that from the seventh century to the sixteenth century there were two false starts for the implantation of Christianity in China before the Christian presence became permanent. I will deal with both of them in the remainder of this introductory chapter. As we will see, from the verifiable beginning of the transmission of the Christian religion in the seventh century, the form in which it entered China was both replicated and transformed in varying degrees. We will probably never know just how close the Roman empire and the Later Han Dynasty in China (25–220 CE) came to linking up and establishing direct contact at the end of the first century. The peace which facilitated communications between the two great empires made possible commercial exchange along the Old Silk Road, which crossed central Asia and today's Turkestan. But the trade remained in the hands of Middle Eastern or central Asian middlemen. Rome ruled all to the west of the Caspian Sea, and Han envoys made it as far as the east side of the Caspian. Conceivably Christianity could have entered China during these years, but there is no real evidence that it did so. Ironically, the same period of relative order along the Silk Road which enabled Rome and China to have a near-miss in contact did make possible the first significant foreign missionary movement successfully to arrive in China that of Buddhism, brought from India. Who can say what might have resulted if Christianity had been successful in establishing itself in China at the same time as Buddhism? There would have been two foreign religions competing for attention and converts. Of course that did not occur, and from the early third century China was in chaos and the Silk Road practically nonfunctional. To the west of China, as Rome's empire dwindled over the next few centuries and competition grew between the Roman church and the Eastern church, first arose the Syrian Church of the East, and then the Persian empire in the Sassanid period (225–651) developed as the geographical base for Eastern Christianity. The Eastern Christians, who after the fifth century were called by some Nestorians or Nestorian Christians, succeeded in establishing a secure minority position vis-à-vis the Zoroastrians and Manicheans, their main competitors in the Persian religious marketplace.[4] Despite the waning of the power of the Sassanid state, and strong competition from other branches of Eastern Christianity, the Persian Nestorians continued vigorous in their identity, especially in their missionary outreach to regions beyond the Persian empire. In the sixth and seventh centuries, a dynamic missionary movement emanated from the Patriarch of the church in Persia through the metropolitans and bishops of the ecclesiastical structure. The result was tens, perhaps hundreds of thousands, of converts among the diverse peoples of central Asia. India also became a metropolitanate for the first time; and finally in 635 the first carriers of the Christian gospel, a band of Persian Nestorian Christians, arrived in China.

Nestorian Christians in Tang China

In either 1623 or 1625, either in today's Xi'an or in an area about 75 km to the west of Xi'an, a nine-foot high marble stele (a commemorative slab, tablet) was dug up which told a remarkable story.[5] In the more than 1800 Chinese characters and in the smaller number of Syriac letters carved on it, allegedly a Christian monk named Jingjing, claiming to be writing in the year 781, gives a detailed history of Nestorian Christianity from its beginnings in China in 635. He also (in Syriac) records the names of the bishops and priests of the Da Qin (vaguely countries of the west, probably meaning Persia or Syria, or even the Roman empire) monasteries around the empire. The title at the top of the stele translates as "A Monument Commemorating the Propagation of the Da-Qin (Syrian) Luminous Religion in China." A slightly freer translation might be "The Story of the Coming of the Religion of Light from the West to China." At the very top is a Christian cross rising from a (Buddhist) lotus blossom.[6] It is hard to overstress the impact this discovery had on Christian history in China, after it was generally accepted as authentic. In the 1620s, the Jesuit missionaries in China, who had been there only 40 years, were often confounded by the claim that Christianity was entirely foreign and too new to have any appeal in China. As far as anyone knew, Roman Christian envoys were the first; they had come to Mongolia and then China in the thirteenth century, and were gone already just over a century later. But here in this massive stone tablet seemed to be proof positive that Christianity had been firmly established early in the Tang, more than six hundred years before the first European emissaries came in the thirteenth century. Moreover it survived for well over two hundred years. It was a member of the Chinese social and political elite, a Christian convert, who heard about the stele and alerted the Jesuits to its discovery. But this leads us to events to be covered in the next chapter, so we will leave the stele and return to the story it helps to clarify concerning the beginnings in early Tang.

The Tang dynasty (618–907) was young and vigorous in 635. Its second emperor, Taizong, presided over a capital city (Chang'an, today's Xi'an) larger, richer, and more magnificent than any in the world. The Tang armies,

Figure 1.1   The Nestorian stele. Credit: dk/Alamy.

this early in the dynasty, were stronger than those of any neighbors, and Tang jurisdiction stretched farther west than that of any previous Chinese authority. With relative peace re-established in the area between China and Persia, a booming international trade revived on the Old Silk Road, of which the terminus was Chang'an. Some of the Middle Eastern and central Asian merchants who participated in the trade surely were Christian, but they were not missionaries. Yet Taizong may have learned a bit about their following a different religion and was curious; in addition to Buddhism being a fairly recent import, there were among the many foreigners in cosmopolitan Chang'an Zoroastrians from Persia, Manicheans, inner Asian tribal groups with their own practices and rituals, and Jews. And Guangzhou, already by this time an important south China coastal entrepôt, had a large number of Arabs, of diverse religious identities, engaged in maritime trade. So when a delegation of Nestorians, led by their bishop, Alopen (or Aluoben), dressed in white robes and carrying their scriptures and icons of Christ, Mary, and the saints, arrived in dignified procession at the city gate after months on the Silk Road, they were formally greeted and escorted in dignified procession to the emperor. At least this is the story told on the stele. The court certainly knew they were coming, and must have known something about them, because (again, according to the inscription on the stele) Taizong ordered the Christian scriptures which the Nestorians had brought with them to be translated. It is implied that Alopen himself was heavily engaged in this work. After familiarizing himself with the basic doctrines, three years later, in 638, the emperor issued an edict of approbation for the Christians:

> The way does not have a common name and the sacred does not have a common form. Aluoben, the man of great virtue from the Da Qin empire, came from a far land...his message is mysterious and wonderful beyond our understanding. The message is lucid and clear; the teachings will benefit all; and they shall be practiced throughout the land.[7]

In the same year, 638, the group of Nestorians around Alopen built the first Christian church in China, in Chang'an. There were 21 Nestorian monks in China, probably all Persian. For the period down to its creation in 781, the stele itself is the primary source of what is known about Tang Nestorian Christianity. It records a pattern of expansion and growth, with perhaps two or three dozen monasteries being established during that century and a half. There was also some persecution, especially during the late seventh century when Empress Wu reigned (685–704) and favored the Buddhists. For centuries there was very little known of events after the 781 stele. And the theology of the Nestorians is not described in detail on the stele. But early in the twentieth century, at Dunhuang (in the far West, on the northern route of the Silk Road in today's Xinjiang), thousands of manuscripts were discovered stored in sealed grottoes in approximately the year 1005. They had been preserved by the dry climate. Among them were several early Nestorian documents, including scriptures translated very early, some perhaps by Alopen himself.[8] From these documents we can see the remarkable combination of Christian ideas and concepts mixed with Daoist and Buddhist terms that constituted Nestorianism in China. One scripture found at Dunhuang, "The Treatise of Veneration," even includes a Manichean scripture.[9] Other titles of these scriptures and liturgies include: "The Book of Jesus-Messiah," "Sutra of the Teachings of the World-Honored One," "Discourse on

Monotheism," "Da-Qin Luminous Religion Hymn in Adoration of the Holy Trinity," and several others.[10] The first two of these are thought by several scholars to have been, as the documents themselves claimed, translated into Chinese between 635 and 641. If so, then Alopen himself may well have been the translator. According to scholars who have analyzed them, they show a clearly discernible Christian core, not any significant deterioration of the essential dogmas of Christianity, although there is little emphasis on the crucifixion of Jesus, and considerable admixture of Daoist and Buddhist terms and images.[11] Yet the whole question of the extent to which Christianity and Daoism (more so than Buddhism) might have been compatible with each other still awaits systematic treatment by scholars conversant with both traditions.[12] In other words, we still do not have a good grasp of the "religious content" of Nestorian Christianity in China.

We do know, in broad outline, the fate of Tang Christianity. After a massive internal rebellion which nearly toppled the state in the 750s, the cosmopolitanism of the early Tang ebbed, and nativist elements revived. The court was weaker (its writ not extending as far), poorer (unable to subsidize religions as it had before), and more vulnerable to the cultural conservatives, many of them ardent Confucianists, who in the ninth century created a rising chorus of anti-foreignism and demands for a crackdown on "foreign religions." This culminated in 845, with a decree from the throne which was aimed mainly at cutting back the wealth of Buddhist monasteries and restricting use of them as tax shelters, laicizing many of the clergy, and drastically tightening overall control of Buddhism. Monks were now required to register with the state, and the state itself took on the authority to ordain new clergy (in this regard, obviously one is reminded of the imperatives of the present Chinese state in maintaining a system of official registration of church buildings and clergy). Near the end of the edict, almost as an afterthought, the emperor added, "We have ordered more than 2,000 men of the Nestorian and Mazdean religions to return to lay life and to cease polluting the customs of China."[13]

This was a severe enough blow to Buddhism to check its growth for some time, although it made a comeback fairly quickly. It seems to have been a truly disastrous event for the Christians, and as a matter of fact for all other foreign religions as well, except Islam. We do not know the health of the overall Christian church in China as of 845, although it must have had several monasteries in order to have so many monks laicized. But apparently it was moribund by the end of the dynasty in 907. Snippets of sources, a handful of scattered references, in the tenth century indicate that no Christians were left in China.

There is not full agreement on the most important cause of the decline and disappearance of Tang Christianity. Some theologically oriented scholars stress the alleged amalgamation, even syncretism, between Christian dogma and Daoism or even Buddhism, and blame this for Christianity's loss of doctrinal integrity and its fading from the scene. Some stress the change in context, that is, the loss of the openness of Chinese society and the imperial court which had characterized the cosmopolitan seventh century. Others point out a related factor: there is very little evidence anywhere in the sparse documentation on the Nestorians that ethnic Chinese became converts or monks. In fact the evidence, such as it is, indicates that virtually all of the clergy and converts were foreign, both Persian and several other identities. Only a handful of Christians could have conceivably been Han Chinese. Thus we are probably justified in judging Nestorian Christianity in Tang China to have been a marginal religion, not central to the processes of Chinese history and society. Yet what is most noteworthy and portentous for the future, perhaps, despite the relative paucity of documentation, is the alacrity with which the Christian faith took on distinct Chinese characteristics, as seen in the cross-fertilization of Daoism and Christianity in some of the early scriptures and liturgical pieces which have survived. This feature of Christianity in China, the process of cross-cultural movement and the simultaneous replication and transformation of the faith in a new cultural setting, is one to which we will frequently return.

Christians and Mongols (Thirteenth to Fourteenth Centuries)

Just as the "pax Romana" during the first two centuries imposed sufficient security on the Mediterranean basin for the apostles to make missionary journeys far and wide, the "pax mongolica" imposed by the Mongols made possible the first direct European Christian contacts with China. But when the European friars who were the first emissaries of the Western church arrived among the Mongols a few decades before the 1271 Mongol conquest of all of China, they discovered many Nestorian Christians among them, including among the Mongol elite and their tribal allies. This is a chapter of China's Christian history that is often overlooked or given short shrift. We will try concisely to do it justice here.[14]

Nestorian Christianity remained prevalent in its core area of Persia, and many Persian Christian merchants plied the trade routes of central Asia, where they had considerable contact with a Turko-Mongolian tribe called the Keraits. In the early twelfth century the Keraits, who numbered about 200,000, began to convert to Nestorian Christianity, and by the thirteenth century were virtually entirely Christian. Other tribes, such as the Ongut, the Naiman, the Merkit, and others, converted in smaller numbers. In the late 1100s the Christian Kerait were an early ally of the Mongol subclan which produced Genghis (or Chinggis) Khan (1162–1227) as its leader. When Genghis Khan began to amalgamate the Mongol tribes into the greatest fighting machine the world had ever seen, he took many of his leaders and officials from the Kerait. Despite a falling-out with the Kerait chief, which cost the latter his life, Genghis took three daughters of the Kerait royal family as wives – one each for himself, his oldest son Jochi, and his fourth son Tolui. This wife of the fourth son, Sorkaktani-beki (or Sorghaghtani), a Kerait Christian princess, became the mother of three emperors: a Great Khan of the Mongols, an emperor (ilkhan) of Persia, and the founding emperor of the Yuan dynasty in China, Khubilai (1216–1294).

At the halfway point of the thirteenth century, as Pope Innocent IV (1243–1254) and other strategists of Western Christendom surveyed the world which confronted them, they were concerned about both the Moslem occupation of the Holy Land and the memory of Europe's recent (1230s) providential escape from being ravaged by the fearsome Mongol war juggernaut. Thus for strategic reasons of realpolitik the Vatican wished to make contact with the Mongol rulers in order to avoid future hostilities and to explore forming an alliance which could oust the Islamic defilers of Jerusalem and the Holy land. There was also an authentic religious motivation at work. In recent decades two new missionary-minded orders had been founded, the Dominicans and the Franciscans, Why not send missionaries from among these enthusiastic priests to try to convert the Mongols to Christianity in addition to the politico-strategic purpose?

Accordingly, between 1245 and 1253 Innocent IV commissioned two different Franciscan-led diplomatic-religious missions to the Mongols.[15] Both friars made it to Qaraqorum (Karakorum), the Mongol capital before it was moved to China proper. And both returned to Europe after two years, each writing a description of what he had seen and experienced, even though the hope of achieving an alliance with the Mongols had evaporated and there was no success in converting them to Christianity. The friars also alerted the European world to the success and prominence of the Nestorian communities among the members of the Mongol coalition. There were no more Christian emissaries sent by Rome until the 1290s, by which time the forces of Khubilai Khan had defeated the last Song Dynasty resistance, destroyed the old regime, and in 1271 set up a new dynasty, the Yuan, ruling all of China. Several years before that, Khubilai had already moved the Yuan capital from Qaraqorum to Khanbaliq (also called Dadu), the site of today's Beijing. Thus until 1293 the Nestorians, still largely non-Chinese, maintained a monopoly on the institutional Christian religious presence in China. Indeed, there is scattered documentary and archaeological evidence (tombstones, tablets with inscriptions and images) that there were small groups of Han Chinese converts among the Nestorians, although the preponderance of the members of these Christian communities remained non-Chinese.

It is just at this juncture of the Christian story in China that we should acknowledge the story of the Polo brothers and Marco Polo's famous

Description of the World (published circa 1298). They are representative of the presence of several Italian traders, Roman Christians, in Yuan China. The Venetian brothers Niccolo and Maffeo Polo left Venice about 1252, and they managed to make it to Khanbaliq in 1265, where they had at least one audience with Khubilai. After a return to Europe, they set out on their second voyage in 1271, accompanied by Niccolo's son Marco (1254–1324/5). They reached Khubilai's summer capital Shangdu in 1275, and then remained in China for the next 16 years, apparently in the employ of Khubilai and the dynastic government. Only in 1291 were they given permission to leave China, accompanying a mission to the Khanate in Persia. They left the rest of their traveling companions at Hormuz, and were back in Venice in 1295. Marco's *Description of the World* has unique and valuable information on the distribution of Nestorian Christians in Yuan China.

There were other Italian merchants, who were residents in several cities, and who were sometimes helpful to the Roman Catholic missions which existed in a handful of places in Yuan China. The first papal envoy since the 1250s, Friar Giovanni da Montecorvino, was accompanied by an Italian merchant from Venice, Pietro de Lucalongo, arriving at Quanzhou on the southeast coast and coming to Khanbaliq in 1293 via the Grand Canal. De Lucalongo also a few years later bought for Friar Giovanni a piece of land in the capital on which to build a church. Italians in other cities assisted the small number of Catholic missionaries in various ways.

Del Carpini and van Rubroek had observed the established Nestorian presence in the Mongol capital of Qaraqorum in the 1240s and 1250s, but did not stay long enough to get into competition with the Nestorian hierarchy. Giovanni da Montecorvino, however, had considerable success, so much so that it prompted the Roman Church to send several more missionaries, a few Dominicans as well as Franciscans, to China. The result was direct competition between Catholics and Nestorian Christians. Montecorvino claimed as many as six thousand baptisms by about 1305. One group was from the Nestorian Ongut tribe, whose chief (whom the missionaries called Prince George) converted with many of his fellow tribesmen. Several thousand Armenian Christians and Byzantine Alans in the capital city also came into the Catholic fold, partly because they had no clergy of their own nearby and they were not permitted in the Nestorian churches without converting. As far as we can tell, Montecorvino, who was consecrated archbishop of Khanbaliq in 1313 by newly arrived priests bringing instructions from the Holy See, was a dedicated and enthusiastic representative of the Franciscans, and preached and evangelized with perseverance, so much so that he sparked active and voluble opposition, even threats, from the Nestorians.[16] Tension and conflict between Catholics and Nestorians were frequent in these circumstances.

From the 1320s until the end of the dynasty in 1368, both varieties of Christianity persevered, but without signal success. In addition to two churches in the capital, a few Catholic missionaries and as many as three churches were present in the port city of Quanzhou. Fujian Province, and Hangzhou and Yangzhou, for a time had Franciscan residences. After Montecorvino's death in 1330, instability in the empire, and uncertainties of transport in sending more missionaries, slowed the Catholic efforts, and by the 1350s virtually all of the European Catholic priests were gone.

What of an overall verdict on Christianity in Mongol times? We know more about its presence and nature than we do about Christianity in the last part of the Tang, but that is still not a great deal. We do know that Nestorianism was sufficiently successful along the Silk Road that the Patriarchy in Baghdad established several metropolitan provinces on the way to China, two of them, including Khanbaliq, in China proper. Almost nothing concerning Christianity appears in Chinese sources of the Yuan. There is not even a specific Chinese language term for Christianity, Nestorian or Catholic. There is also very little evidence of interaction between either Catholics or Nestorians with Buddhism and Daoism. Over the time of the century from the 1240s to the 1340s, there were only a handful of clues: a Buddhist-Christian "debate" in which Willem van Rubroek participated in May 1254; conflict in 1304 between Nestorians in Jiangnan (lower Yangzi R. delta) and the local Daoist clergy whom the Christians were evangelizing; and the restoration of two Nestorian monasteries to the Buddhists in 1311. It seems that there was more trouble between Montecorvino and the Nestorians in Khanbaliq over his alleged stealing of Nestorian sheep than occurred between either version of Christianity and native Chinese religions. One inference that may be drawn from this is that none of the Chinese religious traditions saw Christianity as a religious or ideological threat.

Thus we must conclude that, much as in the case of the Tang Nestorians, in the Mongol period, despite the Roman church joining the Church of the East in missionary work in China, the elements of Christianity present seem to have been so closely tied to the foreign presence that there was almost no influence on indigenous persons and institutions. Even though the Franciscans, for example Montecorvino, preached to the Chinese and wanted to convert them, there is no evidence that any responded in verifiable numbers, at least not in sources that are at present available.

What became of Christianity in China from the mid fourteenth century? Ming dynasty sources have no reference whatsoever to Yuan Christians' fate. The demise of the Yuan dynasty in 1368 did not necessarily have to entail an end to the faith in China, but it created severe restrictions on missionaries. Their primary source of protection and funding was the Mongol ruling clan and the foreign merchants, most of whom retreated north with the Mongols; or, if they stayed, they were expelled by the somewhat xenophobic politics of the new Ming. Still, the establishment of a new dynasty alone, however xenophobic, cannot account fully for the decline of the missions which now occurred, in the East in general as well as in China. By the mid fourteenth century the Franciscans had become crippled by internal contention and strife, and they were hit very hard by the Black Death in 1348. Moreover, the original strategic goal of the Papacy for the China Mission, to bring Mongol firepower into a joint campaign against the Saracens in the Holy Land, dissipated as the great Khanates of the Middle East, central Asia, and South Asia as well as the Yuan dynasty, collapsed into the annals of history.

Notes

1. I am indebted to Professor Liam Brockey for information on the early Portuguese chroniclers of the church in India.
2. The recent French work is Pierre Perrier and Xavier Walter, *Thomas Fonde L'Eglise en Chine (65–68 Ap. J-C)* (Paris: Editions du Jubilé, 2008).
3. Pierre Perrier and Xavier Walter, *Thomas Fonde L'Eglise en Chine (65–68 Ap. J-C)* (Paris: Editions du Jubilé, 2008). Conservative Catholic groups, for example, very much like this Thomas-in-China angle because it serves to elevate Christianity against other religions and tends to be triumphalist in general.
4. These events are well chronicled in Samuel Hugh Moffett, *A History of Christianity in Asia, Vol. I: Beginnings to 1500* (Maryknoll, NY: Orbis, 1998), Chs. 4–12. Moffett believes that the severe condemnation of Nestorius and his followers as heretics at Ephesus in 431, during the third of the great ecumenical church councils of the early church, was unwarranted. Another very competent general account is Jean-Pierre Charbonnier, *Christians in China A.D. 600 to 2000*, trans. M.N.L. Couve de Murville (San Francisco, CA: Ignatius Press, 2007; original French edition, Paris, 2002), pp. 21–67.
5. A thorough discussion of the uncertainties of date and place is in Nicolas Standaert, ed., *Handbook of Christianity in China, Vol. 1: 635–1800* (Leiden: Brill, 2001), pp. 12–15. There is no favorite between the dates, but most scholars think the site was Xi'an. Since 1907 the stele has been in the Beilin Museum in Xi'an, where it has a prominent place. Visitors can purchase rubbings of either the title phrase at the top, on a smaller piece of marble, or one of the entire thing, which stands about eight feet tall.
6. The stele is variously referred to as the Nestorian monument or the Nestorian tablet. "Luminous religion" or "the religion of light" are translations of jingjiao.
7. From Martin Palmer, *The Jesus Sutras: Rediscovering the Lost Scrolls of Taoist Christianity* (New York: Ballantine, 2001), p. 43. The text of the edict is from the Nestorian stele itself, not official Tang records.
8. These are described in Nicolas Standaert, ed., *Handbook of Christianity in China, Vol. 1: 635–1800* (Leiden: Brill, 2001), pp. 4–7.
9. The Manichean inclusion is noted in David Bundy, "Missiological Reflections on Nestorian Christianity in China in the Tang Dynasty," in Frank K. Flinn and Tyler Hendricks, *Religion in the Pacific Era* (New York: Paragon House Publishers, n.p.).

10. Translations of these titles vary extremely widely. Palmer, *The Jesus Sutras* translates the second in the above list as "Sutra of the Teachings of the World-Honored One," where Jean-Pierre Charbonnier translates it as "Discourse of the Master of the World on Almsgiving." Jean-Pierre Charbonnier, *Christians in China A.D. 600 to 2000* (San Francisco, CA: Ignatius Press, 2007), pp. 47–50.

11. Recent treatments of the content of Tang Christianity are Samuel Hugh Moffett, *A History of Christianity in Asia, Vol. I: Beginnings to 1500* (Maryknoll, NY: Orbis, 1998), pp. 302–314, Nicolas Standaert, ed., *Handbook of Christianity in China, Vol. 1: 635–1800* (Leiden: Brill, 2001), pp. 33–38, Jean-Pierre Charbonnier, *Christians in China A.D. 600 to 2000* (San Francisco, CA: Ignatius Press, 2007), Chs. 2–3, and Martin Palmer, *The Jesus Sutras: Rediscovering the Lost Scrolls of Taoist Christianity* (New York: Ballantine, 2001), *passim*.

12. Two essays which move in this direction are Livia Kohn, "Embodiment and Transcendence in Medieval Taoism," and John H. Wong, O.S.B.Cam., "Tao-Logo-Jesus, Lao Tzu, Philo, and John Compared," in Roman Malek, SVD, ed., *The Chinese Face of Jesus Christ*, Vol. 1, Monumenta Serica Monograph Series, no. 50 (Sankt Augustin, Ger.2002).

13. For the full text of the imperial edict see Wm. Theodore de Bary and Irene Bloom, comp., *Sources of Chinese Tradition, Vol. I: From Earliest Times to 1600* (New York: Columbia University Press), pp. 585–586.

14. Unless otherwise noted, the narrative in this section is based mainly on Samuel Hugh Moffett, *A History of Christianity in Asia, Vol. I: Beginnings to 1500* (Maryknoll, NY: Orbis, 1998), pp. 399–420, 442–475, and Nicolas Standaert, ed., *Handbook of Christianity in China, Vol. 1: 635–1800* (Leiden: Brill, 2001) pp. 43–112, *passim*. Despite being outdated, a still very useful broad but detailed account of Christianity in China is Kenneth Scott Latourette, *A History of Christian Missions in China* (London: SPCK, 1929). Pages 61–77 are on the Mongol period.

15. Giovanni dal Piano del Carpini, and Willem van Rubroek.

16. Montecorvino was the last archbishop consecrated in China until modern times.

2

The Jesuit Mission of Early Modern Times and Its Fate

Prologue

The second ring road in today's Beijing is where the old city wall was, until the mid 1950s when Mao Zedong had the wall demolished. Just west of the former wall, only a short walk along Chegong E. Road, is a large compound which contains the Chinese Communist Party's Administrative College. Here officials on the fast career track receive training for high positions in the Party. In the middle of the courtyard is a walled-in graveyard, which many visitors are surprised to learn has the remains of over 60 Catholic missionaries of the Ming and Qing periods. The most prominent is the grave of Matteo Ricci, given pride of place in the arrangement of the tombstones. It was not always thus. Ricci (1552–1610), an Italian Jesuit who was the first Westerner to reside permanently in Beijing, after his death was honored by the Ming emperor with a gravesite outside Fuchengmen (the Fucheng gate). Ricci was joined by other Jesuits and missionaries of other Catholic orders over the next two or three centuries, including Adam Schall von Bell (1592–1666) and Ferdinand Verbiest (1623–1688), among other luminaries. In the violence of the Boxer Uprising in 1900 xenophobic mobs toppled the tombstones and desecrated the grounds. Then during the violent Red Guard phase of the Cultural Revolution in late 1966, youthful iconoclasts spurred to action by Mao's call to "destroy the 'four olds,'" inflicted another round of mindless

A New History of Christianity in China, First Edition. Daniel H. Bays.
© 2012 Daniel H. Bays. Published 2012 by Blackwell Publishing Ltd.

Figure 2.1   Graves of Ricci, Schall von Bell, and Verbiest. Credit: Lou-Foto/Alamy.

violence upon the site. In the "reform and opening" period since 1979, at first the cadres running the party school would occasionally arbitrarily permit well-known or well-connected visitors, including foreigners, to view the site, which was still in a disordered state. But then they realized their courtyard could be a source of income, even a cash cow. With the assistance of some foreign organizations and governments, many of them Italian, extensive repairs and restoration were done. And of course admission began to be charged. Today visitors and groups are systematically shown a 40-minute English DVD (also for sale) called simply "Matteo Ricci in China," which praises Ricci for his commitment to "East-West cross-cultural exchange" without ever mentioning Christianity. Then the visitors are given a tour of the site and encouraged to take pictures. A foreign visitor who actually knows something about the historical events and personages represented in this fashion today can only shake her head and think, "the irony of it all."

Background and Context

The third advent of Christianity in China, in which Christianity in China became a permanent part of the Chinese religious landscape, took place in the sixteenth century. It constituted a key transition in the worldwide serial movement of the Christian faith to parts of the non-West. It also was an important part of the first cross-cultural learning experience of the West.[1] All this occurred as an extension to East Asia of historical forces sweeping Europe, most importantly the repercussions of the Protestant Reformation and the creation of the Portuguese and Spanish seaborne empires. These two factors combined to facilitate an unprecedented number of Christian missionaries coming to China in the late Ming and early Qing, and even more importantly the creation within China circa 1600–1900 of a surprising number of Christian communities, many of which proved quite resilient when the young Chinese church was outlawed and persecuted in the eighteenth century. This is the first period in which Chinese Christians start to become part of the historical record, visible in both Western and Chinese sources from about 1600 onward.[2]

The Protestant reformers of the early sixteenth century were a mortal threat to the Roman church, which responded to the challenge by mobilizing its most capable representatives and itself engaging in substantial institutional and ideological reform. This was the "Catholic Reformation," which had many elements and purposes, one of which was to infuse the hierarchy and personnel of the Roman church with renewed piety and a rekindled missionary spirit. Ignatius of Loyola (1491–1556), fired by a dramatic conversion experience, gathered a few like-minded colleagues and in the 1530s organized a confraternity of individuals which in 1540 was regularized by the Pope as a new religious order, the Society of Jesus, or Jesuits. Jerusalem, not East Asia, was the first goal of the Jesuit founders. When going there proved impossible, the rest of the known world came into strategic missionary focus, and Jesuits, who under the charismatic inspiration of Ignatius multiplied dramatically in number, began setting off for destinations worldwide. Francis Xavier (1506–1552), who had been with Ignatius one of the founders of the Jesuit order, was assigned to the East Indies mission and went to Goa in India for a time. He then pioneered the mission to Japan in 1549, and finally died of sickness on an island off the southern coast of China in 1552, frustrated by the Chinese refusal to permit entry and long-term residence of missionaries. It took more than thirty years after his death for the first European Catholics to gain secure entry to China.

The other European development which shaped Christianity in China was the rise of the first of a succession of seaborne empires beginning in the early 1500s. The Portuguese led the way. It is important to remember that neither the Pope nor the Jesuits had ships of their own. But Portuguese merchant shipowners and ship captains, although occasionally behaving like pirates, were willing to do what would today be called pro bono work for the church by transporting Jesuit missionaries around the world – preferably fellow Portuguese Jesuits, but also Italians and those of other nationalities. By the 1550s–1560s a network of Portuguese settlements had been implanted on the seacoast from the Indian Ocean to Japan: in 1510–1511 came Goa in

India and Malacca in Southeast Asia on the Straits of Malacca. Then in 1557 Macau (Macao) in south China was granted to the Portuguese by local officials as a place to reside year round because Westerners were not permitted to reside permanently in China, only to go to Guangzhou (Canton) for the trading season.[3] About the same time as Macau, Nagasaki in far western Japan became the foreign trade center in Japan. The basic trade pattern, set by the predictable monsoon winds, involved ships coming from Portugal around the Cape of Good Hope, making rest stops in Goa and Malacca, before coming to Macau. In Macau they took on items that would sell well in Japan (varieties of tea, fine porcelain, some foodstuffs), then went on to Nagasaki to sell those goods and amass a boatful of Japanese products and a substantial amount of silver. The silver was mined in Japan, where it was plentiful, and in the 1500s it was needed in China to provide liquidity for the expanding economy. Back in Macau (trading was actually done in Guangzhou), the silver would finance purchase of the popular items from China (silk, porcelain) which would bring multifold profits in Lisbon or other European cities.

From the 1540s on, part of the eastbound cargo on Portuguese ships going from Europe to Asia was an increasing number of Catholic missionaries. These were nearly all Jesuits, and most were Portuguese in nationality. The reason for this was the *Padroado*, the agreement between the governments of Spain and Portugal, brokered by the Vatican, which divided most of the non-European world between the spheres of influence of the two respective powers.[4] This division was first applied to the Atlantic in the Treaty of Tordesillas in 1494, and then to the Pacific, including China and the rest of Asia, in the Treaty of Saragossa in 1529. Thus most of the Americas and the Philippines were in the Spanish sphere, and most of Africa and Asia in the Portuguese. A corollary of these events, and a fact of the world scene, was that in the sixteenth century, Lisbon and Madrid were essentially the energizing core of the world missionary movement. Their ships not only dominated the trading routes, but the (at least simulated) piety of the rulers and the ship owners and captains as well meant that when needed, transportation for missionaries to get to their assigned mission field would be available. Another factor was at work in the close three-way cooperation of merchants, representatives of the crown, and missionaries. It was assumed by all that European Christianity (there was hardly any other kind at this historical juncture) would be a big part of the template for cultural change among the new peoples being "discovered" as Europeans sailed around the world. All agreed on the unitary nature of Christianity and European culture. This was "Christendom," which had a territorial or tribal aspect; unanimity was expected of all who were part of the tribal unit – just as the tribes of northern Europe had Christianized by territorial unit.[5]

What were the results on the ground of the early Jesuit mission? In the last decades of the sixteenth century, it appeared to all observers that Christianity was a booming success in Japan, which had opened to missionaries in 1549, and a non-starter in China, where missionaries were unable to settle permanently until 1583 – and even then in only very small numbers until well after 1600. Success in conversion and social and political influence seemed to be showered on the Japan mission; in 1571 the regional feudal lord even put the port city of Nagasaki in western Japan under the jurisdiction and administration of the Jesuits. And there were well over 100,000 converts by the 1590s.[6] Meanwhile China seemed like a stone wall; from 1552 to 1583, over 50 missionaries, mostly Jesuits but also including a number of Franciscans from Spanish territory in the Philippines (despite the *Padroado*'s allocation of China to Portugal), made a total of about 60 failed attempts to settle in China.[7]

The breakthrough did not come until 1582–1583, when the Italian Michele Ruggieri (1543–1607) won permission from Guangdong provincial officials to reside in a city other than the provincial capital, Guangzhou, and learn the Chinese language. He was joined by a fellow Italian, Matteo Ricci (1552–1610), who at age 30 had spent several years at Goa and Malacca. It is useful to note that Ricci was not the first Jesuit to establish himself in China, nor the first to study the language seriously. That distinction goes to Ruggieri. But Ricci was specially picked to join Ruggieri in pursuit of competence in the language. And in many ways Ricci is the most interesting and impressive of the early China missionaries. He is also, out of all the thousands of individual missionaries who ever went to China, the one person whom many educated Chinese today are able to name.

Ricci, the Jesuits, and the Larger China Mission

Ricci is certainly not without his biographers, but most of what has been written on him is hagiographic or at least highly admiring.[8] He is an extremely attractive historical figure, who in many ways exemplifies the best of the Jesuit approach to missions and attitude toward Chinese culture. But he was only one of hundreds of Jesuits in China in the approximately two hundred years from the 1580s to the 1780s. All were well educated and many made noteworthy contributions, both spiritual and secular. Ricci did, however, put into very effective operation the policies first articulated by Alessandro Valignano (1539–1606), Jesuit high-ranking "Visitor" with authority over all of the Asia missions.[9] Very concisely, these policies were:

- Accommodation and adaptation to Chinese culture.
- Evangelization from the top down, addressing the literate elite, even the emperor if possible.

- Indirect evangelism by means of science and technology to convince the elite of the high level of European civilization.
- Openness to and tolerance of Chinese moral values and some ritual practices.[10]

It was also Ricci who early on set his sights on Beijing and the imperial court and determined to gain permission himself to live there on a permanent basis. This he finally did in 1602, the first missionary to do so since the Mongols left China. Perhaps best exemplified by Ricci, these strategies overwhelmingly characterized the Jesuit mission for the first few decades, when almost all of the Jesuits (and there were no non-Jesuits until the 1620s) had an urban mission, excellent language abilities, and followed the above principles. It is this group, from Ricci to Schall to Verbiest and on to seventeenth-century figures, mainly in Beijing, that has been the focus of most scholarship on the Catholic mission. On the other hand there were only from 5 to 15 missionaries in China at any one time in those near-fifty years, so it is not surprising that they mostly remained in major cities. Moreover, there is no doubt that chances of meeting and befriending the highest level officials were best in major cities, especially in Beijing. Success in converting the "three pillars" of the church – Xu Guangqi (1562–1633), Li Zhizao (1565–1630), and Yang Tingyun (1562–1627) – all high degree-holders and officials of the late Ming, seemed to validate this Beijing-centered strategy.[11]

In the 1630s, after the Jesuit monopoly ended, Spanish Franciscans, Dominicans, and Augustinians began arriving and the average number of missionaries went up to a range of 30–40. It remained at that level for about another half-century, to 1680. Remarkably, the number of missionaries was hardly affected by the Manchu conquest of the Ming in 1644 and the establishment of the Qing Dynasty. The Jesuits in Beijing, led by Adam Schall von Bell, at the changeover in authority in 1644 employed fast footwork to show the new rulers their usefulness in the fields of astronomy and other areas of science and technology.[12] There was, however, a short hiatus in the upward trend, when from 1665 to 1671 the missionaries almost all were exiled to Guangzhou or Macau during a crackdown inspired by xenophobic forces at court pandering to the insecurities of the Manchu rulers. When the young Kangxi emperor took the throne in 1669 he purged many of the hidebound officials and relaxed strictures on the missionaries, who resumed their work around the country. In the 1680s missionary numbers rose again, and then there was a doubling in the 1690s. In the one year of 1701, 30 new missionaries arrived, bringing the number to about 140, where it remained for a few years, until the Rites Controversy struck with its deleterious effects. The increased numbers partly reflected new sending orders, for example the Missions Etrangères de Paris, French Jesuits, Lazarists, and others. And it was partly due to the increased attraction of

China as a successful mission field, which seemed to be amply proven by the Kangxi emperor's 1692 edict of toleration for missions and Christianity. The success in gaining this decree from Kangxi semed to augur well for the mission, and kept active the longstanding hope that the emperor himself would convert to Christianity. In fact Kangxi, although he rather liked the Jesuits, and valued their services to him, never seems to have seriously considered becoming a Christian. But missionary hopes remained high.

A comparative observation seems appropriate here. Approximately a century previous, in the 1590s, the Japan mission was still prospering, as it had since the 1550s, and there were probably well over 200,000 Japanese Christians, including large numbers of daimyo and samurai. Meanwhile, although Ricci was edging his way toward Beijing, he had yet to get near it. Moreover, there were as yet no prestigious or even any elite Chinese converts, and there were a mere handful of missionaries in the country. A century later, in the 1690s, with the decree of toleration in force and over one hundred missionaries in country, China was (relative to a century previous) booming. Now there were probably more than 150,000 faithful in China, and steady growth, whereas in Japan, due to an especially fierce and thorough eradication campaign beginning in the 1620s, there remained very few Christians, and none visible in public.[13]

In my view, some of the interesting aspects of these patterns of numbers and composition of missionaries include: 1) how few the Jesuits were and yet how totally they dominated the scene for the first half-century, until about 1630; and 2) How complex and diverse the mission became in the next 60–70 years, as the Spanish friars of the mendicant orders (Dominicans, Franciscans, Augustinians) established themselves, almost entirely out in the provinces. And many of the newly arrived Jesuits were also assigned to the provinces, where in several areas conversions were on the increase. It is ironic that the attention of scholars has remained fixed on the missionaries at court, who were still hoping to convert the emperor. But the real action, and I would claim the real significance, was elsewhere. The relative newcomers on the mission field, including many of the Jesuits arriving in the last decades of the seventeenth century, were not so wedded to the now century-old strategies of Valignano and Ricci. In 1700, there were still many Jesuits working (as technicians, map-makers, even casting cannons for Qing military campaigns) at the court and elsewhere in Beijing and in a handful of other large cities (Nanjing, Fuzhou). But a great many Jesuits, and virtually all of the mendicant friars, were scattered across the empire creating and maintaining local rural-based Christian communities. These communities consisted largely of commoners and low-ranking elites, and it took considerable time and energy for administering the sacraments, carrying out the duties of training and encouraging local catechists, hearing confessions on a regular basis, performing funerals and weddings, and so forth. In short, these were the tasks of community-building, and the Jesuits were especially good at it. As we know from recent scholarship, the rigorous training in human personnel management methods, leadership skills, and practical experience in teaching and training that all Jesuits received back in Europe was impressive. The long common course of study, in science and languages as well as theology, learning to function in a group, and multi-year "apprenticeships" in teaching younger confrères, made for a remarkably effective cadre of personnel.

When this kind of experience was added to their superior Chinese language training and language facility, it often resulted in the missionaries in the field succeeding in running ahead of missionary theology and facilitating the formation of dynamic, cohesive Christian multi-family social units. As Liam Brockey puts it, the product of the Jesuits' labor was Christianity becoming less the "religion of converts" and more "the faith of families."[14] The missionary friars also established such communities, but they were not as skilled as the Jesuits in human resource management; most of the well-rooted Christian communities, those that would prove able to survive in the trials of the dawning eighteenth century, were products of the Jesuit mission. Most Jesuits in fact created a heavy work load for themselves. Because of the Europeans' fear that the purity of teaching and ritual might be compromised in Chinese hands, they were slow to ordain Chinese as priests, or even to turn over many duties to their Chinese catechists. As a result they had more work on their own shoulders. Nevertheless, they could not do everything themselves, and had no choice but to train catechists and lay leaders as helpers, and eventually to support a few bright and pious Chinese young men to undergo training in overseas seminaries to become priests. But they graduated and were ordained only at a slow rate.

Chinese Christians and Christian Communities

I will come back to the story of the Catholic mission before 1800 in the next section of this chapter. But I wish to stop and attempt to delineate what we know, or can surmise, about the Chinese Catholics of this time, that is, the Chinese flock being shepherded by the missionaries. One of the general impressions of Chinese Christians from the early 1600s to the present is that for the most part they were poor, of lower status, and marginalized.[15] It is true that there were not many higher elite degreeholders or officials who were Christians in the late 1600s and 1700s; no equivalents to the "three [or four] pillars" of the late Ming. One of the few exceptions was in Hangzhou, where the literatus Zhang Xingyao (1633–after 1715) after his baptism in 1678 wrote many essays and poems reconciling Christianity and Confucianism.[16] Yet in fact the scattering of lower, if not higher, degree holders among the Christian communities was not negligible. A close analysis of this question shows that the percentage of those with this status among Christians was extremely close to the percentage of the elite in the entire population (from 0.6% to 0.8%). Thus it is true that in contrast to the 1620s almost no officials were Christians in the early 1700s, but a number of non-office holding lower gentry (degree-holders) were. These constituted a reservoir of social capital and often of practical leadership experience which stood the Christians in good stead when the missionaries left.

The religious life of these parishes at some distance from Beijing, especially of those in rural areas led by non-Jesuits, was rather different from the cerebral world of most of the urban Jesuits. The religious consciousness of Catholic congregations in the countryside was to a great extent drenched in the world of miracles, visions, and other manifestations of the supernatural. In some ways it was the world they had always known, with new actors and Christian gods, and employing rituals which appeared to be similar to those of traditional village popular religion. At times, in the eyes of officialdom, especially after the proscription on Christianity in 1724, rural Christian communities appeared not only to be suspiciously heterodox in their ideology, but also liable to lapse into sedition.[17] Festivals and holy days sometimes would be occasions of believers fired by so much zeal that they wept uncontrollably, engaged in acts of self-mortification, and generally gave themselves over to emotional release. It was difficult enough for the European priests to control or keep within acceptable bounds this tendency when the foreigners were themselves present. Later in the eighteenth century, when the missionaries were gone or in hiding, there was little to prevent a steady slide toward incorporation of traditional religious practices and ideas into Catholic practice.

This phenomenon of adaptation to Chinese tradition has caused a leading Sinologist, Jacques Gernet, to conclude that the "conversions" to Christianity in this period were not authentic because they were often the result of the converts looking for benefits (healing, effectiveness, power) and not understanding the doctrines or meaning of the catechism or the sacraments.[18] And the Chinese Christians do seem to have instinctively looked for the same manifestations in Christianity that they were familiar with in their native religions. Gernet quotes Father Louis Le Comte at the end of the seventeenth century: "What the Chinese need, even when it comes to an object of worship, is something that strikes their senses. Magnificent ornaments, singing, processions, the sound of bells and musical instruments and Church ceremonial – all this is to their taste."[19] Today not many scholars would agree with Gernet's general thesis. Throughout the history of world Christianity, not all Christians have had a clear intellectual grasp of their faith, for example of the theological meaning of baptism or an orthodox conception of the Trinity. Moreover, in looking back at this period of history it should also be remembered that the missionaries themselves, including the Jesuits, were still in part products of late Medieval Europe and Scholasticism, and were not devoid of sensibilities to miracles and the supernatural.

Thus in many ways there was a spectrum of Christianities present in eighteenth-century China. As we survey the national scene from the 1580s to the early 1800s, several different centers of Catholicism are apparent:

Beijing

Ricci's original target, the capital city was over time rather hospitable to the resident missionaries. The Jesuits built up a Chinese Christian community of several thousand, including more than one hundred members of the extended Ming royal family. Some of the missionaries accompanied the Ming court in its flight to the south, and several more of the deposed ruling house, including a claimant to the throne, were baptized in south and southwest China in the 1640s and 1650s before the final demise of the refugee court. After the handover of power to the new Qing regime, and the Jesuits' success in maintaining residence in Beijing, the congregation of believers continued to grow. By 1700 it included a small but increasing number of ethnic Manchus. Several of these were from the Sunu family (Sunu was a cousin of the Yongzheng emperor, who reigned 1723–1735). After Yongzheng's prohibition of Christianity in 1724, he punished the Christians in Sunu's clan over the next few years, and Manchu converts seem to have disappeared, except perhaps for a handful. Despite the hostile atmosphere, a small number of converts, 2000 or so, continued to exist in Beijing through most of the eighteenth century. Two churches, the Nantang (South Church) and the Dongtang (East Church), were used on and off by the remaining missionaries and the Chinese Christians. A surprisingly large number of Jesuits and from time to time a few other missionaries stayed in Beijing because they were employees of the emperor. Even after the Catholic church's abolition of the Jesuit order in 1773, the old Jesuits ensconced at the emperor's court continued their work, still hoping for the elusive imperial conversion which would be the key to a Christian China. They quietly shepherded as best they could the Chinese believers as well, until they gradually died off and the number shrank to almost none.[20]

Jiangnan

In Ming times, Jiangnan was a province containing both Anhui and Jiangsu of later times. It refers to the lower Yangzi region, also including Zhejiang Province. After Ricci's death in 1610, Jiangnan became a fertile field for the Jesuits, starting with one of the "three pillars," Li Zhizao, inviting three missionaries to establish a residence in his native city of Hangzhou in 1611. The church which spread out from there established itself in the second capital

Nanjing as well as in lesser cities, and the Jiangnan area quickly became the richest and most important region for the church. Xu Guangqi, the highest ranking Ming Christian official, was buried outside of Shanghai and his descendants built a chapel there in his memory. But Shanghai did not become the nerve center of Jiangnan Catholicism until later, in the nineteenth century. The pattern for expansion, which was also followed in other areas, was that the missionaries would be invited to an area by Chinese converts, then they would go and settle there with the help of the best-connected among the converts, and launch more localized mission efforts from the approximate geographical center of the area. By 1700, about 65 percent of Chinese Christians lived in Jiangnan.

Fujian

This coastal province, just across the Taiwan Strait from Taiwan, was first missionized by the Jesuit Giulio Aleni (1582–1649) in the 1620s. Again the pattern was that an important convert made the first settlement possible. Aleni settled in and remained based in Fuzhou, the provincial capital. Soon Dominicans and Franciscans from the Philippines, some coming directly and some coming via Taiwan (until the Spanish were expelled from the island by the Dutch in 1642), were also active in Fujian. There were established communities all over the province, although Fu'an in northern Fujian became the most important Dominican center and sending point for further mission ventures.[21]

Zhili

Since 1912 this geographical entity, which contains Beijing, has been called Hebei Province. In the late 1600s, the number of Christian communities in southern Zhili expanded rapidly. Although they were all managed by Jesuits except for one or two, it is apparent that the old Jesuit "convert from the top" strategy was not being followed closely, as it still was in Beijing. Large numbers of converts and mass baptisms were not uncommon in south Zhili.

Shandong

Abutting south Zhili on the east is the northwestern region of Shandong Province. This area was nearly all under the direction of the Franciscans in the late 1600s, though there were missionaries from the Propaganda Fide in Shandong as well. There were dozens of churches built and communities formed, and thousands of converts were made. [22]

In all these areas and even in others with a smaller presence of Christianity the multiplication of centers of Christian activity meant for the missionaries a heavy load of pastoral duties: giving the sacraments, hearing confessions, training catechists and other helpers. And at the turn of the century they still were not receiving much direct assistance in priestly duties from Chinese confreres. Of the approximately 140 missionary priests in China in 1701, 130 of them were Europeans.

The Rites Controversy

The so-called "rites controversy" is one of the most commonly discussed events in Chinese Christian history, but it has not been researched systematically in archives by scholars until recent years. This is because between 1704, when the "rites" were prohibited by the Holy See, to 1939, when they were again approved, the subject matter was off limits to Catholic scholars and the materials were unavailable to non-Catholic scholars.[23]

To summarize very briefly, the controversy began with the Valignano-Ricci "accommodation policy" and the opposition it aroused among other Europeans, and culminated with a papal condemnation of the rites and a rejection of the Jesuits' policy in 1704 (a rejection reiterated by papal decree in 1715 and 1742, lest there be any doubt).

The specific issues encompassed by the controversy were:

- Whether certain established traditional Chinese terms, for example those that might be used to translate the name of God, the soul, and so forth, should be used or new ones coined. For example, both *tian* (heaven) and Shangdi (lord on high) were commonly used terms with many religious connotations. Ricci and the Jesuits had no problem in using these terms.
- The essentially civic or essentially religious nature of the ceremonies performed, especially by the degree-holding elite class, in honor of Confucius and their own families' ancestors, the latter represented by tablets in an "ancestral hall" in the home. These rituals included incense burning, prostrating one's self, or offering food. Should these acts be considered religious observance or civic duty? And should Chinese Christians be permitted or forbidden to participate? The Jesuits considered them civic functions, and permitted them.
- A related set of questions centered on relationships with non-Christians. Could mass be said for the souls of Christians' non-Christian ancestors? And could Christians be permitted to support and participate in community festivals or entertainments in honor of non-Christian gods? The Jesuits and their accommodation policy basically said "yes" to both questions.

The Jesuits were well set in their ways on all these questions ever since the time of Ricci. But the Jesuit position on these, and on the many related sub-issues, did not sit well with the mendicant priests who followed the Jesuits and had a more culturally limited Euro-centric view of how extensively the Chinese Christians should participate in these non-Christian (or "pagan") activities. Beginning with a Dominican who returned to Rome and launched an attack on Jesuit policy in the 1640s, the tide of dispute ebbed and flowed for more than sixty years, with the Vatican going back and forth depending on who was the most recent emissary from China presenting the case for or against the Jesuits. In the 1690s, ironically just after the Kangxi emperor's 1692 toleration decree for all Christians, the Pope became increasingly involved, and both the critics' attacks and the Jesuits' defense became increasingly strident.

Charles Maigrot MEP, Vicar Apostolic of Fujian, who had been in China since 1684, in March 1693 issued a Mandate from his jurisdiction formally indicting the use of the rites by Christians. This was after years of guerrilla warfare between Maigrot and pro-rites proponents. The latter included Bishop Gregory Luo Wenzao (1619–1691), a Dominican ordained in the Philippines in 1654, who then came to China, and who became the first Bishop of Nanjing, with the distinction of being the first and the last Chinese to be consecrated bishop until the twentieth century. Pope Clement X appointed him bishop in 1677, but he was not consecrated until 1685 because many of the European missionaries were opposed. Luo ordained several Chinese priests during the six years of his bishopric.

When Maigrot's indictment of the rites reached Rome, it set off several years of complex judicial proceedings, and stormy debates at the Sorbonne and other academic centers between advocates and opponents of the Jesuits over the issue. The Pope became thoroughly personally invested in this issue, as well. Finally a commission of cardinals recommended against the rites, and the Pope agreed, issuing a decree in November 1704 that ruled decisively against the rites. This was a watershed in early modern Sino-foreign relations, not just because of the content of the decision, but because of the Chinese emperor's reaction to the highly counterproductive manner in which it was conveyed to China. A papal legate was dispatched to China in 1705, to inform both the missionaries and (as it turned out) the Chinese emperor of the decisions. This was Charles-Thomas Maillard de Tournon (1668–1710), who turned out to be an unhappy choice. Tournon behaved highhandedly toward the missionaries and disrespectfully toward the emperor Kangxi. Kangxi had been puzzled for years by this issue festering among the missionaries. Curious, in July 1706, he invited Tournon to the summer capital north of Beijing for a discussion. Tournon took along Maigrot, champion of the rite-haters, and they had disastrous interviews with Kangxi, during which Maigrot showed himself incompetent in the Chinese language even after more than 20 years in China. And the emperor grew increasingly irritated, then angry, at the message from the Vatican. In fact, as far as can be determined he was quite outraged by what he saw as gratuitous interference in his state and culture, with foreigners who spoke no Chinese presuming to dictate to him the meaning for his subjects of Chinese rituals and cultural practices. In December 1706, Kangxi laid down the gauntlet by decreeing that all missionaries would have to undergo an examination, and only those who agreed with "the policies of Matteo Ricci" would receive a certificate (piao) which permitted them to remain in China. Those who refused were to be deported. Tournon, who was then in Nanjing, rejoined with a decree of February 1707, dictating the exact answers the missionaries were to give to the questions of the emperor, threatening with excommunication those who dared to be disobedient. The emperor soon banished Tournon to Macau, where he languished under house arrest until he died, soon after receiving news of his appointment as a cardinal.

There were in fact a number of missionaries who were deported in the next few years, but nothing like a clean sweep was made. The status of Christianity as a legitimate religion was not (yet) rescinded; that would not come until 1724, under Kangxi's son, the Yongzheng emperor (r. 1723–1735). Moreover, Kangxi exempted all the 15–20 Jesuits in imperial employment around the court, as well as ignoring the continued presence of a number elsewhere who kept a low profile. Some missionaries deported after 1707 managed to sneak back into the country, and new ones were always arriving. Kangxi seemed rather lax on this issue in his last years, so that provincial officials had no great incentive to enforce rigorously the requirement of the piao. Near the end of his life, however, in 1721, he was again angered by an envoy from Rome, the papal legate Mezzabarba, who attempted to mitigate somewhat the anti-rites stance of Rome by granting "eight concessions" to the local missionaries in Beijing. But this was viewed as woefully insufficient by Kangxi, and at any rate the "concessions" were all soon annulled by Rome.

When the Yongzheng emperor took the throne in 1723, he tightened the reins of central control over both state and society. He was of course also alert to possible sedition and departures from imperial Confucian ideological orthodoxy, very conscious of who was dependably loyal and who might not be. For reasons that are not entirely clear, he made Christianity illegal early in 1724, labeling it an "evil cult" or "heterodox sect" (xiejiao), subversive of Chinese culture and values. He also renewed the expulsion of missionaries outside Beijing, calling for all of them to be taken to Guangzhou and held under detention. He also systematically destroyed the clan of his cousin Sunu, in whose family several had become Christians in recent years. The doom of the Sunu clan was probably also due to rumors that some of its Christian members, perhaps with the connivance of foreign priests, had been active in attempting to turn the process of determining the succession to Kangxi in a different direction, away from Yongzheng. Withal, these developments put Christianity into the legal and political category of illegal religion and/or heterodox sect, which label it would keep until the 1840s.

Despite the measures of Yongzheng, which on their face seem rather draconian, and which were continued by his successor Qianlong (r. 1735–1796), several dozen foreign missionaries managed to remain in the country. Thus in the years between about 1710 and 1750, covering the reigns of all three of the great emperors, there were still usually more than eighty missionaries in China, a bit more than half of the high point of the early 1700s. The sharp nationwide persecution of 1784–1785, however, reduced the number of foreigners considerably, although as late as 1800 there were still about 25 foreign priests in the country, half of them in employment at the court. The Jesuits were all aging and weakening since the Jesuit order had been dissolved by order of the Pope in 1773. Meanwhile, as all the orders with personnel in China realized, there was no way to maintain even this small number of European priests. Thus all the orders developed plans to increase the number of Chinese clergy. And indeed the number of native priests increased steadily, to 40–50 by 1800.

Historians' assessments of the importance of the rites controversy vary widely. One pole of the spectrum, stressing unrealized technology transfer as well as religious factors, is that it was a major turning point in China's non-modernization, or aborted modernization. A corollary is that the outcome of the dispute ruined the prospects to adapt Christianity to China on a large scale, making it impossible to make China a "Christian" nation, which otherwise might have been the case. The other end of the spectrum of opinion among historians is that these events of the seventeenth and eighteenth centuries are in the end not really part of Chinese history at all, but an episode in European intellectual history or Western church history. But that stance ignores the prominent participation of Chinese priests and lay people in the controversy. They had large stakes in the issue, because of the extremely important role which ritual, that is "the rites," played in traditional Chinese culture and society.

The outcome of the rites controversy was certainly a setback for the growth and public life of the church in China; there seems little doubt of that. However, the extreme shortage of priests and of European Christian leadership after 1710 did not result in wholesale collapse of the Chinese church for the next century. Remarkably enough, the nationwide number of converts, perhaps 200,000 or more in the early 1700s, despite a dip to 120,000 in mid century, steadily increased again and climbed back to approximately 200,000 in the early 1800s. This was a result both of:

- the effective job of organizing local communities and rooting them in faith and the life of the church done by foreign missionaries, to be sure, but also by Chinese priests and catechists; and
- the internal dynamics of these communities once they got operating under their own power, as it were.

We will pursue this phenomenon, because it seems to be the first instance in Chinese Christian history that a certain amount of local agency occurred over a long period of time.

On their Own: The Long Eighteenth Century and the Life of the Church in China

Christianity in China was proscribed, categorized as a heterodox ideology, and officially forbidden to be practiced for about 120 years, from 1724 to the 1840s. This was almost the same number of years as from Matteo Ricci's establishing residence in Beijing in 1600 until Yongzheng's decree, during most of which time Christianity was legally or by practice sanctioned. But this long period of time after 1724 was not uniformly one of persecution. In some ways, just as today, Christianity was, on the one hand, constantly vulnerable to persecution, arrests, and other forms of harassment; but on the other hand, in normal times, especially in regions far from the capital, Christians practiced their faith openly. The foreign priests were more vulnerable to arrest and (usually) deportation because it was harder for them to hide their identity.[24] But even they were not usually molested as they made their peripatetic rounds from one Christian community to the next. A priest could stay only a few days in each locality, ministering to the Christians with confession, baptisms, and the eucharist before hurrying on to the next group of Christians eagerly awaiting his arrival. It was easier for Chinese priests to travel, of course, but there were not very many of them until late in the eighteenth century. The important point here is that except for Beijing, where the aging Jesuits were at any rate restricted in the religious functions they could perform, there was virtually no locale in China where a priest was permanently present.

This general situation in the empire as a whole meant that during these decades, as Christianity became more localized, foreign oversight perforce declined, and some interesting cases of hybridity or inculturation occurred.[25] Until the recent past, historians have had only fuzzy notions of what happened to Chinese Catholics and the local church in China during this 120-year period. The European records are scarce because the priests were fewer and were often out of touch with what was going on at the local level. But some excellent scholarship of recent years has provided us with considerable insight into both the practice of Catholicism and the perceptions of the scholar-official class and the Qing state.

The work of Lars Laamann shows the remarkable degree to which Christianity at the grass-roots level adapted itself to Chinese traditional culture. An example of this was grass-roots Christians' emphasis on expressions of filial piety and family solidarity, including use of ancestral tablets; despite the seeming finality of the Vatican's rejection of ancestor tablets, they continued to be used by many Chinese Christians. All that was required was a willingness to make a few adjustments to the terminology used in the ritual.[26] Another, for example, was the lack of a close connection between being converted and baptized and having a sense of sin and need for redemption; Christians often had to be coerced by the priest into receiving the sacrament of confession and absolution. Yet another was the strong millenarian tradition of Chinese popular religion, which had a tendency to insinuate itself into the fabric of the local church. Other gaps between practices of the Europeans and their Chinese charges included the intense practicality and materialism of the converts. Well-off Catholics, because of the cultural obsession with sons, were often quite willing to compromise the church's insistence on monogamy. Aberrations and departures from orthodoxy were often abetted by local Catholic leaders, especially the catechists, who had sometimes received only a modicum of training from the nearest harried European priest and interpreted the catechetical texts as they pleased. In short, before long the theological components of the faith of the converts in some areas were in tatters, and the core of Christian identity became religious symbols and ritual behavior, especially filial respect for the Christian ancestors.

This considerable cultural overlap between popular Christianity and the practices of indigenous society was sufficient to alarm the state. The Qing Dynasty was in its heyday during the eighteenth century, but it was deathly afraid of popular movements which might challenge the state.[27] Enough Christian communities behaved sufficiently like sectarian rebels such as the anti-dynastic White Lotus Society that Qing officials were alarmed. So whenever sectarian popular religion came under scrutiny and persecution, so did the Catholics. This occurred on a national scale in the late 1740s, 1784–1785, again in 1805, and after the shocking near-success of the Eight Trigrams Society's conspiratorial rebellion in 1813, which fought its way inside the outer wall of the Forbidden City in Beijing. Many other cases of temporary crackdowns, with local as well as national officials classifying the Christians as followers of a heterodox "evil cult," occurred during these decades. All in all, it can be said that in the late eighteenth and early nineteenth century, Catholicism was doubly suspect: it was a "foreign religion," closely associated with the Europeans, and very few Chinese, including Chinese Christians, understood how it worked. Yet at the same time Catholics behaved much like native Chinese sectarians, with sacred scriptures, charismatic leadership at times, and always with a whiff of apocalypse about, deriving from the millenarian component of both.

One region of China shows very well the paradox of significant growth during this century of proscription. That is the province of Sichuan, in southwest China. Several aspects of Sichuan's emergence as a Christian center reveal the dynamics of expansion.[28] More recently settled than the rich provinces of the eastern part of China, it was fertile and prosperous; but it had suffered a terribly destructive sequence of events during the Ming-Qing transition in the 1640s. A series of bandits and, in effect, warlords, devastated the land and cities of the province, decimated the population by senseless wholesale slaughter, and laid waste to vast swathes of the countryside. For decades, until late in the eighteenth century, Sichuan was a recipient of population movements from all over China. Many of these recent immigrants had no family or other social network nearby. This recent history seems to have helped to set the scene for church growth in the province. Indeed, Sichuan had remarkable growth in the last half of the century, and had probably about forty thousand Christians by 1800. Other regions with longer-established Christian communities did well during the eighteenth century to minimize losses or at best hold their own. Sichuan was virtually the only place where significant growth occurred. How was this accomplished with so few European missionaries present in the province?[29] One reason was that more Chinese priests were available after mid century. They studied usually at one of three sites: the College of the Propaganda Fide in Rome; a seminary established in Naples in 1732 to train Chinese clergy; or the seminary which had been established in Siam in 1666 by the Société des Missions Etrangères de Paris. André Ly (1693?–1774), one of the best-known Chinese priests of the mid eighteenth century, was trained at the latter institution.[30]

The pattern in Sichuan seems to have been that the European priests came through just often enough to monitor the state of health in doctrine and ritual of the community, whereas the Chinese priests increasingly took responsibility for administering the sacraments and other pastoral functions. But not many Chinese priests were available until late in the eighteenth century; for some years in mid century Andre Ly was the only Chinese priest in the entire province. For training and maintaining the local faith community, the Chinese catechists (*jiaotou*) or congregation head (*huizhang*) were crucial. These were local men who taught the classes leading to baptism, and did much more; they also functioned as lay leaders able to represent the Catholic community in relations with officials and the local elite. In fact they often played a key role in the conversion process. The *jiaotou*, as well as the *huizhang*, appear to have been extraordinarily important in the eighteenth century.[31]

Christians in Sichuan were targets of official repression several times during the eighteenth century, for reasons both local and national. Two instances of arrests and interrogations of Christians were in 1746 and 1755, when provincial officials were alerted by the court to be vigilant for rebellious sects, especially the White Lotus. Christians were already on the list of illegal sects, and were potentially vulnerable to being accused as an actively rebellious sect. This is exactly what happened in 1746 and 1755, when such accusations were lodged by other locals who had personal or legal disputes with the Christians and denounced them to the authorities. This resulted in several members of the community being arrested, interrogated, and suffering some mistreatment in the judicial system. Yet the interrogators were at bottom concerned only with whether these sectarians, whose beliefs they neither understood nor cared about, were in fact White Lotus or had similar treasonous intentions. When questioning revealed the differences between the groups, the investigating officials almost always decided that the Christians, while illegal, were not dangerous, and dismissed the case or meted out token punishment. There were exceptions to this pattern, however. Sometimes Christians were treated more harshly, for example being exiled to Turkestan.

Compared to such local and provincial cases of persecution, a greater danger inhered in the larger-scale nation-wide campaigns against Christians and the constant stream of foreign priests illegally entering the country.[32] These occurred in 1784–1785, when many priests and *jiaotou* were put in prison, in 1805, with a scare about surreptitious activities of illegal foreigners and rumors of espionage, and of course the court's visceral reaction to the 1813 Eight Trigrams rebellion, which occasioned a national crackdown. It could almost be argued that at its most aroused, the central government in 1800 was capable of a scale of arrest, interrogation, and detention of suspects (or anyone caught up in a security sweep) nearly as great as that of today's government, given the comparative difference in communications technology.

Despite their vulnerable legal status, occasional local or national campaigns of suppression, and periodic expulsion of the dwindling number of European missionaries, Chinese Christians more or less maintained their numbers, and developed several generations of loyalty to their Catholic communities. It can fairly be said that the Jesuit missionaries (and some from other orders, to be sure) had built well in the seventeenth century. The edifice they had constructed was still standing in the early nineteenth century. But the missionaries were essentially gone by then, with just a handful still sneaking in from Macau. All over China, longstanding groups of Christians, their faith rooted often in well over a century of loyalty to the church and its marks of identity – especially baptism, marriage, and funeral rites – were unable to receive these sacraments and other pastoral services provided by the clergy. For many communities, neither foreign nor Chinese priest was available. Into this void stepped natural leaders of these communities: the jiaotou and/or *huizhang*, the heads of wealthier Christian families, parents and siblings of those who had become ordained priests and were highly respected for that vocation, all took up at least a part of the slack created by the absence of priests. Like an organic being adapting to its environment, these Christian communities created their own version of Christian identity, with traditional rhythms of village life intertwined with the festivals and holy days of the church year. They created a natural hierarchy and themselves arranged for and conducted rituals of identity, markers between their world and that of their non-Christian neighbors. The priest was still highly respected and his visits were occasions of excitement, but in normal times the community carried on by its own resources.

One aspect of Christian life in these decades which derived from the dynamics of Chinese society and eventually made some of the foreign missionaries very nervous was the role of women, especially those with a religious vocation. From the start there was implicit tension between habitual practices of the European church and aspects of the traditional place of women in China. Priests could not visit Chinese women in their homes, or have any direct physical contact. This made confession and some other rituals awkward. Traditional Chinese gender segregation in public also resulted in the missionaries conducting separate masses for men and women, or even separate churches.[33] These features of Chinese society as they played out in the church resulted in women having separate associations, and in effect their own networks of communication. Some women were trained as catechists, to deal with dying infants or to prepare women for baptism, explaining doctrine and coaching them for the examination to be given by the priest on one of his visits.

Missionaries themselves applauded Chinese women who chose not to marry, made a vow of chastity, and lived to serve the church. But the assumption probably was that such a woman would lead a life of contemplation, not public activism. But for some women the unmarried state and the vow of chastity were a path to leadership in the Christian community. In Sichuan in the mid 1700s an Institute of Christian Virgins was formed with missionary encouragement, and within a few years its members had moved from a stress on seclusion and prayer to evangelism and social service in their communities.[34] By the late 1700s they were not only functioning as catechists, preparing women for baptism, but dispensing famine relief and medical care and, perhaps most important in terms of social impact, establishing and teaching in schools for girls. In some places in China these virgins were given custody of churches and other property when missionaries and Chinese priests were deported and exiled. This phenomenon of activist Christian virgins was most visible in Sichuan, but it occurred in many places. It is another index of the adaptability of Christianity to a local culture when the guiding hand of the missionary is (voluntarily or involuntarily) partially removed.

Thus by the early decades of the nineteenth century the long history of Catholic missions had resulted in a small but resilient Chinese church, which was forced by the circumstances of its illegality to do without hands-on European management. Not surprisingly, the Chinese Christian communities made their own way forward, reconciling Chinese culture with their Christian identity as instinct and practical experience led them. This in turn led to a certain amount of confidence on the part of local priests, catechists, and Christian literati, especially in Jiangnan, where the eventual return of the European clergy in the 1840s would be occasioned by open conflict (see Chapter 3).

In the meantime, forces of historical change were gathering. Just as the rise of the first European seaborne empires brought the first Jesuits to East Asia in the mid sixteenth century, the industrial revolution and new maritime technology in the first decades of the nineteenth century brought new participants in Sino-foreign relations. The foremost new player was the British seaborne empire, in the form of the British East India Company (BEIC), which with other Europeans and Americans was limited to the same restricted market as were the Portuguese and Dutch before them – that is, trade limited to several weeks per year in Guangzhou, the rest of the year residing in tiny Macau.

The China Christianity scene also became more complex when the first Protestant missionary from English-speaking lands, Robert Morrison, came to Guangzhou in 1807. European Protestants for almost three centuries, with a few exceptions, had not emphasized the need or desirability of systematically sending missionaries to "heathen" lands.[35] The modern English Protestant missionary imperative arose in the 1790s, first among British Baptists. Morrison was followed by a handful of other missionaries during the next three decades, mainly British or American. All lived in the Macau-Guangzhou axis, and all, along with the foreign merchants doing an increasing but still frustratingly restricted business, longed for the time when they would be able freely to enter China to preach the gospel to all Chinese. Their situation was rather like that of the pre-Ricci Catholic missionaries stuck in Macau for over thirty years waiting for the Ming dynasty to permit residence in China. But since there was no contact between Protestants and the established Catholic mission, no Protestant would have had occasion to reflect on this historical parallel.

With the arrival of the Protestants and the continued growth of trade in and near Guangzhou (the opium cargo had to be offloaded outside the city, because it was contraband), the backdrop was being assembled and the actors were gathering to raise the curtain on the modern history of Christianity in China.

Notes

1. These concepts, the serial movement of Christianity in world history and the Western missionary movement as a cross-cultural learning experience, are fully developed by Andrew Walls in his writings, for example, "The Nineteenth-

Century Missionary as Scholar," in Andrew Walls, ed., *The Missionary Movement in Christian History* (Maryknoll, NY: Orbis, 1966).

2. Of general sources, the most encyclopedic and detailed is Nicolas Standaert, ed., *Handbook of Christianity in China, Vol. 1: 635–1800* (Leiden: Brill, 2001), part 3, "Late Ming-Mid Qing," pp. 113–689; other recent general treatments are Jean-Pierre Charbonnier, *Christians in China A.D. 600 to 2000*, trans. M.N.L. Couve de Murville, original French edition, Paris, 2002 (San Francisco, CA: Ignatius Press, 2007), pp. 123–318, and more concisely Samuel Hugh Moffett, *A History of Christianity in Asia, Vol. II, 1500–1900* (Maryknoll, NY: Orbis, 2005), pp. 105–142. Although dated, Kenneth Scott Latourette, *A History of Christian Missions in China* (London: SPCK, 1929), pp. 78–198, is still useful.

3. Officials at the Ming court in Beijing were not aware of this grant of Macau to the Portuguese for several decades.

4. Much later, in the late nineteenth and early twentieth centuries, Protestant denominations sought through "comity agreements" to divide up Chinese territory into areas assigned to different mission groups, in order to avoid unseemly competition.

5. Again, Andrew Walls has done the classic analysis of this phenomenon. Andrew Walls, "From Christendom to World Christianity," in *The Cross-Cultural Process in Christian History*, ed. Andrew Walls (Maryknoll, NY: Orbis, 2001).

6. Some claim as many as 300,000 by the early 1700s.

7. In 1585 the Pope would issue an order that only the Jesuits could send missionaries to China and Japan. And the Jesuits decided that only Portuguese Jesuits would go to China; Jesuits from other countries who wanted to go to China had first to come to Portugal and join the Portuguese service. Nicolas Standaert, ed., *Handbook of Christianity in China, Vol. 1: 635–1800* (Leiden: Brill, 2001), p. 296.

8. The glowing treatment of Ricci began with the publication of his memoirs, or *Historia*, within a decade after his death. Ricci, *Fonti Ricciane*. Pasquale M. d'Elia, S.J., ed., *Storia dell'Introduzione del Christianesimo in Cina* 3 vols. (Rome, 1942–1949). Recent examples are Vincent Cronin, *The Wise Man from the West* (London: 1955); George H. Dunne, S.J., *Generation of Giants: The Story of the Jesuits in China in the last Decades of the Ming Dynasty* (Notre Dame, IN: U. of Notre Dame Press, 1962). A more balanced account but very sympathetic is Jonathan Spence, *The Memory Palace of Matteo Ricci* (NY: Viking, 1984).

9. Valignano is an understudied figure, in my view.

10. Nicolas Standaert, ed., *Handbook of Christianity in China, Vol. 1: 635–1800* (Leiden: Brill, 2001), pp. 310–311.

11. Nicolas Standaert, ed., *Handbook of Christianity in China, Vol. 1: 635–1800* (Leiden: Brill, 2001), pp. 404–405, suggests that Wang Zheng (1571–1644) should be included in this small group of very highly placed and well connected men.

12. Jonathan Spence has a fine short essay on Schall von Bell, in *To Change China: Western Advisors in China 1620–1960* (NY: Little, Brown, 1969), pp. 3–22.

13. Actually the figure of 150,000 for the late 1690s is an estimate. It could as well have been put at 200,000. Nicolas Standaert, ed., *Handbook of Christianity in China, Vol. 1: 635–1800* (Leiden: Brill, 2001), pp. 380–393, has an excellent

discussion of the sources for various figures, charts of alleged statistics at different times, and the whole issue of numbers before 1800.

14. Liam Matthew Brockey, *Journey to the East: The Jesuit Mission to China, 1579–1724* (Cambridge, MA: Harvard University Press, 2007), quotations from p. 115.

15. A classic example is Paul A. Cohen, "Christian Missions and their Impact Until 1900," in John K. Fairbank, ed, *The Cambridge History of China*, Vol. 10, *Late Qing, 1800–1911, Part I*, pp. 545–590 (Cambridge: Cambridge University Press, 1978). Another classic analysis with an interpretation that Christianity cannot be really understood by Chinese society is Jacques Gernet, *China and the Christian Impact*, trans. Janet Lloyd (Cambridge: Cambridge University Press, 1985).

16. Zhang's identity as both Christian and Confucian is the focus of David E. Mungello, *The Forgotten Christians if Hangzhou* (Honolulu: University of Hawaii Press, 1994).

17. An excellent local and provincial study is David E. Mungello, *The Spirit and the Flesh in Shandong, 1650–1785* (Lanham, MD: Rowman and Littlefield, 2001).

18. Jacques Gernet, *China and the Christian Impact*, trans. Janet Lloyd (Cambridge: Cambridge University Press, 1985, French edition 1982), esp. pp. 82–104.

19. Jacques Gernet, *China and the Christian Impact*, trans. Janet Lloyd (Cambridge: Cambridge University Press, 1985, French edition 1982), p. 87.

20. One of the very few scholarly treatments of the Beijing Christians is John W. Witek, S.J., "The Emergence of a Christian community in Beijing During the Late Ming and Early Qing Period," in Xiaoxin Wu, ed., *Encounters and Dialogues: Changing Perspectives on Chinese-Western Exchanges from the Sixteenth to Eighteenth Centuries* (Sankt Augustin, GER: Nettetal, 2005), pp. 93–116. As yet unpublished is an excellent and more detailed account of the vicissitudes of the missionaries and Christians in Beijing from the late 1700s to 1840. Xiaojuan Huang, "Christian Communities and Alternative Devotions in China, 1780–1860" (Ph.D. dissertation, Princeton University, 2006), Ch. 3.

21. A fine study of the Dominicans and Fu'an Christians is Eugenio Menegon, *Ancestors, Virgins, and Friars: Christianity as a Local Religion in Late imperial China* (Cambridge, MA: Harvard University Asia Center, 2009).

22. A nice treatment is in David E. Mungello, *The Spirit and the Flesh in Shandong, 1650–1785* (Lanham, MD: Rowman and Littlefield, 2001).

23. All major sources discuss the controversy, but in-depth research is more recent. Differing points of view are found in James S. Cummins, *A Question of Rites: Father Domingo Navarette and the Jesuits in China* (Aldershire, Hants: Scolar, 1993); George Minamiki, *The Chinese Rites Controversy: From its Beginning to Modern Times* (Chicago: Loyola University Press, 1985); and especially the essays in David E. Mungello, ed., *The Chinese Rites Controversy: Its History and Meaning* (Nettetal: Steyler Verlag, 1994).

24. Sometimes the transgressing priests were imprisoned or even executed, usually at a time of heightened suspicion or worries about treason.

25. I purposely am not using the term "syncretism" at this point.

26. This and following discussion, see Lars Laamann, *Christian Heretics in Late Imperial China: Christian Inculturation and State Control, 1720–1850* (London:

Routledge, 2006). Interestingly, what Jacques Gernet saw in the 1980s as insufficient understanding of Christianity on the part of these Christians, whose faith would therefore be suspect, is seen by Laamann as a simple process of inculturation.

27. An example is Philip A. Kuhn, *Soulstealers: The Chinese Sorcery Scare of 1768* (Cambridge, MA: Harvard University Press, 1990). The Qianlong emperor's phobia here was the danger of wandering mendicant monks, which would appear to the throne to be very like the wandering Catholic priests performing pastoral duties for the scattered Christians. Today's Chinese government is also made very nervous by the hundreds of Christian traveling Protestant evangelists, who are ubiquitous.

28. Robert Entenmann has devoted his career to in-depth study of Catholicism and Sichuan. Just two of several seminal articles are: "Chinese Catholic Clergy and Catechists in Eighteenth Century Szechuan," *Actes du Vie colloque international de sinology, Chantilly 1989* (Variétés Sinologique, 78) (Taibei: Ricci Institute, 1995), pp. 389–410; and "Catholics and Society in Eighteenth-Century Sichuan," in Daniel H. Bays, *Christianity in China: From the Eighteenth Century to the Present*. (Stanford, CA: Stanford University Press, 1996), pp. 8–23.

29. In the eighteenth century, Sichuan was in its entirety under the jurisdiction of the MEP.

30. Ly is especially important because his journal, later translated into French, is a valuable resource for historians, Andre Ly [Andreas Ly or Li Ande], *Journal d'Andre Ly, pretre chinois, missionaire et notaire apostolique, 1747–1763*, ed. Adrien Launay (Paris: Alphonse Picard et fils, 1906).

31. Another term for this local Catholic leader who was liaison with the priest was *huizhang* (congregation or assembly head). More on this later.

32. The irritation of the authorities at the constant trickle of foreign priests across the border from Macau, and the government's occasional spasm of alarm and anger, may remind some of the irritation of today's government at constant Bible smuggling across the border and occasional crackdowns on it.

33. Sectarians such as the White Lotus were frequently accused of "mixing the sexes" in their worship.

34. See Robert Entenmann, "Christian Virgins in Eighteenth-Century Sichuan," in Daniel H. Bays, *Christianity in China: From the Eighteenth Century to the Present* (Stanford, CA: Stanford University Press, 1996), pp.180–193.

35. These included the German Pietists and the Moravians.

3

Protestant Beginnings, Catholics Redux, and China's First Indigenous Christians, 1800–1860

Prologue

As we edge from late imperial toward modern Chinese history, several historical sites catch our attention as identifying milestones of China's Christian history.

For example, Morrison's grave. Robert Morrison (1782–1834), pioneer Protestant missionary and longtime factotum of the British East India Company (BEIC), died young at 52, like all foreigners still unable to reside permanently in any place in China except Portuguese-run Macau. He was buried in the small cemetery assigned to non-Catholics behind the tiny chapel where the pious among the foreign community (all too few, according to the missionaries), met for worship. Piety notwithstanding, the missionaries and the traders were about equally frustrated by the Chinese government's refusal to discuss expansion of trade and scope of missions work. Today one can visit freely both chapel and graveyard, and have one's photo taken at the well-shaded Morrison grave (there are no guards or barriers).

The British treaty of 1842

On the bank of the Yangzi River at Nanjing, onetime capital of all of China and still capital of Jiangsu Province, a simple but ideologically charged small

A New History of Christianity in China, First Edition. Daniel H. Bays.
© 2012 Daniel H. Bays. Published 2012 by Blackwell Publishing Ltd.

museum commemorates the British "defeat" of the Qing forces after three years of intermittent warfare (the museum presents it as more of a stalemate) and the signing of the first Anglo-Chinese treaty in 1842 just here, on a British warship in the river. The captions of all exhibits and their descriptive plaques make it clear that these historical events are never to be identified except as the "Opium War" (Yapian Zhanzheng) and the "unequal treaties" (*bupingdeng tiaoyue*). As we will see, the foreign missionary movement in China was highly complicit in and, some would insist, profited from these events.

The American treaty of 1844

Two decades after Morrison's death and two years after the British treaty, the young American nation, looking to the Pacific for its future, sent an envoy, Caleb Cushing, as minister plenipotentiary to sign its own treaty with China. The Sino-American negotiations, in which American missionaries played an important part, were held on the outskirts of Macau. The American treaty added considerably to the accumulation of foreign special privileges in China. The temple where the negotiations were held, and the stone table in the courtyard of the temple where the official copies were signed, can still be seen as a tourist site today.

The Qing summer capital, 1860

If we were to go to the Opium War museum in Nanjing (mentioned earlier) and then go to the city of Chengde, north of the Great Wall, which was the summer capital of the Manchu ruling house, our tourism would have nicely bracketed the formative period (1842–1860) of the framework for modern China's interaction with the outside world, including Christianity. For at the heart of the palace, in the emperor's private quarters, we can see clearly the table and chair (and on the table, allegedly the very writing brush) used by the Xianfeng emperor to sign the Convention of Peking in 1860 after the flight of the court, the Anglo-French occupation of the city and the destruction of the Summer Palace.

As a reminder that there was an internal dimension of Christianity's presence in China in the mid nineteenth century, one could take a walk on top of the massive old city wall of Nanjing, the capital of the Christian Taiping rebels in the 1850s. On a quiet night, going through one of the stretches of the wall that still today is visibly scarred and blasted from the incessant cannon-fire during the ten-year siege of the city, one can almost hear the ghosts of the Taiping fighters in desperate struggle, defenders of the Christian faith fighting to the death against the Qing government, the enemies of Christ.

All of these phenomena characterized the mid century presence of Christianity. The nineteenth century started slowly in China, but in the 1830s picked up the pace in the runup to the Opium War. By 1860 there was heavy Christian involvement both in a massive political rebellion led entirely by Chinese Christians and in the new political institutional arrangements that would underpin the foreign Christian presence for nearly a century to come. But let us go back to the beginning of the story.

Waiting on the China Coast

In the first decades of the nineteenth century, the Qing court cracked down on sectarians, owing to its fears of popular anti-dynastic agitation accompanying the growth of sectarian religious movements. The court was shaken by, among other disturbing events, the apparent near success of the White Lotus rebellion in central China at the turn of the century, and by the Eight Trigrams uprising of 1813, which came close to penetrating the Forbidden City in Beijing. The emperor ordered more vigilant monitoring and surveillance of religious groups, especially those on the "most wanted" list of illegal "evil cults" such as the White Lotus Society – and including Catholic Christianity. Thus Catholics in the early nineteenth century had a difficult time, and the number of foreign priests grew ever smaller through attrition in Beijing and capture of most of those who continued to enter China surreptitiously. In the last years of the eighteenth century and the first years of the nineteenth, several foreign priests were executed after capture. There was no danger of the Catholic church in China wasting away to nothing; it remained resilient. But it could not flourish under these circumstances.

In these decades after 1800, Protestantism appeared for the first time. In 1807 Robert Morrison (1782–1834) of the London Missionary Society (LMS) arrived in Guangzhou. His life and work was emblematic of several features of the early Protestant effort in China.[1] Morrison, of working-class personal background and with only a modest education, was caught up in the evangelical enthusiasm for missions which characterized some parts of British society in the late eighteenth century, especially in the Nonconformist churches. The Baptist Missionary Society (est. 1792) predated the interdenominational LMS (1795). The Baptists sent their first missionary, William Carey, to India. Morrison, the first LMS representative to China, began to prepare himself in 1803, attending the Missionary Academy at Gosport, then studying Chinese in London for two years with a tutor – a young Chinese man who happened to be in London. Here Morrison showed the capacity for hard work and self-discipline that he displayed all his life. His efforts on the language gave him a head start when he finally arrived in China, and he started translating the Bible within a few months.

When Morrison finally embarked for China in late 1806, he did not receive the courtesies which the seventeenth-century Portuguese and Spanish merchant vessels extended to their missionary compatriots, that is, a free ride to Asia. The British East India Company (BEIC) was above all mindful of its purpose, which was not to support missionary endeavors but to run India efficiently and to make a profit in the China trade, to part of which (tea imports into Britain) the Crown had granted the BEIC a monopoly. Thus the BEIC did not want missionaries in India or China, and refused Morrison passage on its ships. As a result he traveled on an American ship, as guest of the pious owner. After arrival in Canton he found a teacher and set about learning the language well, although it was still forbidden by Chinese law for foreigners to study Chinese. Within two years he had made a fair beginning on compiling a Chinese dictionary, and in translating the Bible into Chinese. He had also become a very competent translator, resulting in his being hired by the BEIC (despite the BEIC's bias against missionaries) to be its official translator. In gaining this post, Morrison thereby secured his position on the China coast for the long term, although at times his missionary role was cramped by his official duties.

From today's perspective we can appreciate the multiple roles Morrison played successfully. He was a pioneering scholar, with several pathbreaking publications, in some of which he was assisted by an LMS colleague, William Milne (1785–1822), who joined Morrison in 1813. These publications included the first systematic grammar of Chinese, a three-volume Chinese–English dictionary, the Bible in Chinese, many miscellaneous writings, and an English-language newspaper in Canton. Morrison was also an educator, active in establishing the Anglo-Chinese College at Malacca in 1817, probably the most important of several initiatives taken by the early Protestant missionaries among the overseas Chinese in Southeast Asia. From time to time he served as interpreter for the British government as well as for the BEIC. He was the official translator for Lord Amherst's fruitless diplomatic mission to Beijing in 1816 in search of an easing of restrictions on foreign trade. In his lifetime he was a major, if not the foremost, Sinologist of his day, and the leading interpreter of China to Western nations. He was pious and serious-minded, something of a loner, and his capacity for sheer hard work and perseverance are inspiring, though a bit daunting. After his death in 1834 he was buried in the Old Protestant Cemetery of Macao, where his grave and tombstone have been well preserved and quite open to view.

One reason Morrison spent so much time on his dictionary and his Bible translation was the instinctive ingrained Protestant conviction that every people needs to have the scriptures in their own language; indeed his formal instructions from the LMS were a manifestation of that conviction. But another reason was that there was not much else to do. Open propagation of Christianity was still illegal under Qing law, and the BEIC did not want any taint of Christianity, with its unpredictable consequences, to interfere with its commercial activities. Moreover, the foreign community on the China coast

Figure 3.1 Morrison's grave in Macao. Credit: Imagestate Media Partners Limited - Impact Photos/Alamy.

lived very restricted lives. Merchants and missionaries alike could only reside in Guangzhou during the trading season, at other times perforce retiring to the tiny enclave of Macau on the coast. And they could not set foot on the streets of the metropolis of Guangzhou, but instead were confined to their tiny plot of land along the river.

The Protestant fraternity of missionaries gradually grew, but only slowly. William Milne was a useful co-worker for Morrison after his arrival in 1813, but he died young, in 1822. Another LMS representative, Walter Henry Medhurst (1796–1857), arrived among the Chinese diaspora in Southeast Asia in 1819, where he worked on many of the same projects (the Anglo-Chinese School, writing or translating tracts and other literature and printing it) as Morrison and Milne had done earlier in Batavia, Malacca, Singapore, and Penang.

Before 1830, among Protestants, besides the LMS only the Netherlands Foreign Missionary Society made an assignment to China. That was the redoubtable and charismatic Karl Friedrich August Gutzlaff (1803–1851), who arrived in Southeast Asia in 1827 and on the China coast in the 1830s, by which time he had long since left the Netherlands society in order to operate independently.[2] In 1830, Elijah Coleman Bridgman (1801–1861) became the first American China missionary, sent by the ecumenical American Board of Commissioners for Foreign Missions (ABCFM)[3]. In addition to several publications in Chinese, Bridgman edited an important English-language monthly periodical, *The Chinese Repository*, from 1832 to the late 1840s. The *Repository* had a mixture of informational articles and opinion pieces relevant to the China coast foreign community. Considering that it was written on the China coast in isolated circumstances, the *Repository* was notably comprehensive, informative, and objective in its coverage of China.[4] Later in the 1830s the ABCFM appointed to China Samuel Wells Williams (1812–1884), a printer who later was a US diplomat and who in the 1840s wrote a two-volume treatise on China which remained the standard reference for several decades.[5] Peter Parker (1804–1888), the first medical doctor on the China mission field, was a 1834 ABCFM appointee who established China's first modern hospital, the Canton Ophthalmic Hospital, in 1835.[6] The lives and work of all of these and many others are amply documented in Western missionary sources. Those same sources are quiet on descriptions or even identities of the Chinese associates and colleagues of the missionaries. Indeed, only a few names are discernible among those Chinese who consti- tuted the Chinese church before 1840. Before that time there was only a single Chinese ordained Protestant evangelist, Liang Fa (1789–1855). Liang, who was converted about 1815, worked as a helper to William Milne until the latter's death in 1822, and later worked for the LMS in Malacca and on the China coast, where he had the distinction of writing the Christian treatise that launched the Taiping Rebellion. He Jinshan (Ho Tsun-sheen or other ver- sions), the second ordained Chinese evangelist, was not ordained until 1846.

Before the outbreak of the Opium War in 1839, altogether from 1807 a total of about fifty Protestant missionaries had been assigned to China, but only a handful had stayed for any length of time. The China mission was scattered from Guangzhou-Macao to Singapore and Batavia. The cost of the efforts to advance this enterprise had been great: the labors and tedium of language study and development of basic language learning tools; the frequent illnesses of themselves, spouses, and children, and the high toll of lives; and the frustrations of living within the narrow parameters of the restrictions imposed on foreigners by Chinese government policy. Even more troubling was the small number of converts, fewer than one hundred total for the entire Protestant effort as of 1839 – and many of them were in the employ of a mission. The missionaries were certain that if they could only obtain access to the interior of China, conversions would increase dramatically.

As with the 30-year period from the death of Francis Xavier off the China coast (1553) to 1583, when Ruggieri and Ricci were finally permitted to enter and take up residence, it was 32 years from Morrison's arrival to the 1839–1842 event we usually call the" Opium War." Ricci and Ruggieri had to wait until the provincial officials were willing to let them live in China; they had no military threat to brandish or other leverage with which to coerce the Chinese. The missionaries of the 1830s, however, Protestant and Catholic alike, were in different circumstances. They chafed at the increasingly intolerable (in their eyes) constraints put upon them by the Chinese authorities, preventing access to China's "heathen" (or at least "lost") millions. Of course the other categories of foreigners on the China coast, especially the merchants of both the BEIC and those among the private ship owners who had a stake in the trading system, with few exceptions wanted if necessary simply to bludgeon the Chinese government with sufficient military force for them to open up the system for regulating foreign trade.

The Treaties (I)

During the first decades of the nineteenth century, the crux of the foreign trade standoff between the British and other Western interests and the Qing government became the opium trade. In a way, the problem was simple – opium was an illegal substance in China, and the foreigners who sold it were lawbreakers. Tensions grew between the British and the Qing over the mounting scale of the illegal opium flow into China, brought by foreign traders. These tensions escalated in the late 1830s and resulted in war in 1839. The war, fought sporadically from 1839 to 1842, was viewed by Britain as a fight for fair open trade and access to the Chinese domestic market, and by the Chinese as a struggle to maintain sovereign control over its foreign trade and not be pushed around by the Western powers. The fact that the war seemed to be prosecuted for maintenance of the privilege of British ships to continue transporting contraband opium to China presented the China coast missionaries with something of a moral quandary. Most missionaries were not insensitive to the physical and social damage done by extensive use of opium, and none favored its sale by their countrymen in China, although some, for example Gutzlaff, did distribute tracts from opium vessels along the China coast. Although the salience of the opium issue caused some dissent and protest on the floor of the House of Commons in London, with critics of government policy decrying the criminality of the opium trade, no China coast missionary was sufficiently concerned about the morality of the opium issue actually to oppose the war and its settlement. They recognized the immorality of the trade, but they were certain that the war was the hand of providence opening China to the Gospel.

The diplomatic settlement of the war, manifested in the treaties China signed first with the British in 1842 and then with the Americans and the French in 1843 and 1844, was a milestone in modern Chinese history. It was the first scaffolding upon which the entire system of China's foreign relations, foreign trade, and even intellectual discourse with foreigners, would be built; this system would last a full century, to be ended only in 1943, in the midst of World War II. It is usually called the "treaty system" by Westerners. Chinese almost always call it the "unequal treaty system," because in fact it was an inherently unequal set of arrangements forced upon China by the superior military power of the Western nations, led by the British.

For our purposes, the most important provisions in the first set of treaties in 1842–1844 involving Christianity included the following. 1) extraterritori-ality (foreign citizens coming under their own consular authority, not Chinese jurisdiction, for any sort of crime or other legal action.); this was a provision applying to all foreigners; 2) provisions secured by the French in 1844 indicating that Christianity would be no longer be legally outlawed; and 3) opening up five coastal cities for trade and residence by foreigners, including the right to build churches, missionary residences, schools, and other elements of Christian communities; and 4) the foreigners right to reclaim the use of former church buildings wherever they had formerly existed before the proscription of 1724, and no matter what the present use of the property. Thus, for example, a former Catholic church that might have been a Buddhist temple for over a century after 1724 could be turned back over to the French missionaries, with the French consul prepared to support the foreign seizure of such properties. This provision only benefitted Catho-lics, of course; Protestants had no such properties.[7]

Between Treaty Rounds

In the years from 1842 to 1860, foreign missionaries had much wider scope for their actions. And several new denominations appeared on the list of Protestant missionary societies present in China. In 1842 there had been seven, including five American, one British, and one from the Netherlands; between 1842 and 1860, 20 more societies were represented, six American and the other 14 divided between Britain and continental Europe. Most of these sooner or later made their headquarters in Shanghai, as did the majority of trading or commercial enterprises that set up business on the China coast. Well before 1860 it was apparent that Shanghai was destined to become the queen of the treaty ports, and almost all foreign institutions in China had either headquarters or major offices there. In Hong Kong (which had been ceded to Britain in perpetuity as a crown colony in the 1842 treaty) and the five "treaty ports" designated by the treaty (Guangzhou [Canton], Xiamen [Amoy], Fuzhou [Foochow], Ningbo, and Shanghai), small congregations of Chinese Protestants began to form under missionary leadership. But there was still dissatisfaction with the continuing restrictions, which limited missionaries to these five cities and their immediate suburbs (all foreigners were permitted to travel only a half-day's journey outside the city; they had to return the same day). Protestants again were more hampered than Catholics, who were accustomed to clandestine illegal entry into China to visit their communities. Catholics had networks of Chinese believers to hide them, and also had the treaty provisions legalizing Christian belief for Chinese and returning Catholic properties, which rendered a bit uncertain their status in the interior, although technically they were not supposed to be there. As I will show later, the reappearance of European Catholic bishops and priests caused problems in some Catholic communities in several places.

Protestant missionaries, temporarily stymied in their desire to move beyond the five treaty ports, nevertheless found ways of keeping themselves occupied. They preached to the urban population which surrounded them, they trained helpers and Chinese evangelists to take up part of the work load (although these Chinese helpers are often not visible in the missionaries' reports and documentation), they established day schools and boarding schools for boys and girls, and they offered medical services to the Chinese.[8] And they also engaged in extensive written communication. In addition to the copious letters and reports to the mission society general secretary or corresponding secretary in the home office, and private letters, all of which constitute a treasure trove of historical documentation for scholars today, missionaries wrote or translated tracts and other reading matter, both religious and secular, and published them on their own presses. Some of these presses became full-fledged publishing houses.[9] This continued the practice of writing and publication in Chinese firmly established by the earliest Protestants, Morrison and Milne and others, a habit that continued well into the twentieth century.[10]

The Bible

Among the several issues dealt with by missionaries in the 1842–1860 period in the category of "literary work" was the continuing major problem of the translation of the Bible into Chinese. Robert Morrison's pioneer translation, while monumental, was not very good. Even before his death in 1834 there was general acknowledgment of the need for a new one. In the mid 1830s two veterans, W.H. Medhurst and Karl Gutzlaff, collaborated to produce, in only four years, an intended revision of Morrison's Bible which turned out to be a new translation. Although the directors of the LMS and the British and Foreign Bible Society, the original sponsors of the Morrison Bible, in 1836 refused endorsement because of their loyalty to the memory of the recently departed Morrison, nevertheless when the Medhurst–Gutzlaff translation was completed, most thought it an improvement and it was used extensively for several years. This was also the Bible translation used by the Taiping rebels in the great rebellion which was brewing in the 1840s.[11]

What most exercised the missionary Bible translators in the 1840s was a series of debates on the proper Chinese terms for "God," "baptism," and a few other basic Christian concepts. These debates were embedded in the cooperative approach to making a new translation by each mission designating a delegate to participate. This ambitious project began in 1843. The single largest issue centered on the deity itself. Was God best translated as Shangdi, "lord on high," with connotations of monotheism in the religion of ancient China? Or was it best expressed by Shen, a generic term for gods which here meant the single God? Then there were Catholics, who long since had decided on Tianzhu, "Lord of Heaven." Because Chinese ideographic characters all carry intrinsic meanings, there were no characters that were entirely devoid of meaning, no matter how they were pronounced. These issues had already been debated extensively by the Catholics in the seventeenth century, but as in most things, no Protestant would believe that he could learn anything from the Catholics. The Baptists were particularly focused on the term for baptism, wanting one which would imply or connote baptism by immersion, not sprinkling. These problems, in some ways insoluble, eventually resulted in two major accepted versions of the Bible in Chinese, one using Shangdi and the other Shen.[12] The Baptists pulled out of the joint translation project and used their own version. Nevertheless, the joint efforts of the committee produced a new version of the New Testament by 1851, written in more classical style than previous or later translations.[13] This, called the "Delegates' Version," was admired by many for its more elegant style, and was extensively used throughout the rest of the century, though its classical flavor made it more difficult for commoners to read with easy comprehension. There were several versions of the Old Testament which were paired with the Delegates' Version New Testament. The success of the Delegates' Version reflects the role of capable Chinese assistants for the missionary translating team, although their names seldom appear in the records. This lack of public recognition for the Chinese scholars was true as well of the later large multi-decade project to do a Mandarin colloquial translation. This aimed at creating a version of the Scriptures that would be accessible to the modestly educated but would still be acceptable to the well educated. The project began in 1890 and resulted in the "Union Version" Bible of 1919, which even today is the standard translation used by Christians in China and in overseas Chinese communities.[14]

In addition to the several missionary scholars focused on Bible translation, a handful of them began to translate Chinese works into European languages. Foremost among these was James Legge (1815–1897), a Scotsman who found the "Chinese Classics" (the Four Books and the Five Classics) fascinating to read and also able to provide many insights into Chinese character, social behavior, and values. Although technically still an LMS missionary (for example, he served on the "Delegates' Version" translation committee), Legge became estranged from the mission in the 1860s and eventually went to Oxford in the 1870s as its first chair of Chinese.[15]

In complete contrast to the measured steps of Legge, Karl Gutzlaff in the mid 1840s threw himself into what became the first significant attempt, Protestant or Catholic, to give agency to Chinese in the missions effort. Through his one-man organization, called the Chinese Union, Gutzlaff collected resources from Europe not via missionary societies but directly from the crowds he addressed in trips back to Europe and from the individuals whom he charmed with rosy depictions of Christianity's growth in China.[16] Back in China he sent dozens of Chinese evangelists and colporteurs, with thousands of Bibles and Scripture tracts, into the interior beyond the sub-urban environs of the five treaty ports, to which the foreigners were limited. By 1850, evidence abounded that many if not most of the Chinese agents had failed spectacularly to warrant Gutzlaff's trust in them. They did not distribute Bibles but sold them as bulk scrap; they did not go to their assigned places but disposed of their cargo on the road; some never even left Hong Kong. The entire affair was a scandal and an embarrassment, and probably contributed to Gutzlaff's untimely demise in 1851, at age 48.[17] The loudly voiced criticisms of Gutzlaff's Chinese Union in the foreign missionary community had the unfortunate result of casting a shadow of suspicion on the policy of giving extensive responsibilities to indigenous personnel, which subtly colored the relationship between missionaries and Chinese Christians for the rest of the century. Yet in truth the Chinese Union had not been a total disaster. Some Chinese evangelists from the Union were hired by the LMS; others worked with the early missionaries of both the Rhenish and Basel missions in itinerating (journeying around) the interior of south China in the 1850s. Some of these Chinese workers went further afield on their own, evangelizing their own kin and Hakka villages where Christianity took root even before the Basel missionaries established themselves in the area after 1860.[18]

By mid century the Protestant missionary movement had been in existence for more than 50 years, and in China for more than 40. There was consid-erable reflection on philosophies or strategies of missionary work on the part of some, especially mission society executive administrative officials in the growing home offices of the societies. Was there a "theory of missions" evident in China? The general secretaries of two of the major British and American sending agencies had a similar philosophy of overall missions strategy. Henry Venn (1796–1873) and Rufus Anderson (1796–1880), longtime secretaries of the Church Mission Society (Anglican) and the ABCFM, respectively, agreed that it was: 1) more important to preach the Gospel than to educate or heal non-Christian peoples (though they did not oppose the latter); and 2) supremely important to put native converts in charge of new churches as soon as possible – that is, the foreign missionary should step to the side sooner rather than later.[19] This was emphasizing "native agency." Anderson was known for his stress on what later was called the "three-self" principle much talked about in China since 1950: "self-support, self-governance, and self-propagation."[20] But actual conditions and trends in China differed. Already visible in the Protestant missionary approach to their work in Hong Kong and the five treaty ports before 1860 was a tendency to create institutional structures for the general improvement of Chinese society (schools, medical clinics, newspapers, knowledge of hygiene, and such). However, in China in the mid and late nineteenth century there was not a major proportion of missionary opinion that actively promoted Anderson's "three-self" principles. In addition to factors I will describe in Chapter 4, this is not really surprising. In the urban areas to which they were confined in these decades, Protestants did not attract very many middle class or well educated converts, the sort to whom it would be easy to pass on leadership responsibilities. And of course the fiasco (as the foreign residents of the treaty ports saw it) of Gutzlaff's Chinese Union did not inspire foreign confidence in Chinese Christian personnel. Hong Kong was something of an exception here. As early as the 1840s, the church in Hong Kong began to attract some elements of the social elite classes (of course Hong Kong was a fully colonial situation, the treaty ports were not; the normal Chinese avenue to status and power, the civil service examination, did not apply in Hong Kong).[21] As a result, in Hong Kong the names of some individual Christians begin to appear in the historical records in the 1840s.

Roman Catholics

The first few decades of the nineteenth century were a time of lying low for the Catholic church in China. The old missionaries still in China had almost died off by the 1830s, and only a handful had crept into the interior and survived the vigilance of the Qing surveillance system. Without much direct knowledge of the congregations, Rome and church officials were nevertheless alarmed at stories of local Catholic communities behaving in unorthodox ways of worship, family life (such as continued use of the ancestral rites), the role of women in the church, and management of relations with the state. The prospect of women evangelizing, training new converts for baptism, and otherwise playing leadership roles in the Chinese Catholic church was anathema to the European priests. Thus one of the first things that the Catholic missionaries – Jesuits, Franciscans, and others alike – did upon their return to sites of surviving Catholic communities was to reestablish control over these communities. For example, the returning missionaries restricted or did away with much of the accustomed activities of the Christian Virgins by invoking the powers of the larger church and the Vatican.[22] Some of the sharpest conflict between returning missionaries and the local lay leadership which had sustained these Catholic communities for over a century took place in Jiangnan (Jiangsu Province plus parts of Anhui and Zhejiang

Provinces). The several tens of thousands of faithful Catholics of this area, including many well-to-do families of long pedigree (such as the descendents of Xu Guangqi in Xujiahui [Zikawei] in suburban Shanghai – now one of the central districts in today's Shanghai), at first welcomed the Jesuits back, and missionaries of other orders as well, in the early 1840s. But they found the missionaries so domineering and contentious, and so determined to change the habits and practices of the locals in the name of "reform," that by the late 1840s their local leaders wrote up several formal grievances and sent emissaries to take them in person to Rome and Lisbon.

These documents, only recently discovered in archives in Rome and Lisbon, shed considerable light on what seems to have been a blatant power grab by the Europeans. The Jiangnan petitions claim transgressions by not only the Jesuits but Franciscans, Lazarists, and representatives of the Missions Etrangères de Paris as well.[23] This is one of very few expressions of Chinese Christians' views extant for pre-1900 history. The protests seem to have availed little. By the 1860s the foreigners, especially the French, were in a commanding position of authority in the Chinese Catholic church. In Jiangnan in particular, in the 1850s and 1860s the Taiping Rebellion wrought such devastation in the prosperous areas where some of the prominent old Catholic families had their properties, that it weakened these old lineages and made them dependent on the missionaries for relief.[24] Allied with French diplomatic power, French missionaries were often a powerful element of local communities until well into the twentieth century. Nevertheless, the local lay leadership of the church remained extremely important as well, continuing to play a key role as evangelists, catechists, and managers of the local community.

The Taipings: China's first indigenous Christian movement

Arguably the most significant set of events involving Christianity and China in the 1800–1860 period was the Taiping Rebellion (1850–1864). The Taiping movement was inspired by Hong Xiuquan, a Hakka failed scholar who received his Christian ideas from bits and pieces of the Bible, a personal audience with the Christian God, and a few weeks' study with an American Baptist missionary, Issachar Roberts, in Hong Kong in 1847. By this time Hong had organized a faith community (or "church"), the God Worshippers' Society, whose communitarian principles and institutional practices were proving to have an appeal to the disinherited of southwest China. These included a variety of ethnic Hakkas, out-of-work miners and charcoal workers, women attracted by the gender equality of the movement, and a few members of secret societies such as the Triads. All was held together by Hong's religious prophetic vision and the conviction that he was literally God's son, Jesus's brother, and had been given a mandate directly by God the father to eliminate idolatry and false religion from Chinese society. The main Christian inputs into Hong's movement, besides the short time spent with the Baptist Issachar Roberts, were from the Bible itself, the 1830s translation by Medhurst and Gutzlaff.

Scholars still debate whether the Taipings had an ideology that was essentially Christian or not. Probably most would say definitely not, but I think we should consider the formal Taiping articles of faith to be Christian enough. For example, the Taiping version of the Ten Commandments, written by Hong Xiuquan himself in the early 1850s, appears to be standard nineteenth-century Christian fare.[25] The main problems of historical judgment come after the God Worshippers, under Qing government pressure, escalated to open rebellion in 1850 and set their sights on replacing the alien and antiquated Qing dynasty. Then in behavioral terms the Taipings appeared more akin to Chinese folk or popular religion. Early in the rebellion, the Protestant missionaries of the day were delighted at the prospect of a Taiping victory and a "Christian ruler" for China. Western governments also thought it possible that the Taipings might be more amenable to fostering trade and foreign intercourse than was the decrepit Qing regime.

However, both political and religious hopes came to naught. In 1853 British, American, and French vessels carrying diplomats and officials made separate journeys from Shanghai upriver to the Taiping capital of Nanjing. They were disappointed that the Taiping leaders showed no willingness to abide by the terms of the treaty system, and in fact insisted on assuming that foreigners would naturally have a subordinate status in future relationships. This experience was sufficient to quench any positive feelings toward the Taipings in Western diplomatic and commercial circles.[26] The missionaries, at least some of them, for a few years tried to give the Taipings the benefit of the doubt and some continued to regard them as fellow Christians despite the unusual Taiping beliefs. But as time passed and more missionaries in the late 1850s and early 1860s made the short trip up the Yangzi River from Shanghai to Nanjing, a steadily increasing number of them turned away from Hong and his movement. This was partly because of Hong's seemingly bizarre display of concern for making the Bible conform to traditional Confucian "family values," leading to his insistence on rewriting the Bible in several places. It was also due to the chaotic and murderous military and civilian administrative practices and behaviors of the Taipings.[27]

When a new round of treaties was signed between China and the Western powers in 1858–1860, that also seemed to dampen any remaining missionary sympathies for the Taiping rebels. The new treaties with the Qing promised what the missionaries had wanted for years – full and free access to the interior of China – and there was no guarantee that the Taipings would grant the same rights if they won. There was a strain of nationalism, or at least a prototype of it, visible in the religious as well as the political-commercial aspects of Taiping leaders' attitudes towards foreigners. They presumed Christian equality for themselves with the foreigners, because both Chinese and Westerners were after all children of the same God, and all are equal before Him (although because of the Taiping king Hong's special family relationship with God the Taipings were if anything more equal). It was difficult for even the most pious and generous of attitude among the missionaries, however, to view the Taipings, or any Chinese Christians, as real equals, because of their sadly benighted state of civilization; despite being Christians, they nevertheless were still heathens in comparison to the model of civilization in the West. In the end there was almost no sympathy for the Taipings in missionary circles, and scarcely a missionary could have been found who considered the Taipings' beliefs and practices to be anything like authentic Christianity.

Although missionary observers considered the Taipings outrageously un-Christian, it is doubtful that the missionaries realized the full extent to which Taiping ideology constituted a mortal threat to the traditional socio-political order. One aspect of this threat was the Taiping critique of the imperial state itself and its rationale all the way back to the First Emperor of Qin more than 200 BCE Hong and the Taipings, positing the equivalence of the Christian God and the Chinese Shangdi of Shang and Zhou times (circa 1600–1000 BCE), condemned the first emperor and all his successors to the dragon throne since for usurping from God himself the self-appellation "di." The divine nature thus claimed by the ruler constituted the "blasphemy of empire," and rendered illegitimate the imperial power structure that had prevailed during the previous two millennia.[28] The other aspect of Taiping ideology which constituted a danger to the old order was the degree to which members of the scholar-elite class, or "gentry," steeped in Confucian values of hierarchy and particularistic loyalties, were threatened by the egalitarian universalist values of Taiping monotheism.[29] The problem here for the position of Christianity in China was that what missionary opinion had judged to be hopelessly deficient, the strange and twisted ideas of Hong and his movement which by no means could be considered authentic Christianity, was in fact considered to be precisely that by Chinese Confucian elites.

These civilian elites mobilized themselves to form armies and command troops to fight the Taipings to the death in order to rescue the monarchical-imperial system and their own dominant class position within that system. The writings and proclamations of, for example, the Hunanese Zeng Guofan, the chief Qing defender and Taiping-slayer, who spent over a decade pursuing the extermination of the Taipings, left little doubt that he saw the contest between the Taipings and the Qing as a war of civilizations, Christian vs. Confucian. Zeng, in an 1854 proclamation, for example: "The [Taiping] bandits have stolen a few scraps from the foreign barbarians and worship the Christian religion...Scholars may not read the Confucian classics, for they have their so-called teachings of Jesus and the New Testament...This is not just a crisis for our Ch'ing dynasty, but the most extraordinary crisis of all time for the Confucian teachings..."[30] Zeng went on to rail against the sacrilegious and despicable destruction of temples and ancestral altars by the iconoclastic Taipings, and vowed in this public proclamation that he personally would "sleep on nettles" until he had exterminated them.[31] This attitude of Zeng Guofan was typical of those Confucian elites who remained loyal to the regime of a foreign occupier (the Manchus) despite its dysfunctionality, because of the ideological and cultural heterodoxy of the native Chinese Taipings – and that heterodoxy was viewed as Christianity, the same as that of the foreigners from the West. As a result, for decades after the fall of their capital Nanjing in 1864 and the wholesale slaughter by Zeng's Qing loyalists of as many Taiping adherents as possible, in the eyes of the elite the Taiping threat continued in the guise of foreign missionaries. And it is true that there were some links between Taipings and missionaries in south China during and after the rebellion. Two relatives of Hong Xiuquan worked closely with Hong Kong missionaries for a time.[32]

The Treaties (II)

Christianity and the second round of treaties, 1858–1860

Even as the Taiping Rebellion continued in the late 1850s, the Qing court was confronted with another military action by the British, this time including the French as well. The European powers were hoping to settle once and for all the issues left unresolved by the 1842–1844 treaties. These issues included, among others, the legal status of opium, foreign diplomatic representation at the court in Beijing, the levying of internal transit taxes on foreign goods, the constant pressure for the opening of more treaty ports including on inland waterways, opening up the entire country to foreign travel, and protection for Chinese Christians peaceably to practice their faith. It was the last two items that were of particular interest to missionaries in China and missionary agencies in Britain, France, and America. War broke out in 1856 between China and Britain, with the latter using a pretext to start the war. The French also joined, and their combined military, including British command under Lord Elgin, in 1858 forced the Chinese government to agree to a peace accord, the Treaty of Tianjin. This, like the treaties of 1842–1844, was lopsidedly unequal, with China giving all the concessions and the Europeans receiving all the benefits (and, due to the multiplier effect of the "most favored nation" clause in all the treaties, the Americans and other non-belligerents as well).[33] All of the diplomatic and commercial issues mentioned earlier were addressed and settled to the foreigners' advantage. Unrestricted travel outside the treaty ports was granted, and the right of Chinese to believe and practice Christianity was directly or indirectly included in all the treaties. The 1858 treaties, however, had no provision that in their travels throughout China foreigners could freely rent or purchase property wherever they pleased and erect buildings thereon.

There was no foreign inclination for a continuation of the war beyond 1858, but for the unwillingness of the Chinese Emperor Xianfeng and his court to ratify the Treaty of Tianjin and permit the changes for which it provided to be implemented. The emperor was especially adamant about foreign diplomatic representatives not being permitted to reside in Beijing. In 1859 when the British and French diplomats accompanied by a small military force returned ready to exchange official copies of the ratified treaties they were fired upon and repulsed by the Chinese coastal forts; then in 1860 a foreign negotiating party under a white flag was detained and some of them killed by the still-recalcitrant Chinese authorities. These acts of "treachery," as they were seen by the Europeans, brought Lord Elgin and several thousand British troops posthaste back to the China coast. They and a French force quickly marched to Beijing and on Elgin's orders systematically destroyed and burned the Yuanmingyuan, the Summer Palace northwest of the city which existed for the private enjoyment of the emperor and the royal family. The hapless Chinese court fled north beyond the Great Wall, to Chengde, while British and French troops occupied Beijing for a time. Prince Gong, the emperor's brother, stayed behind in Beijing and signed the Convention of Peking, a document that basically reaffirmed the terms of the Treaty of Tianjin of 1858 but added a few extra penalties, including an indemnity. It did, however, also include an important addition to the clause permitting foreign travel throughout the empire, which was added by the French (probably by Delamarre, a missionary who was the chief French interpreter) to one draft of the document and resulted, almost unknowingly, in general acceptance. This French maneuver reiterated more explicitly an 1846 Chinese promise to promulgate throughout the country toleration of Chinese Catholics and the restoration to custody of the French legation in Beijing of all buildings or property confiscated from Catholics earlier. But the phrase concerning unrestricted travel was expanded to include the words that it would be "permitted to French missionaries to rent and purchase land in all the provinces and to erect buildings thereon at pleasure."[34] This phrase was contested later by Chinese authorities, but it was for the most part implemented for both Catholics and Protestants, and resulted in a great many cases of conflict and local problems in the decades after 1860.

At any rate, thus was brought to nearly final form the treaty system, which was to remain in place for well over half a century to come with minimal further changes except for the increase in the number of designated treaty ports, the increased practical autonomy of the foreign territories, called "concessions," in the larger treaty ports, and the steady increase in the number of foreign residents living in the concessions.

Missions and the diplomacy of inequality

Looking back to 1839 from the vantage point of 1860, it seems evident that the foreign missionary community in China, though small, was not a simple bystander to the military and political events on the China coast during these years. First, they were substantial beneficiaries of the new framework of relationships between China and 'the West. Their longtime goal, to be able to go anywhere in the Chinese empire to preach the Gospel and to establish residences and other facilities including churches and schools, was substantially met by 1860. It is not surprising that there were no missionary protests in either the war of 1839–1842 or that of 1856–1860 against the means by which the British government and its military forces advanced foreign interests in China. Beyond this, however, the second factor is that they were not only beneficiaries of the results, but some were active participants in the process of forcing the treaty system on China. Actually the tradition of missionary involvement in Sino-foreign diplomacy and politics goes back to the Jesuits at court in the Qing dynasty, and the more than twenty-year employment of Protestant pioneer Robert Morrison as interpreter-translator for the BEIC from about 1810 to the 1830s. He also was a part of the British government's failed 1816 Amherst embassy to Beijing. Morrison was succeeded at the BEIC by his son John Robert Morrison after his father's death in 1834.

Some missionaries did considerably more than interpret or translate. During the Opium War, the ubiquitous Karl Gutzlaff was very busy from 1840 to 1843 working as interpreter for several British ships and for the government of Hong Kong. Most interesting was that the British military forces at various times installed Gutzlaff as civil magistrate for the occupation regimes in three important cities in central China – Dinghai, on Zhoushan (Chusan) Island off the Zhejiang coast; Ningbo, a commercial center in Zhejiang Province; and Zhenjiang (Chinkiang), a strategic city on the lower Yangzi River at the point where the Grand Canal, a crucial means of strategic transport, crosses the Yangzi on its way to the north.[35] This was a remarkable feat for a missionary, and it resulted in the Chinese in the areas in which Gutzlaff served viewing him with a combination of fear and awe. During his magistracy at Ningbo, a local poet wrote a poem about his regime, referring to him as "Daddy Guo":

Up to his high dais Daddy Guo comes.
If you are in trouble, He'll get things straight.
If you have been wronged, He'll come to the rescue,

If you have gotten into difficulties He'll arrange things for you.
He's a master at speaking the Chinese language,
Daddy Guo is nothing short of a genius![36]

Several American missionaries worked closely with the US government in its pursuit of its interests in China. Elijah Coleman Bridgman, who came to China in 1830 as the first American missionary and was editor of the respected *Chinese Repository,* became translator and adviser to Congressman Caleb Cushing and his diplomatic delegation to negotiate the first Sino-US treaty between 1842 and 1844. S. Wells Williams wrote the American bestselling book of the nineteenth century on China, then in the 1850s he joined Admiral Perry in his voyages to open Japan to foreign trade and intercourse. Later he served as secretary-interpreter to the US legation to China, in which position he helped to fashion the Treaty of Tianjin of 1858. He had resigned from the ABCFM in 1857. In 1862 he joined the US legation in Peking, where he served until 1876, several times acting as head of legation. A second US missionary, W. A. P. Martin, a Presbyterian who had come to Ningbo in 1850, also played an important role with Williams in the fashioning of the 1858 treaty. It was Williams and Martin who were adamant about including a paragraph in the American version of the treaty specifying freedom of both foreigners and Chinese converts to practice and teach Christianity anywhere in the interior. Ambassador Reed, the American envoy, was not disposed to be inflexible on this point, but Williams and Martin persuaded Reed to insist that it be included in the treaty.[37] Another example of missionary-government collaboration was Peter Parker, the pioneer medical missionary who came to China in 1834, and in 1844 succeeded Bridgman as part-time secretary and interpreter to the first US legation to China. He severed ties with the ABCFM in 1847, but continued work at his Canton hospital and a diplomatic role as US chargé d'affaires until 1855. After a brief sojourn in the US he returned to China in late 1855 as US commissioner plenipotentiary until his recall in 1857.[38]

What are we to make of this pattern of missionary service merging into and even being overshadowed by government service? Some scholars would not find anything particularly unusual or sinister about this phenomenon. It was a natural thing for governments sorely in need of language-competent fellow nationals in carrying out essential tasks of diplomacy and commerce to enlist the assistance of those citizens. And at the time, missionaries undoubtedly constituted the largest available group of potential translators and interpreters. At least this was still true in the mid nineteenth century.

Yet from the longer perspective, it is striking how natural it was for missionaries to enlist themselves in a project that essentially put China permanently in a handicapped position of inequality, unable to pursue her own national goals. What seemed a natural thing in 1860, however, 60 years on would be labeled "imperialism," with all the negative connotations that the term still has today. The missionaries of mid century saw only the furtherance of the cause of the Gospel in the edifice of the treaty system which had been erected by 1860. They plunged into institution-building with enthusiasm, expending increasing resources of personnel, finances, and material, as Chapter 4 will describe.

The Chinese role

What can be said of the body of Chinese Christians as of 1860? First, the Catholics: by this point most of the old Catholic strongholds dating back to the seventeenth century, such as those in Jiangnan between Shanghai and Suzhou, in Shandong Province, and in Zhili, had recovered their numbers and more.[39] In 1860 there may have been as many as 250,000 to 300,000 Catholics, mainly in rural areas and often living in communities that constituted entire villages or significant portions of a village. Catholic institutional endeavors were modest in aim: orphanages, a few simple clinics, primary schools. No names of widely recognized Chinese Catholic leaders have come down to us from these decades. Ma Xiangbo (1840–1939), a future important Catholic figure, in 1860 still had several years of training ahead to become a Jesuit priest.

Protestants were more urban than were Catholics, but there were precious few of them. There were only a few hundred Chinese Protestant converts before 1860, almost all in small congregations pastored by missionaries in one of the five treaty ports. There was only a handful of ordained Chinese, perhaps only two, and very few distinguished or notable Chinese Christians. Liang Fa, the first ordained Chinese, who had written the tract which had contributed to the inception of the Taiping Rebellion, had died in 1855. He Jinshan, the second Chinese Protestant to be ordained (1846), in 1860 was working as an LMS evangelist in Foshan, Guangdong Province, where he had been posted for years, but he would not become a pastor of the Foshan church until 1870, only a year before his death. A future important leader of the Chinese Anglican church, Yen Yung-king (Yan Yongjing), in 1860 was still an undergraduate at Kenyon College in Ohio, where he would graduate in 1861 and then return to China in 1862. Yen will appear again in Chapter 4.[40]

There were two important Christian laymen during these years, although they were not very active in church affairs. One was Yung Wing (1828–1912), who was educated at a school run by the wife of Karl Gutzlaff and then at the Morrison Education Society School in Hong Kong. After being taken to the US by one of his teachers, he graduated from Yale in 1854, became a naturalized US citizen, and returned to work in Hong Kong, Canton, and Shanghai.

Another was Wang Tao (1828–1897), a classically trained scholar and Christian convert who made a considerable impact on two of the major literary projects of the missionary community in the 1850s and 1860s. One was the Delegates' Version of the Bible, which was completed by a small subcommittee in Shanghai chaired by Walter Henry Medhurst working from 1847 to 1853. During the last year of this time Wang Tao was working closely with Medhurst as his Chinese teacher. Wang's biographer Paul Cohen believes that much of the credit for the felicity of this translation should go to Wang, because Medhurst was acknowledged by all to be the main shaper of the Delegates' Version.[41] The other major project was James Legge's monumental translation of the Chinese Classics. Legge had already published Volumes I and II of this huge work when Wang Tao came to Hong Kong and Legge hired him as assistant in 1862. The two men had a ten-year collaboration, three of them in Scotland, where they constituted an extremely effective translation and annotation team. Legge was quick in his praise for Wang's role, giving his Chinese partner credit for his major contribution to this remarkably durable translation which, after almost 150 years, is still considered to be one of the best. Such explicit commendation also appeared in the published volumes. When Legge became Oxford's first Chair of Chinese in 1877, he invited Wang Tao to return to Britain and join him, but by this time Wang was well into a career as a journalist, and declined.[42]

Conclusion

This brief overview of the events of mid century leaves us with the conclusion that one of the most important developments for Christianity in these years was the embedding of itself into the developing treaty system as the framework of its own existence in China. This was true for Chinese Christians as well as foreign missionaries, because the space to exist of the former was based on the legal status of the latter. After this point, it became increasingly difficult to imagine Christianity being present in any other political and legal context. In this regard as in many others, China's experience can be profitably compared with that of Japan. Japan was entirely successful in limiting the influence of foreign missionaries after the late 1800s, China was not. Another conclusion is that the most important single event of these decades was the Taiping Rebellion. For decades to come, the Taiping experience shaped Chinese government and elite perceptions of Christianity, and gave an example (albeit an untypical one, perhaps) of what an indigenized Christianity might look like in China. Indeed, a century and a half after the Taipings, several of today's sectarian movements in the countryside deriving from Protestantism bear some resemblance to them, in my opinion.

Notes

1. Morrison has been somewhat neglected as a research topic in recent decades, but he is well served by a new biography by Christopher Hancock, *Robert Morrison and the Birth of Chinese Protestantism* (London: T&T Clark, 2008).

2. The best work on him is Jessie Gregory Lutz, *Opening China: Karl F. A. Gutzlaff and Sino-Western Relations, 1827–1852* (Grand Rapids, MI: Wm. B. Eerdmans, 2008).

3. The ABCFM was formed in 1810; it sent missionaries first to the Middle East, India, and the Sandwich Islands (Hawai'i), only in 1830 making its first assignment to China.

4. Among Bridgman's Chinese writings was a short history and geography of the United States. Fred W. Drake, "Protestant Geography in China: E. C. Bridgman's Portrayal of the West," in *Christianity in China: Early Protestant Missionary Writings*, ed. Suzanne Wilson Barnett and John King Fairbank (Cambridge, MA: Council on East Asian Studies, 1985), pp. 89–106.

5. S. Wells Williams, *The Middle Kingdom*, 2 vols. (New York: Putnam, 1848, rev. ed. 1883).

6. For two very different portraits: Edward V. Gulick, *Peter Parker and the Opening of China* (Cambridge, MA: Harvard University Press, 1973); and Jonathan Spence, *To Change China: Western Advisers in China 1620–1960* (New York: Penguin, 1969, 1980), pp. 34–56.

7. There were many other provisions of the early treaties, of course, but none impacting directly on the Christian endeavor in China. Ironically, although the French treaty provided that old churches should be returned to the Catholics, it was still illegal for French missionaries to go beyond the environs of the treaty ports – a rule routinely ignored by Catholic missionaries, accustomed as they were to sneaking into China.

8. A look at establishing basic missions apparatus in Fuzhou in the 1840s and after is Ellsworth C. Carlson, *The Foochow Missionaries, 1847–1880* (Cambridge, MA: Harvard University, East Asian Research Center, 1974).

9. Here I am thinking of the American Presbyterian Press, already important by 1860, and later the Christian Literature Society, One of several works on these is Adrian A. Bennett, M*issionary Journalist in China: Young J. Allen and his Magazines* (Athens, GA: University of Georgia Press, 1983).

10. Suzanne Wilson Barnett and John King Fairbank, eds., *Christianity in China: Early Protestant Missionary Writings* (Cambridge, MA: Committee on American-East Asian Relations, Dept. of History, Harvard University, 1985).

11. For the Medhurst–Gutzlaff version, Jost Oliver Zetzsche, *The Bible in China: The History of the Union Version or the Culmination of Protestant Missionary Bible Translation in China* (Sankt Augustin, Ger.: Institut Monumenta Serica, 1999), pp. 72–74.

12. Tianzhu was never seriously considered by Protestants.

13. "Classical" means shorter, using fewer characters for the same thing, and using a specialized vocabulary and grammar not used in the vernacular.

14. Jost Oliver Zetzsche, *The Bible in China: The History of the Union Version or the Culmination of Protestant Missionary Bible Translation in China* (Sankt Augustin, Germany: Institut Monumenta Serica, 1999), covers the Delegates' Version and the Union Version in some detail.

15. The best study is Norman J. Girardot, *The Victorian Translation of China: James Legge's Oriental Pilgrimage* (Berkeley: University of California Press, 2002).

16. One who heard Gutzlaff in England during his last tour and was greatly influenced in his own China missions career was Hudson Taylor, founder of the China Inland Mission.

17. See Jessie Gregory Lutz, *Opening China: Karl F. A. Gutzlaff and Sino-Western Relations, 1827–1852* (Grand Rapids, MI: Wm. B. Eerdmans, 2008), for Gutzlaff's role and his fate.

18. Several examples are in Jessie G. Lutz and Rolland Ray Lutz, *Hakka Chinese Confront Protestant Christianity, 1850–1900* (Armonk, NY: M.E. Sharpe, 1998). Also a good summary is in R.G. Tiedemann, "Indigenous Agency, Religious Protectorates, and Chinese Interests: The Expansion of Christianity in Nineteenth-Century China," in Dana L. Robert, ed., *Converting Colonialism: Visions and Realities in Mission History, 1706–1914* (Grand Rapids, MI: Wm. B. Eerdmans, 2008), pp. 206–241.

19. Articles on Venn and Anderson, by Wilbert R. Shenk and R. Pierce Beaver, respectively, in G. Anderson *et al.*, eds., *Mission Legacies: Biographical Studies of Leaders of the Modern Missionary Movement* (Maryknoll, NY: Orbis Books, 1994).

20. The Protestant movement in S. Korea in the twentieth century also very self-consciously applied the three-self principles to its situation.

21. Carl T. Smith, *Chinese Christians: Elites, Middlemen, and the Church in Hong Kong* (Hong Kong: Oxford University Press, 1985).

22. The Jesuits as an order had been abolished by Rome in 1773, but re-established in 1824. It must be said that the nineteenth century Jesuits fell well short of those of the seventeenth century in quality of education and in breadth of spirit. For the Virgins, see Robert E. Entenmann, "Christian Virgins in Eighteenth Century Sichuan," in *Christianity in China: From the Eighteenth Century to the Present*, ed. Daniel H. Bays (Stanford, CA: Stanford University Press, 1996), pp. 180–193.

23. David E. Mungello, "The Return of the Jesuits to China in 1841 and the Chinese Christian backlash," *Sino-Western Cultural Relations Journal* XXVII (2005), pp. 9–46. For more use of these documents, Xiaojuan Huang, "Christian Communities and Alternative Devotions in China" (Ph.D. dissertation, Princeton U., 2005).

24. R. G. Tiedemann, "Indigenous Agency, Religious Protectorates, and Chinese Interests: The Expansion of Christianity in Nineteenth-Century China," in *Converting Colonialism: Visions and Realities in Mission History, 1706–1914*, ed. Dana L. Robert (Grand Rapids, MI: Wm. B. Eerdmans, 2008), pp. 217–218.

25. A full version of this is in Pei-kai Cheng and Michael Lestz, *The Search for Modern China, A Documentary Collection* (New York: Norton, 1999), pp. 139–143.

26. Jonathan D. Spence, *God's Chinese Son: The Taiping Heavenly Kingdom of Hong Xiuquan* (New York: W.W. Norton, 1996), pp. 192–209.

27. Many insights into Hong's thought are in Jonathan D. Spence, *God's Chinese Son: The Taiping Heavenly Kingdom of Hong Xiuquan* (New York: W.W. Norton, 1996). Pages 255–261 have examples of Hong's excising from the Bible or rewriting what he considered scandalous parts of several Old Testament stories, including Noah's drunkenness, incest between Judah and Tamar, and Jacob's deception of Isaac to steal Esau's birthright.

28. This is extensively argued in Thomas A. Reilly, *The Taiping Heavenly Kingdom: Rebellion and the Blasphemy of Empire* (Seattle: University of Washington Press, 2004).

29. For some stimulating ideas here, see Joseph R. Levenson, *Confucian China and its Modern Fate,* Vol. 2, *The Problem of Monarchical Decay* (Berkeley, CA: University of California Press, 1964), pp. 87–118.

30. From Pei-kai Cheng and Michael Lestz, with Jonathan D. Spence, *The Search for Modern China: A Documentary Collection* (New York: W.W. Norton, 1999), pp. 147–148.

31. Pei-kai Cheng and Michael Lestz, with Jonathan D. Spence, *The Search for Modern China: A Documentary Collection* (New York: W.W. Norton, 1999), p. 148.

32. R. G. Tiedemann, "Indigenous Agency, Religious Protectorates, and Chinese Interests: The Expansion of Christianity in Nineteenth-Century China," in *Converting Colonialism: Visions and Realities in Mission History, 1706–1914,* ed. Dana L. Robert (Grand Rapids, MI: Wm. B. Eerdmans, 2008), pp. 226–227.

33. The US and Russia both also signed treaties at Tianjin in 1858.

34. Kenneth Scott Latourette, *A History of Christian Missions in China* (London: SPCK, 1929), p. 276.

35. See discussion of these fascinating episodes in Arthur Waley, *The Opium War Through Chinese Eyes* (New York: George Allen & Unwin, 1958), Ch. 5; in Peter Ward Fay, *The Opium War, 1840–1842* (Chapel Hill: University of North Carolina Press, 1975); and Jessie Gregory Lutz, *Opening China: Karl F. A. Gutzlaff and Sino-Western Relations, 1827–1852* (Grand Rapids, MI: Wm. B. Eerdmans, 2008), *passim*.

36. Arthur Waley, *The Opium War Through Chinese Eyes* (New York: George Allen & Unwin, 1958), p. 230. The poem goes on for several more stanzas. Gutzlaff's Chinese name was Guo Shili.

37. Kenneth Scott Latourette, *A History of Christian Missions in China* (London: SPCK, 1929), p. 275.

38. Jonathan D. Spence, *To Change China: Western Advisers in China 1620–1960* (New York: Penguin, 1980), pp. 54–56, has a deft portrait of Parker's decline into frustration, bitterness, and belligerence by 1857.

39. Actually the Jiangnan community was delayed in its recovery by the devastation of the Taiping Rebellion, which laid waste to the wealth of many Catholic communities and which was still raging in 1860.

40. The careers of Liang, He, and Yan are described in Zha Shijie, *Zhongguo Jidujiao renwu xiaozhuan* (biographies of leading Chinese Christians) (Taipei: Chinese Evangelical Seminary Press, 1983), pp. 1–4, 9–14, 27–32.

41. Paul A. Cohen, *Between Tradition and Modernity: Wang T'ao and Reform in Late Ch'ing China* (Cambridge, MA: Harvard University Press, 1974), pp. 22–23.

42. Paul A. Cohen, *Between Tradition and Modernity: Wang T'ao and Reform in Late Ch'ing China* (Cambridge, MA: Harvard University Press, 1974), pp. 59–61.

4

Expansion and Institution-Building in a Declining Dynasty, 1860–1902

Prologue

The custodians of Chinese history in China today, the propaganda organs of the Party and the state, have long memories, at any rate longer than that of the Vatican. On October 1, 2001, China's national day, when the Party leads the country in celebration of the founding of the PRC in 1949, and almost everyone receives a week's vacation, the Holy See announced the beatification of more than one hundred foreign martyrs, mostly clergy, slain by the "Boxers" in the anti-foreign and anti-Christian violence of the summer of 1900. This statement from Rome elicited a scathing denunciation of the Vatican by the Chinese government for "hurting the feelings of the Chinese people," as well as a gratuitous accusation that all these murdered missionaries were just imperialists anyway, and deserved to die. This incident symbolizes very well the ambiguous role and legacy of Christian missions and Chinese Christianity in modern Chinese history. At no time in Chinese Christian history was the problem of violence being directed at missionaries and Christians more salient than during the four-plus decades covered in this chapter. Yet this was also a time when the young Chinese Protestant church, and in different ways the Roman Catholic church as well, put down roots of community that constituted a solid foundation for the future.

A New History of Christianity in China, First Edition. Daniel H. Bays.
© 2012 Daniel H. Bays. Published 2012 by Blackwell Publishing Ltd.

This period of more than 40 years was marked by rapid growth of the foreign missionary establishment and, for Protestants, a more diverse spectrum of mission organizations present in China by the end of the century. The Chinese Protestant church also grew rapidly in percentage terms, though in absolute numbers it was still tiny, approximately 100,000 communicants in 1900. During these decades several Protestant urban congregations served by Chinese pastors developed the capacity to support themselves financially and to operate on their own, without being under close mission supervision. In fact during these years Protestant Christianity became a true Sino-foreign endeavor, though the role of the Chinese was often in the shadows.

There was growth among Roman Catholics as well, but fewer cases of real Chinese and foreign cooperation. The Catholic missionaries were more often than their Protestant colleagues likely to be involved in the recurring *jiaoan* ("missionary cases" or "missionary incidents") that were a great irritant in Sino-Western relations during these decades. And the European, mainly French, hierarchy in the Chinese church maintained a fairly airtight control, denying the Chinese priests a voice in managing church affairs, despite the fact that their role in the growing church was essential.

Broad Patterns of the Times

There was an immediate reaction to the clauses of the 1858–1860 treaties which opened the entire country to foreigners' travel, to their acquisition of property by rental or purchase, and to the erection of buildings thereon. This affected the Protestants the most. First, new missionaries set up new operations in the half-dozen additional internal riverine cities which had been designated as official "treaty ports" in the recent diplomatic agreements. Thus, for example, the Welshman Griffith John (1831–1912) of the London Missionary Society (LMS), in late 1861 relocated from Shanghai to Hankou, gateway city and entrepot of the central Yangzi River valley, to set up an LMS station there. Hankou, while it was not actually the provincial capital of Hubei Province, was the dominant economic force of the tri-cities, which also included Hanyang and Wuchang, the latter being the provincial capital and also seat of the governor-general who supervised both Hubei and Hunan – the province directly to the south. Griffith John and an LMS colleague, R. Wilson, made their first trip to Hankou in June 1861, and established the LMS station in October. Two of John's children and Mr. Wilson died in the first year, and Mrs. John and Mrs. Wilson took their remaining children home to the UK. Now the only Protestant missionary in all the tri-cities, John urged the English Wesleyan Methodist Missionary Society (WMMS) to assign a missionary to Wuhan. Later in 1862 Josiah

Cox was sent to Hankou by the WMMS. Within a year much-needed additional missionaries were sent to Hankou/Wuchang by both of the two societies. Later in the 1860s the American Protestant Episcopal Church (Anglicans) began their mission in Wuhan, and the CIM and yet others did so after 1870. Indeed, in the years after 1860 all over China the number of Protestant missionaries in China exploded, from barely 100 in 1860 to almost 3500 in 1905.[1] It was an astounding increase, considering that it had taken more than 50 years from Morrison's arrival in 1807 for the number to reach 100. These 3500 now represented dozens of missionary societies, some of which focused their efforts solely on China, and some of which, despite few personnel and a thin resource base, used extensive publicity and sometimes romantic depictions of events and achievements in their publications.

This massive increase in Protestant missions was partly due to the increasingly efficient and professionalized mission societies based in the homelands of Europe and North America.[2] While this process characterized most of the denominational societies with missionaries in China, some reacted negatively to this twin process of bureaucratization and institutionalization of the mission, both on the mission field and in the home office. One who did so was J. Hudson Taylor (1832–1905).[3] Taylor, from Yorkshire, England, went to China in the 1850s inspired by Karl Gutzlaff on one of the latter's stirring European tours, but had to return to England in 1859 for health reasons. After thinking through several issues in missions strategy, in 1865 he founded the China Inland Mission (CIM). From the start, the CIM was a 'faith mission" (that is, no finances guaranteed, and no real budget; all confidence was placed in God's provision). The CIM had other practices and policies which were unprecedented, some of them at first controversial:

- Taylor appointed mainly laypersons, not ordained clergy, as missionaries.
- The CIM avoided creating large operations in cities, seeking to penetrate the countryside and unreached places;
- As a result of the non-urban strategy, the CIM developed relatively few schools, hospitals, printing establishments, and other institutions.
- The CIM was the first mission to adopt the practice of wearing native dress as a general policy.
- Taylor's was among the first missions to accept large numbers of single women as missionaries, even sending some of them to work in the countryside with no males accompanying them. This was seen as scandalous by many at the time.
- The power structure of the CIM evolved into the primacy of a China-based "council" or headquarters based in Shanghai, not in London or elsewhere in the West.

Taylor's first group of 22 missionaries, none of them ordained, went to China with him in 1866. Taylor's system, as well as his personal charisma, increased the CIM to 322 missionaries in 1888 and 825 in 1905. By that time it was almost three times larger than the next largest group, the British Church Missionary Society (CMS).

Like Karl Gutzlaff in the 1840s, Taylor excited audiences in the UK and North America in the late 1860s and beyond. His pleas on behalf of the unsaved Chinese moved many to respond. The middle and lower middle class evangelical recruiting base of the CIM was broadened by Taylor's success in recruiting seven aristocratic young Cambridge graduates, the "Cambridge Seven," to join the mission in 1884.[4] This event, "one of the grand heroic gestures in nineteenth-century missions," catapulted the CIM "from comparative obscurity to an almost embarrassing prominence."[5] The CIM, ever alert for good press, made the most of "the Seven" by sending them on tours all over England, Scotland, and Ireland before they embarked for China. Taylor also worked closely with YMCAs and YWCAs, and the publicity machinery of the CIM based in London churned out very effective publications, such as its widely distributed magazine, *China's Millions*. All of this fueled the stunning growth of the CIM.

Institution-building

A strong compulsion to establish and operate in China the main institutions of "Christian civilization" (meaning "Western civilization") characterized the Protestant China missionaries after 1860. With only a few exceptions (such as Hudson Taylor's CIM), they plunged into building, organizing, and regularizing not only schools but an entire educational system capped by "colleges" (at the level of secondary schools until the twentieth century).[6] Statistics gathered in 1906, in preparation for the centennial conference of 1907, revealed 57,000 students in more than 2500 Protestant schools. Missionaries were also persevering providers and improvers of medical care. Hundreds of physicians were appointed as medical missionaries (300 were in China in 1905), a third of them women; and by the turn of the century there were training sites for Chinese nurses and other medical personnel. To deliver care, some large (and expensive) modern hospitals were built and staffed by highly qualified physicians and researchers. Another humanitarian vocation which called forth the commitment of several missionaries was famine relief. The famine in North China in the late 1870s was so bad that dozens of missionaries took leave of their normal jobs and moved to the famine districts of Shanxi Province west of Beijing. Some of these, such as Timothy Richard and David Hill – being fluent in Chinese – increasingly had contact and interaction with the local elite class in the famine districts. Working jointly with the missionaries in relief activities, some members of the elite class softened their hostility to the missionaries, and popular agitation against them in these areas abated.[7]

Other institutional developments that underpinned the Protestant missionary effort in these decades were in the areas of printing, translations, and journalism. Some missions, especially the US Presbyterians, who expanded their Shanghai printing press to a large capacity, stressed publication of not only Bibles, shorter portions of scripture, and religious items such as devotional materials, but a considerable number of secular works as well, including many translations of Western treatises on science, law, and other subjects.[8] Translations were also commissioned by Chinese government offices.[9] Missionary scholars remained active in writing language texts and reference works for academic work on Chinese history and society, such as A Dictionary of Chinese Buddhist Terms.[10] From the 1860s on, missionary journalism flourished in the larger treaty port cities. The monthly missions English-language ecumenical publication, The Chinese Recorder, was published in Shanghai from 1867 to 1941. It was the publication of record for the missions community. In Chinese, the Christian newspaper with the most national circulation was the Jiaohui xinbao (The Church News), 1868–1874, edited in Shanghai by the American Southern Methodist missionary Young J. Allen, which was aimed at a Christian audience. Allen changed gears and in 1874 established instead the Wanguo gongbao (The Globe magazine), with coverage of world and national events, and some opinion pieces, intended to appeal to a broader Chinese audience.[11] It was published until well after 1900.

Thus the single most impressive visible result of the missionary labors of the late nineteenth century was the laying of an impressive institutional foundation upon which, it was expected, the Chinese church would build. Looking back more than a century, it is clear that an imposing edifice of institutions, constituting a substantial investment of human and financial resources, was in place by the early 1900s. This achievement was directly related to the fact that the late 1800s generation of China missionaries included many high achievers and strong personalities who lived long lives in China.

Ideologies

Even as the Protestant missionaries grew rapidly in number in the late nineteenth century, and were becoming more diverse in many ways, they remained substantially unified in terms of their basic theology and goals. This was evident in the three great nationwide missionary conferences which took place, all in Shanghai, in 1877, 1890, and 1907. In each, a large percentage of all the missionaries in China attended; almost no Chinese delegates or observers were present – I will discuss this later in the chapter. The diversity of views in the missions community and open disagreement on matters ranging from the value of schools to the use of Biblewomen, from which is the best Chinese translation of the Bible to the proper attitude to assume toward China's native religions, are clearly evident in the "records" of the three conferences.[12] But also evident in those records is an underlying consensus on the basics of theology and sociopolitical assumptions. Not a single missionary society refused to attend any of the conferences, including that of 1907, by which time serious disagreements were rife among missionaries, but the old nineteenth-century consensus still held. It was not until the 1920s that irreparable splits appeared.[13]

With very few exceptions, one thing that the Protestant missions community continued to hold in common throughout the rest of the nineteenth century was the certain conviction that China needed not only Christ, but the norms of Western culture as well. This was a holistic approach which took for granted the identity of Christianity and the cultural-social forms in which it came. This rather triumphalist assumption rejected the views of the two mid century missions executives, Rufus Anderson (US) and Henry Venn (UK), who strongly believed that missions should bring Christ to the culture, and that Christ could dwell in any culture. The few missionaries who liked the "three-self" formula and advocated rapid movement toward native agency were clearly in the minority. These included John Nevius, US Presbyterian (North) of Shandong Province, who was largely ignored in China but made a big impact on the strategy of missionaries in Korea soon after 1900. Indeed the "Nevius method" is still today revered as one of the secrets of twentieth-century Korean church growth. But in the post-US Civil War decades, missionary bodies, and missionaries themselves, were not hesitant to claim a more expansive goal.

Using what William Hutchison has called a "moral equivalent for imperialism," the late nineteenth and early twentieth centuries saw a radical expansion of the missionary goal – not just to save the heathen soul, but to remake his world.[14] As Arthur H. Smith (1845–1932), longtime American missionary in Shandong Province, wrote in the conclusion to his book *Chinese Characteristics* (first published 1890):

> In order to reform China the springs of character must be reached and purified...What China needs is righteousness, and in order to attain it, it is absolutely necessary that she have a knowledge of God and a new conception of man, as well as of the relation of man to God. She needs a new life in every individual soul, in the family, and in society. The manifold needs of China we find, then, to be a single imperative need. It will be met permanently, completely, only by Christian civilization.[15]

Left unspoken here, though sometimes stated directly, is the assumption that the most appropriate model for "Christian civilization" was in the West, and that it was practitioners and purveyors of this model, i.e. the missionary cadre in China, that should be careful about prematurely transferring authority to Chinese Christian leadership. The missionaries wanted to be sure that their Chinese successors did things the same way that they had.

The Student Volunteer Movement

Institutions and ideology came together as mutually reinforcing in the Student Volunteer Movement. The impulse toward systematic institutionalization of China mission modernizing projects, plus the confidence of two or three generations of American college students and recent graduates that they could help those in need and should do so out of Christian duty, produced a unique phenomenon at the end of the century. The Student Volunteer Movement for Foreign Missions (SVM) added a dynamic element to the development of Christian missions in China and in fact all over the world.[16] Formed in the late 1880s, the SVM, with its astoundingly ambitious watchword "the evangelization of the world in this generation," played a major role in recruiting and directing to the foreign mission field thousands of college-educated, idealistic young Americans. Between 1890 and 1920, over 33,000 young people signed the pledge card of the SVM stating that "It is my purpose, if God permit, to become a foreign missionary." About a quarter of them, over 8000, actually took up missions posts, and more went to China than to any other mission field.[17] The SVM was not itself a sending society, but worked with all Protestant missions, from the CIM to the Episcopalians. A large percentage of the China SVM appointees went to the mission field as teachers.

With skilled leaders such as John R. Mott (1865–1955) and Sherwood Eddy (1871–1963), who were good public speakers and well networked into social circles with access to resources, the SVM was a rousing success for nearly three decades. This cadre of capable, well-educated young people arrived in China and other mission fields with clear normative assumptions concerning religious conversion, the characteristics of a Christian life and of a "Christian society," as well as ideas about the nature of a liberal arts education. For those who came to teach at Christian middle schools and colleges, naturally these assumptions affected the schools where they taught.

Its main impact on China was in the years after 1900, but the SVM was already well before 1900 facilitating the linkups between its members and various mission agencies who were recruiting new personnel. The Young Men's Christian Association (YMCA) and the Young Women's Christian Association (YWCA) movement, which was established in China at about the same time that the SVM was picking up steam, that is the 1890s, would become one of the primary beneficiaries of SVM activism on US college campuses. Before 1900 only a handful of Chinese YMCA and YWCSs had been formed, but that formed a foundation for rapid growth after 1900.

Roman Catholics

After the return to China of the European missionaries and the subjugation by them of what they viewed as obstreperous cases of autonomous behavior among the Chinese faithful, the Catholic church, while continuing to grow, did not change much. The Europeans were very much in charge. The Catholics were short of priests; the size of the church outstripped trained personnel. There were available more Western than Chinese priests, and the former yielded very little power to the latter. One of the brightest Catholic intellects of his generation and gifted in many other ways, Ma Xiangbo (Ma Liang, 1840–1939) went through training and was ordained a Jesuit priest in 1870. He was part of a distinguished old Shanghai Catholic family dating back several generations, his own father was head of a school, and Ma himself was an incredibly talented man, with high hopes for a life in the church. But there he came up against the iron grip on power in the church maintained by the European priests, especially the French. Although he had as good an education as any of them, they refused to accept him as an equal. After many conflicts with his superiors, Ma left the priesthood in 1879, and became an important figure in reformist political and educational circles well into his 90s, and himself remained a faithful Catholic withal.[18] Ma Xiangbo's story was symptomatic of the wastage of indigenous talent by the Catholic church in China during these decades. As a result it actually left the front-line job of evangelizing and making the church grow to those local lay leaders and/or catechists who had been performing it for decades.

The depth of the suspicion and mistrust which the European clergy had for their Chinese colleagues is sometimes striking. As R. G. Tiedemann has pointed out regarding the late nineteenth century, "Clearly, by 1880 a significant attitudinal shift had occurred in the missionary community with regard to native agency, with the emphasis on subordination rather than partnership."[19] European priests' commentary on Chinese priests included such phrases as "unreliable, Lazy, hypocritical, proud, arrogant, ungrateful, miserly, and false."[20] Some Protestant missionaries also had negative views of their Chinese co-workers, but the Catholic case seems extreme.[21] To this situation must be added the failure of the Vatican to consecrate a single Chinese bishop since 1676, over 200 years earlier. This in particular was a very sore point for Chinese Catholics, one not addressed until the 1920s.

Jiaoan and Issues of Local Violence

The Chinese elite, or Confucian scholar–official class, made a supreme and in the end successful effort to save the Qing dynasty from the hated "Christian" Taipings. After the rebellion was finally quelled in 1864, the elite suffered a "Taiping hangover" for years or even decades. The Qing court and Chinese officials in Beijing (where foreign envoys could reside after 1860) and the treaty ports had no choice but to defer to the special treatment and privileges that now accrued to virtually all foreigners in China. They did not like Christianity. They thought it a seditious doctrine but had to tolerate it, lest foreign, especially French, political or military power be mobilized. For it was clear that France, despite very thin grounding in the treaties, had declared itself protector of all Catholic missions in China, not just French Catholic missionaries, and was willing to be quite aggressive in exercising its self-proclaimed role. The open-endedness of the scenarios under which the French government (or for that matter any of the Western governments) might take unilateral action to protect foreign lives and property was sobering. Those officials in close proximity to Western military or diplomatic power, therefore, were acutely aware of the treaty rights of foreigners, and did not welcome incidents involving alleged obstructions of Westerners' exercise of their treaty rights.

This situation was aggravated by an imperial edict of 1862 in response to a longstanding French demand, that Chinese Christians be exempt from taxes or subscriptions to support local "pagan festivals" and celebrations.[22] The result of this measure was that in villages where Christians resided, if they refused to pay the usual subscription for an opera company to put on a show at the village temple on the grounds that this was part of a "pagan festival," either their neighbors' costs would rise or the village would have to make do with lower-cost entertainment. The rub was that if, as often happened, the Christians snuck in to the performance anyway, or sat just outside listening, their fellow villagers would understandingly be angry and harsh words or violence might ensue. There was also (again at French demand) an imperial reiteration of the 1840s order that old (eighteenth-century) Catholic properties confiscated at a time when Christianity was proscribed now be returned to the Catholic church (actually, turned over to the custody of the French government representative). The potential for rumor, misinformation, outright fraud, forgery of deeds or other documents resulting in outraged commoners and perplexed officials in these often-complex property cases was almost limitless. The combined headache of just these two factors, the "pagan festival" issue and the "return of property" issue, was immense. Such cases were ubiquitous and frequent.[23]

In smaller cities and towns, and in the countryside, Western treaty rights were not so readily respected, either by the local elite or sometimes by local officials. In cities without a missions presence, the first missionaries to try to establish themselves were often resisted; the rental or purchase of property could be delayed indefinitely or obstructed, and the local elite sometimes mobilized mobs to stone or shout down the aspiring foreign settlers. In places that already had missions present, at times the elite circulated scurrilous placards or pamphlets accusing the missionaries of cannibalism; vile, unnatural sex acts; kidnapping children and gouging out their eyes to make medicine; and other nefarious behaviors.[24] One can infer from the features of typical Catholic religious life where these stories and rumors came from and why they were so persistent—priests hearing confessions, the mysterious ritual of the body and the blood, and especially the Catholic practice of infant baptism of sick or abandoned infants. But at any rate the rumors were remarkably persistent well into the twentieth century. They were all over north China before and during the Boxer Uprising.[25] Like the "Protocols of Zion" in Europe, these ideas had life of their own. In the newly-established People's Republic of China after 1949 there was a sharp and nasty anti-Catholic campaign which did not shrink from trotting out these same old stereotypes of Catholics.[26]

Why were the elite so implacably opposed to the missionaries? One reason was, as I have claimed above, the "hangover" from the Taipings, who were ideologically anathema to the elite. But another reason was the reality that the missionaries were, at bottom, a threat to the cultural hegemony of the elite all across China. John K. Fairbank once said that "missionaries and the gentry (elite) were as naturally enemies as cats and dogs."[27] The elite held economic, social, ideological, and political hegemony in local society, and the very missionary presence was an affront to their dignity and a threat to their status. Missionaries were literate, they established schools, and because of the treaties they often had better direct access to the nearest government official than did the local elite. Since they could not be touched because of the treaties and extraterritoriality, sometimes they attracted the allegiance of commoners involved in lawsuits who used the connection with the mission to their advantage in court. Or they used their links to the mission to claim exemption from contributions to village "pagan festivals," for example a visit by an opera troupe to which the entire village traditionally subscribed. The result was that the last four decades of the nineteenth century witnessed a more or less constant stream of incidents of violence – the elite denouncing Christianity as heterodox and un-Chinese, the commoners angry at the special treatment and privileges accorded part of the local community, which demolished the ritual "wholeness" of the community itself.[28]

There is not total agreement among scholars on the role of the elite in fomenting these frequent cases of violence. It can be argued that much of the tension in local communities was a natural thing, with lineages and other social or economic groups vying for advantage in a situation of scarce resources, and the Christians were just one more participant in this process.[29] Nevertheless, the incidents continued, and foreign diplomatic complaints and demands resulting from these events eventually filled many storage cabinets in the archives of the Zongli yamen, the equivalent of the foreign office of the dynasty. One of the most shocking incidents was the "Tianjin massacre" (as foreigners called it) in the summer of 1870. The combination of months of rumors of vile deeds and sexual perversions among the French Catholics in Tianjin, both missionaries and converts, and a massive new cathedral built on the site of an imperial temple, provided a volatile atmosphere. The spark was given by the rash behavior of the French consul, who, trying to play his role as protector of Catholics, lost his temper and fired his pistol at a government magistrate. The surrounding crowd exploded in violence; the consul, several merchants and their wives, and ten sisters at a nearby convent were slain – altogether 19, 16 of them French. France exacted a high price in compensation, an indemnity plus punishment of the alleged perpetrators by execution or exile, and a humiliating mission of apology to France.[30]

Some high officials in the Qing government, In particular the ministers of the Zongli yamen, saw quite clearly the causes of the general problem. In an 1878 circular to China's ministers abroad, the Zongli yamen made a very astute and perceptive analysis of the major troublesome aspects of the treaties with the West. In addition to problems caused by taxation disputes, extra-territoriality, and the "most favored nation" clause, much discussion was given to the "missionary question." The chief problems identified were the arrogation of official status to themselves by some missionaries and their interference in local government, and the refusal of Chinese converts to abide by the laws of China. This document expressed hope for addressing these issues in treaty revision talks with the Western powers in a spirit of "reciprocal consideration and mutual forbearance."[31] Yet there was never a chance of such treaty revision for several decades to come. China had virtually no leverage to use on the Western powers. Even a Herculean effort by Japan under its new Meiji government in the 1870s and 1880s to reform its laws and social structure to come up to Western standards barely succeeded in treaty revision and equality for Japan. If anything, Western power in China entrenched itself even more securely in the late 1800s and early 1900s. The pattern of aggressive missionaries, volatile crowds of commoners, and a hostile anti-Christian elite, continued to create incidents, with much property damage and occasional loss of life. There were riots and casualties in Chongqing, Sichuan Province, in the 1890s, and an especially bad incident with the loss of several missionary lives in Gutian, Fujian Province, in 1895. Even as late as 1906, by which time such events were becoming much less frequent, there was a major popular violent upheaval in Nanchang, the capital of Jiangxi Province.[32]

Chinese Christians and the Making of a Chinese Church?

It is easier to describe the foreign missionary presence in China before 1900 than it is to draw an accurate picture of the Chinese church, that is, the Chinese Christian converts. The Christian community was small relative to China's size but not insignificant in absolute numbers. Catholics continued to add steadily to their numbers, and the number of Catholic Christians was 700–800,000 by 1900. Protestants were much fewer, but there had only been a few hundred in 1860 and this had grown to about 100,000 by 1900. Why did even this many Chinese willingly affiliate with foreigners and their religion when the government and elite were so hostile to Christianity during these decades? There is a substantial literature on religious conversion by scholars such as Robert Hefner and Lewis Rambo, but I am not going to rehearse it.[33] For our purposes, a recent essay by R. G. Tiedemann presents a useful approach. He answers the question "why did Chinese Christians convert?" with a three-fold answer: 1) material incentives; 2) sociopolitical incentives; and 3) spiritual incentives.[34] Material incentives could mean getting a job at the missionary compound, as cook, doorman, gardener, language tutor, household servant, and such; but could also include access to Western-style medical care, help in a lawsuit, or benefitting from famine relief distributions of food by the mission. Some of the material benefits were enjoyed by the whole community. Building of chapels, churches, missionary homes and schools, all created economic activity which certainly benefitted some in the community. And the ability for the Christian community to opt out of the payments for village opera and other "pagan" activities reduced one's annual budget for ceremonial expenses, even as it may have threatened the social integration of the village.

Sociopolitical incentives, the second category, included formation of a cohesive interest group to fight for access to resources or power at the local level. A small, weak lineage, or those on the margin of a large powerful one, might do better in the competition for resources – both tangible resources and symbolic ones – if it were identified as Christian. That would be especially true if a nearby missionary was wont to intervene in the magistrate's court on behalf of his flock. In fact, that was a reasonable expectation for a local group of Christians to make in the context of local conflict and competition for resources by large, powerful lineages, salt smugglers, bandits, religious sectarians, landlords with their private armies of thugs, and so forth. The same principle applied to the role of the Chinese pastor: in the hyper-competitive world of late-nineteenth-century China, in many cases the lay members of the congregation or the parish would have thought either the mission or the Chinese clergy negligent if in disputes, even lawsuits, they had not tried to intervene and play a mediating role.[35] It was mainly the foreign missionaries who were faced with the choice of intervening or holding back. Chinese pastors or preachers were clearly expected to play the traditional leadership or brokerage role accorded to men of some status in the community, even if their status was not as high as that of the degree-holding elite.[36]

Short-term material benefit could mesh with longer-term social or economic benefit. For example, in the famine districts of Shanxi and Shandong in the late 1870s the relief activities of missionaries, taken at great risk to themselves, truly seem to have opened the door to many more conversions in those districts in the post-famine years. With enough new local believers, a Christian community could be formed. After a church or chapel for worship was built, next would come a school, and children, including girls, from non-elite families could receive an education. This was a key development, for education was crucial in social mobility in traditional China, and Chinese Christians did not remove themselves from Chinese society when they converted. Despite the accusation of losing their culture, and the perhaps well-meaning foreign missionary intention that they adopt "Christian civilization," Chinese Christians on the whole remained thoroughly steeped in their own culture.

I believe that what we can see in the late nineteenth century is the beginning of the process which later, early in the twentieth century, will produce several largely middle class Protestant urban communities growing out of the missionary-initiated institutions. But before 1900, we are in the early stages of this change. Over 30 years ago, Paul Cohen characterized nineteenth-century Christians, saying that they "were confined almost entirely to poor peasants and townspeople, criminal elements and other unsavory types, and deracinated individuals in the treaty ports."[37] If this was ever true, it was no longer so late in the nineteenth century. The Confucian scholar–official elite for the most part continued to shun Christianity and missionaries until the late 1890s, but in schools both in city and country, the Protestant school system did a remarkable job of creating a middle class, and even some wealthy individuals. Two Chinese scholars, Tao Feiya and Liu Tianlu, have carried out a fine study of Christianity and society in Shandong Province, including emphasis on social competition, careers, and mobility of Shandong Christians.[38] Their conclusion is that the Chinese Christians who were educated in Shandong mission schools between about 1880 and just after 1900 became the core of an increasingly prosperous and assertive Shandong Christian community, visible especially in Ji'nan and Qingdao. Although many of the graduates (or attendees – some did not graduate) did enter church work, many others went into secular areas such as private businesses and trade, government agencies (for example, the customs and the post office), interpreting, and teaching in the new Chinese government school system after 1900.

This first generation of Christian school students, whether believers or not, contributed to changes in urban society and economy at the turn of the century and after. Of course, not all school attendees were members of Christian communities. Some never became Christians and others dropped their Christianity as their careers advanced. But apparently a significant number did remain Christian, and they constituted the social and economic foundation of an increasingly confident non-missionary Protestantism in the twentieth century, which I will discuss in more detail in Chapter 5.

There remains the category of "spiritual incentives" as a reason why many Chinese Christians chose to believe. Some Chinese, from the time of Matteo Ricci on, have found personal solace or peace of mind from the basic doctrines of forgiveness of sins and the concept of Jesus's atonement, as well as spiritual strength for striving after moral improvement. Liang Fa, one of the earliest converts in the 1810s and author of the famous tract which influenced the Taiping founder Hong Xiuquan, had a grasp of the doctrinal essentials of Christianity, although power for moral living (by Confucian as well as Christian standards) was at the core of his belief.[39] There were actually two categories of spiritual attraction which Christianity had for Chinese. Both are evident in the story of Protestantism in Fuzhou, Fujian Province. One of the earliest Fuzhou converts, Huang Naishang (1849–1924), who became a patriarch of the Fuzhou Methodist church, was attracted partly because the prospect of belief promised not only salvation for himself, but answered questions not addressed by Chinese religions, and the power to lead a more moral life. But some Fuzhou converts, like many in China today, saw Christianity in the context of the supernatural aspects of Chinese popular religions of the time – belief in ghosts, spirits, supernatural messages, healing of sickness and disease, visions, and out-of-body experiences. Moreover, in the world of popular religion gods contended and competed with one another. In this contest, the Christian god had proven more efficacious than the "false gods" of China. To some of these converts, it seems, perhaps Christianity was not so much a source of moral power but an efficacious set of tools to use for protection in the uncertain world of the unseen.[40]

Women

Another topic related to conversion is the appeal and impact of Christianity on Chinese women. In the late nineteenth century, one of the most important factors here was the operation of schools for girls, giving thousands of Chinese girls a glimpse of worlds they never would have otherwise seen, and exposure to the possibility of life paths different from what they could have previously imagined. And even as the church offered a much longer menu of acceptable public roles for women than did traditional society, most of the new options required education. Many men after their own conversion wanted their wives and daughters to become literate and have some education, and in particular Chinese pastors were expected to have wives who were literate and educated. They often played a key role in their husband's ministry; they established and ran schools for local girls and women in their homes, or assisted the women missionaries in running boarding schools for girls. Some became effective public speakers. Widows in the Christian community played important roles as deaconesses or Biblewomen, some working full-time as traveling evangelists, others working in girls' schools or hospitals. All in all, it seems justified to say that "the impact of the Protestant churches on the life possibilities of Chinese women was enormous."[41] An example was the dramatic story of two Chinese girls who came under the mentoring of a single American woman missionary, Gertrude Howe, in the 1880s. After graduation from mission school, in 1892 Shi Meiyu (Mary Stone, 1873–1954) and Kang Cheng (Ida Kahn, 1873–1930) went to the US, and received their medical degrees from the University of Michigan in 1896. They returned to China the same year and had successful medical practices. Missionaries and Chinese Christian leaders also were early advocates of banning the practice of footbinding of young girls. As for Catholics, in several areas of the country they had orders of Christian virgins, some of whose members played leadership roles in the local community when there was a lack of male priests. The virgins also had an important role as catechists for female candidates for baptism.[42]

Leading Chinese Christians

In the late nineteenth century there were very few Chinese Christians, Catholic or Protestant, whose names would have been widely familiar countrywide. But Chinese collaboration was essential for all missions, especially the Protestants, whose many institutions needed Chinese staff to do most of the real work. In 1905, when fairly reliable statistics were gathered nationwide, there were about 3500 Protestant missionaries. But there were well over 10,000 staff in the various Protestant mission stations and institutions. Of these only about 300 were ordained Chinese clergy. That figure is a bit misleading because unordained evangelists and Biblewomen, who had varying degrees of training and experience, did much of the preaching in the street chapels or just out in the open air.

Missionaries did not usually publicly recognize the essential role of their Chinese assistants. Likewise, there were apparently no Chinese delegates to the big Shanghai missionary conferences of 1877 and 1890, and fewer than ten of the more than 1100 delegates to the nationwide centennial conference held there in 1907 were Chinese. Another example of this lamentable non-recognition was the anonymity of the Chinese scholars who toiled, some for decades, with the missionary translators to create the Union version of the Bible. This task was well under way in the 1890s, although the full translation was not available for use until 1919. By then, some of the missionary delegates to the translation committee had either died or had for other reasons left; in effect some of the Chinese staff of the committee helped to constitute the thread of continuity and its institutional memory. It should be said that in the twentieth century, at a time when other Chinese Christians were beginning to receive more recognition for their achievements in various fields, some of these translators were also recognized for their contributions.[43]

In the late nineteenth century there were only a few Chinese Christians with even a regional reputation, let alone a national one. The previously mentioned women medical doctors Shi and Kang would have had some renown in the Yangzi Valley. In Fujian Province, Huang Naishang was well known as a leader in church and civic affairs.[44] But for truly recognized church or professional Christian leaders, we draw a virtual blank. Yan Yongjing (Y. K. Yen, 1838–1898), who like Rong Hong went to the US at a young age and graduated from an American college (Kenyon College, Ohio), had a brilliant mind and was a great resource for the American Episcopal Church (Anglican) Mission in the Wuhan cities in central China after seminary and his ordination. But Yan's potential for church leadership was never fully tapped by the mission. After a few years in Wuhan, Yan moved to Shanghai and joined the faculty of the newly-established St. John's University (Anglican). He would have made a fine president of St. John's, but never had the opportunity. He also would have made an excellent Anglican diocesan bishop, but that option was not yet possible either. Chinese did not appear in the upper reaches of the Chinese Anglican Church until after the several separate Anglican missions (British, American, Canadian) had combined with each other to form the Anglican (or Episcopal) Church of China (Zhonghua Shenggonghui) in 1912.

Wang Tao, after assisting Medhurst with the Delegates' version of the Bible and Legge with translation of the Classics (see Chapter 3), became editor in the 1870s of a modern-style Chinese newspaper in Hong Kong, and later wrote frequently for the *Shen Bao* in Shanghai. He was fairly well known, but he never wore his Christian belief on his sleeve so practically no one would have known him as a Christian.

Pastor Xi Shengmo ("demon-queller", 1835–1896) of Shanxi Province, although of elite background, came to Christian faith during the Great Famine of the late 1870s, and in the 1880s built a network of Christian opium refuges all across the province. He worked in cooperation with but not ever under the control of agents of the China Inland Mission, including the famed "Cambridge Seven" when they finally arrived in China after the publicity tours following their recruitment. He was an imperious, fiercely opinionated, controversial figure, and perhaps in this regard he prefigured some of the independent Chinese church leaders of the twentieth century.[45]

Christianity at the End of the Century: Reformists, Revolutionaries, and Boxers

Despite the upsurge of energy of the Qing regime during the Tongzhi reign period in the 1860s, called a "restoration" by many, the state itself did not take on the task of reforming its foundations. Reforms were left to the care of regional and provincial officials, who sometimes promoted them and sometimes did not.[46] Thus a coordinated national program of reforms such as was pursued in Japan did not occur. Suggestions for reforms of China's basic institutions were increasing, however. These came from some "Christian reformers," as Paul Cohen has called them, in the foreign-dominated cities of the "littoral" (the coastal edge of China, from Hong Kong to Tianjin), who had acquired a more expansive outlook by association with missionaries or the West. Some of them seem to have been Christian believers, but we cannot be sure. What was important about them at any rate was their advocacy of a Western-inspired set of guidelines for China's development, even though none of them had an official position or much influence in the national power structure through which they might actually implement their suggestions.[47] By this advocacy they did not always intend the Christianization of China, but the Westernization of China was indeed one of their goals.

As time passed, some of the missionaries whose Chinese was excellent and whose writings were well sought, like Matteo Ricci and his Jesuit confrères of three hundred years earlier, tried to influence high officialdom in Beijing with new ideas and strategies for the "salvation" of China. Three of them were especially important:

- Timothy Richard (1845–1919), a British Baptist who spent years in the Shanxi famine districts and in 1891 became secretary (manager) of the Society for the Diffusion of Christian and General Knowledge among the Chinese (SDK), later the Christian Literature Society.
- Young J. Allen (1836–1907), an American Southern Methodist from Georgia who became the foremost missionary journalist of these decades, editing in succession a newspaper for Christians, the *Jiaohui xinbao,* and one for the more general public, the *Wanguo gongbao.* Allen also wrote other essays and books that were widely read among the elite.
- Gilbert Reid (1857–1927), an American Presbyterian who by the 1890s had decided that the opposition to Christianity by the "higher classes" of

China (national and local officials and the local elite) was the most important issue to address, and in 1894 established the Mission among the Higher Classes in China.

These three articulate foreign advocates of Westernizing reform (and implicitly of the Christianity that was assumed to be part of it) were in place in the early 1890s – Richard and Reid in Beijing, Allen in Shanghai.

As the end of the nineteenth century approached, China's national crisis worsened, and increasing numbers of literate Chinese believed that China must emulate Japan and adopt significant restructuring of economic, educational, and military spheres, that is, enact a real reform program. The shocking defeat suffered by China at the hands of Japan in the short Sino-Japanese War of 1894–1895 finally roused a national reform movement centered around a few officials close to the Guangxu emperor, himself a reformist. The leading lights of this reform movement, Kang Youwei (1858–1927) and Liang Qichao (1873–1929), as well as a group of young scholars from elite families, such as Tan Sitong (1865–1898), represent the first time that a significant degree of reform advocacy appeared within the political power structure and the elite itself. From where did these ideas, which ranged from scrapping the old educational system for a new Western-oriented one, to national economic development schemes, to tinkering with the political system and even considering a constitutional system, come? As far as we can tell, at least some of them were introduced by Richard, Allen, and Reid. The writings of all three were clearly influential in the mix of events and personalities that swirled around the court and government between 1895 and 1898, and both Richard and Reid were themselves present in Beijing and able to interact directly with some of the major figures in the reform movement.[48] It is true that the latter two, in their own published accounts later, very likely exaggerated the roles that they played and claimed more influence than they actually had. Moreover, it is a fact that the "100 days' reform" of 1898 prompted a coup by the old Empress Dowager Cixi which squelched the reforms for the time being and sent the main Chinese reformers into exile. Yet this should not obscure the likelihood that there was an extraordinary degree of "Christian" influence at the very center of power in these few years.[49] One of the characteristics of the reform impulse generated by loss of the war with Japan in 1895 and the following escalation of the forces of imperialism to unprecedentedly threatening levels, was a proliferation of study societies and periodical weekly publications all over the country. The model for these was partly the publications of these three missionaries and a few Chinese Christian writers.

These missionary intellectuals, who in fact were using much the same strategy that Matteo Ricci had used three centuries earlier, perhaps came closer than Ricci ever did to influencing the emperor and the court.

Of course for the Chinese principals in these events, to be enamored of aspects of the West or wanting to emulate Japan did not mean acceptance of Christianity. Missionary hopes in this regard, that is, for "conversion from the top," remained unfulfilled.

There was if anything an even more "Christian" complexion in the anti-dynastic revolutionary movement which began to take shape in the 1890s, at least on the surface. Sun Yat-sen himself, future first president of the Republic in 1912, whose career as a revolutionary began with an abortive revolt in Canton in 1895, was a Christian, as were many of the early members of the most important revolutionary organizations, such as the Xingzhonghui (Raise China Society). And, for example, allegedly 30 per cent of the participants in the failed Waizhou uprising in summer 1900 were Christians.

Christians and the Boxers

In the late 1890s, even as 1) some degree of "Christian influence" was seeping through the walls of the imperial palace in Beijing to coalesce around the emperor; 2) newly politicized, urbanized elites became alarmed at China's weakness and vulnerability; and 3) those same elites took the unprecedented steps of organizing themselves and expressing opinions on government policy – two other results came into being as a result of these developments. These were the seeds of modern nationalism, which (I believe) can be identified in the activism of these elites, and a related phenomenon, the emergence of a modern public opinion. The key feature of these new forces was that they were extra-bureaucratic, that is, they were constituted mainly of members of the elite who were not officials – degree-holders or their offspring, but not bureaucrats (though some active officials participated in the reform publications and debates before the coup of September 1898). The more activist, generally younger, members of the elite were among those stimulated by the new published works and study societies spawned by the debates about national survival after 1894, some of which included the writings of Richard, Allen, and Reid. Here, I believe, was the real beginning of what appeared, a few years later, to be the sudden emergence of a nationalist movement and with it a modern public opinion moving toward operating in a public sphere.[50] What seemed later to observers to be a new post-1900 burst of reformist zeal on the part of both the elite and the dynasty actually began in the mid 1890s, and Christian influence upon it was strong.

If 1895–1898 was a period of reform in elite circles and officialdom in which Christianity played at least a small positive role, 1898–1900 was one in which Christianity, foreign missionaries and Chinese converts alike, became targets of mass and official violence on a scale dwarfing that of the "Tianjin Massacre" of 1870. The Boxer Uprising (formerly often called the "Boxer

Rebellion") was a popular movement on the North China plain which was fired by a combination of intense anti-foreign and anti-Christian sentiment and a borrowing of cultural practices from popular culture, especially invulnerability rituals involving spirit possession by the gods of village opera stories.[51] Followers were called "boxers" because they practiced martial arts. A relatively low level of Boxer activity in 1898 and 1899, with (it seems) locally containable violence perpetrated upon missionaries and Chinese Christians, escalated into large–scale incidents in the spring of 1900. This instability building toward a crisis was immeasurably compounded by a terrible cycle of flood and drought which afflicted large parts of Shandong and Hebei Provinces in the years before 1900. Millions of people migrated in search of food, and some of them threw in their lot with groups that in 1900 evolved into a loose alliance of troublemakers that were called by the generic name "boxers." The level of social breakdown feeding into this whole process was significant. It seems clear that the flood-drought-famine cycle of recent years in parts of Shandong and Zhili (Hebei) fused general anti-foreign and anti-Christian sentiments with specific alarm over the foreign presence and rumors that Christians were responsible for the drought, poisoning of wells, and other acts of community sabotage.[52] And the old rumors about nefarious Catholic practices with women and children were also circulated again.

Another factor identified by many scholars wherein Christianity was linked to the origin and development of the Boxers was the behavior of the German missionaries of the Divine Word who entered Shandong in the late 1890s. They are alleged to have been highhanded and imperious, attracting unsavory types as converts and then supporting these converts in lawsuits. This of course also focused popular resentment directly on missionaries and converts.[53]

To this complex but potent socio-economic context was added the political threat of national breakup under control of the Western powers. By 1898 and 1899 the race was on for foreign "spheres of influence" all across the land. What would the government do? The Manchu court hesitated all through the spring of 1900. Its indecision, influenced by troglodyte-like officials around the Empress Dowager, Cixi, brought the Boxers into the streets of Beijing in mid June, where they laid siege to the Legation Quarter not far from the Forbidden City. The empress dowager finally declared war on all the Western powers, and sent imperial military forces to join the siege. The few foreign troops present as legation guards, and civilians as well, pitched in to fortify the Quarter and seal if off with barricades, otherwise all the foreigners in Beijing almost surely would have been killed.

As it was, outside of Beijing the Boxers killed all foreigners and Chinese Christians in north China within their reach. About 250 foreigners died, some in a gruesome manner, and perhaps 30,000 Chinese Christians were slaughtered.[54] Almost all of the murdered foreigners were foreign missionaries, both Protestant and Catholic; the larger part of the Chinese victims were Catholic. The "siege at Beijing" was lifted by a large eight-nation expeditionary force in August 1900, which occupied the city as the empress dowager and the court fled to live in exile in Xi'an until returning to Beijing in early 1902. The foreign military force destroyed the imperial summer palace in the northwest suburbs of Beijing, looted the Forbidden City and many temples and private mansions, and in retaliatory military raids, some extending hundreds of miles from Beijing, destroyed lives and property wherever there had been any Christian casualties. The final toll of Chinese lives lost in these military campaigns included many who were not Boxers or sympathizers, and quite possibly surpassed the approximately 30,000 Chinese Christians who had perished during the summer.

The "Boxer Uprising" is reasonably well known. Its basic elements are in most world history textbooks; a star-studded 1963 Hollywood film, *55 Days at Peking*, was based on it.[55] These versions of events almost always stop with the lifting of the siege of the Legation Quarter in mid August 1900, or at most allude to the diplomatic settlement which China was eventually forced to sign in September 1901, the Protocol of Peking. Other, arguably more revealing, events are ignored or passed over quickly. One is the length of time that the foreign troops maintained a military occupation, in effect a military government, in parts of north China – Beijing was not given back to Chinese control until early 1902. The important commercial and industrial city of Tianjin, astride Beijing's access to the ocean, remained under a foreign military government until 1906. Another is the large number of civilians caught up in retaliatory military action by the foreign troops who remained in north China for well over a year, making raids hundreds of miles away, sometimes to destroy villages or towns, also summarily executing as many as a thousand alleged Boxers or their sympathizers. Some Beijing-area missionaries accompanied these units of marauding Western troops, even suggesting targets for them. Foreign Christian missionaries unfortunately were also extensively involved in the orgy of looting that swept over Beijing with the collapse of Qing authority in the city and the refusal of the foreign troop commanders to stop the widespread and increasingly well-organized lifting of valuable items from both public and private space.[56]

This undisciplined behavior became so extensive by late 1900 that it became disturbing to some newspaper reporters, missionaries, and military personnel, whose reports, when they circulated back in the US and Britain, prompted criticism. The missionary role in these retaliatory and confiscatory activities was an especially controversial issue.[57] I think that the extensive foreign participation in questionable pursuits when Beijing lay prone and defenseless is an index of the loss of morale for those who for years had maintained hopes for China's modernization and even Christianization.

Senior missionaries like Gilbert Reid, W.A.P. Martin, Chauncey Goodrich, and Arthur Smith all expressed disgust and discouragement with the choices made by the Qing court in summer 1900, and expressed little hope that the dynasty could weather the results of this disaster.

However, much to the surprise of most observers, within two years of the Boxer events a new spirit of enthusiasm for reform was gripping the remodeled Manchu government. Even more surprising, the elite class and officialdom was showing more respect for missionaries and Christian institutions than had ever been the case before. The bleak outlook of the Boxer summer gave way to renewed hope among missionaries and Chinese Christians alike that at last China might be turning toward Christianity. Indeed, in retrospect we see here in the immediate aftermath of the Boxer tragedy the beginnings of China's "golden age" of Christian expansion and self-confidence.

Notes

1. In this chapter I will often use statistics for 1905 even when discussing events of the 1890s. This is because in 1905 a very comprehensive statistical survey of Protestant missions was done in preparation for the 1907 centennial conference, and these statistics seem more reliable than those derived from other years between about 1890 and 1915.

2. For a slightly later period, there is much good information in Valentin H. Rabe, *The Home Base of American China Missions, 1880–1920* (Cambridge, MA: Council on East Asian Studies, Harvard University).

3. There are a number of in-house and rather hagiographical accounts of Taylor's life. A recent more objective study is Alvyn Austin, *China's Millions: The China Inland Mission and Late Qing Society, 1832–1905* (Grand Rapids, MI: Wm B. Eerdmans, 2007).

4. One was Charlie Studd, captain of the Cambridge cricket team and member of the All-England cricket team; another, Stanley Smith, was captain of the University Eights crew; one, Dixon Hoste, would be a future CIM director-general. Alvyn Austin, *China's Millions: The China Inland Mission and Late Qing Society, 1832–1905* (Grand Rapids, MI: Wm. B. Eerdmans, 2007), pp. 206–209.

5. Alvyn Austin, *China's Millions: The China Inland Mission and Late Qing Society, 1832–1905* (Grand Rapids, MI: Wm. B. Eerdmans, 2007), p. 206.

6. The thoughts in this paragraph are elaborated nicely in Irwin T. Hyatt, Jr., "Protestant Missions in China, 1877–1890: The Institutionalization of Good Works," *American Missionaries in China: Papers from Harvard Seminars*, ed. Kwang-Ching Liu (Cambridge, MA: East Asian Research Center, Harvard University), pp. 93–128.

7. Paul Richard Bohr, *Famine in China and the Missionary: Timothy Richard as Relief Administrator and Advocate of National Reform, 1876–1884* (Cambridge, MA: East Asian Research Center, 1972).

8. Suzanne Wilson Barnett, and John King Fairbank, eds, *Christianity in China: Early Protestant Missionary Writings* (Cambridge, MA: Committee on American-East Asian Relations, Dept. of History, Harvard University, 1985), several of the chapters.

9. Adrian A. Bennett, *John Fryer: The Introduction of Western Science and Technology into Nineteenth-Century China* (Cambridge, MA: East Asian Research Center, Harvard University, 1967).

10. W.E. Soothill and Lewis Hodous, comps. (London: Kegan Paul, 1937).

11. Adrian A. Bennett, *Missionary Journalist in China: Young J. Allen and his Magazines* (Athens, GA: University of Georgia Press, 1983).

12. *Records of the General Conference of the Protestant Missionaries in China, Held at Shanghai, May 10–24, 1877* (Shanghai: American Presbyterian Mission Press, 1878); *Records of the General Conference of the Protestant Missionaries in China, Held at Shanghai, May 7–20, 1890* (Shanghai: American Presbyterian Mission Press, 1890); *China Centenary Missionary Conference Records: Report of the Great Conference Held at Shanghai, April 5th to May 8th, 1907* (New York: American Tract Society, 1907).

13. James Alan Patterson, "The Loss of a Protestant Missionary Consensus: Foreign Missions and the Fundamentalist-Modernist Conflict," *Earthen Vessels: American Evangelicals and Foreign Missions, 1880–1980*, ed. Joel A. Carpenter and Wilbert R. Shenk (Grand Rapids, MI: Wm. B. Eerdmans, 1990), pp. 73–91.

14. William R. Hutchison, *Errand to the World: American Protestant Thought and Foreign Missions* (Chicago: University of Chicago Press, 1987), Ch. 4.

15. Arthur H. Smith, *Chinese Characteristics*, reprint of 1894 edition with new introduction by Lydia H. Liu (Norwalk, CT: Eastbridge, 2003), pp. 329–330. Smith's book remained the West's bestselling book on China until Pearl Buck's *The Good Earth* was published in 1931.

16. For a general treatment, Michael Parker, *Kingdom of Character: The Student Volunteer Movement for Foreign Missions, 1886–1926* (Lanham, MD: University Press of America, 1998).

17. For the sort of volunteers who came to China, see the excellent analysis by Terrill E. Lautz, "The SVM and Transformation of the Protestant Mission to China," *China's Christian Colleges: Cross-Cultural Connections, 1900–1950*, ed. Daniel H. Bays and Ellen Widmer (Stanford: Stanford University Press, 2009), pp. 3–21.

18. Cohen, *Between Tradition and Modernity*, pp. 251–259 for a short biography of Ma. His post-1900 activities are discussed in chapt. 5. A more recent and in-depth work is Ruth Hayhoe and Lu Yongling, eds., *Ma Xiangbo and the Mind of Modern China* (Armonk, NY: M.E. Sharpe, 1996).

19. R. G. Tiedemann, "Indigenous Agency, Religious Protectorates, and Chinese Interests: The Expansion of Christianity in Nineteenth-Century China," in *Converting Colonialism: Visions and Realities in Mission History, 1706–1914*, ed. Dana L. Robert (Grand Rapids, MI: Wm. B. Eerdmans, 2008), p. 240.

20. R. G. Tiedemann, "Indigenous Agency, Religious Protectorates, and Chinese Interests: The Expansion of Christianity in Nineteenth-Century China," in *Converting Colonialism: Visions and Realities in Mission History, 1706–1914*, ed. Dana L. Robert (Grand Rapids, MI: Wm. B. Eerdmans, 2008), p. 240.

21. See the entries for "native agency" in the *Records* volumes of the 1877 and 1890 missionary conferences.
22. Kenneth Scott Latourette, *A History of Christian Missions in China* (London: SPCK, 1929), p. 307.
23. Roger R. Thompson, "Twilight of the Gods in the Chinese Countryside: Christians, Confucians, and the Modernizing State, 1861–1911," in Daniel H. Bays, ed., *Christianity in China: From the Eighteenth Century to the Present* (Stanford, CA: Stanford University Press, 1996), pp. 53–72.
24. The classic work on this subject remains Paul A. Cohen, *China and Christianity: The Missionary Movement and the Growth of Chinese Antiforeignism, 1860–1870* (Cambridge, MA: Harvard University Press, 1963).
25. See Paul A. Cohen, *History in Three Keys: the Boxers as Event, Experience, and Myth* (New York: Columbia University Press, 1997), pp. 141–172.
26. This happened in several cities. Alluded to in Nara Dillon, "New Democracy and the Demise of Private Charity in Shanghai," in Jeremy Brown and Paul Pickowicz, eds, *Dilemmas of Victory: The Early Years of the People's Republic of China* (Cambridge, MA: Harvard UniversityPress, 2007).
27. John King Fairbank, *The Great Chinese Revolution, 1800–1985* (New York: Harper & Row, 1986), p. 125.
28. Charles A. Litzinger, "Rural Religion and Village Organization in North China: The Catholic Challenge in the late Nineteenth Century," in Daniel H. Bays, ed., *Christianity in China: From the Eighteenth Century to the Present* (Stanford, CA: Stanford University Press, 1996), pp. 41–52.
29. Alan Richard Sweeten, "Catholic Converts in Jiangxi Province: Conflict and Accommodation, 1860–1900," in Daniel H. Bays, ed., *Christianity in China: From the Eighteenth Century to the Present* (Stanford, CA: Stanford University Press, 1996), pp. 24–40.
30. A detailed narrative is found in Paul A.Cohen, *China and Christianity: The Missionary Movement and the Growth of Chinese Antiforeignism, 1860–1870* (Cambridge, MA: Harvard University Press, 1963), pp. 229–261.
31. Pei-kai Cheng, and Michael Lestz with Jonathan D. Spence, *The Search for Modern China: A Documentary Collection* (New York: W.W. Norton, 1999), pp. 157–159.
32. Ernest P. Young, "The Politics of Evangelism at the End of the Qing: Nanchang, 1906," in Daniel H. Bays, ed., *Christianity in China: From the Eighteenth Century to the Present* (Stanford, CA: Stanford University Press, 1996), pp. 91–114.
33. Robert W. Hefner, *Conversion to Christianity: Historical and Anthropological Perspectives* (Berkely, CA: University of California Press, 1993; Lewis R. Rambo, *Understanding Religious Conversion* (New Haven, CT: Yale University Press, 1993).
34. R. G. Tiedemann, "Indigenous Agency, Religious Protectorates, and Chinese Interests: The Expansion of Christianity in Nineteenth-Century China," in *Converting Colonialism: Visions and Realities in Mission History, 1706–1914*, ed. Dana L. Robert (Grand Rapids, MI: Wm. B. Eerdmans, 2008), p. 232.
35. Ryan Dunch, *Fuzhou Protestants and the Making of a Modern China, 1857–1927* (New Haven, CT: Yale University, 2001), pp. 26–29.

36. Ryan Dunch, *Fuzhou Protestants and the Making of a Modern China, 1857–1927* (New Haven, CT: Yale University, 2001), pp. 26–29.

37. Paul A. Cohen, "Christian Missions and their Impact to 1900,"*The Cambridge History of China*, Vol. 10, *Late Ch'ing, 1800–1911*, Part I, ed. by John K. Fairbank (Cambridge: Cambridge University Press, 1978), p. 560.

38. Tao Feiya and Liu Tianlu, *Jiaohui yu jindai Shandong shehui* (Protestantism and Modern Shandong Society) (Jinan, China: Shandong Daxue chubanshe, 1995).

39. Liang Fa's work, *Quanshi liangyan* (Good Words to Exhort the Age), is quoted in Pei-kai Cheng, and Michael Lestz with Jonathan D. Spence, *The Search for Modern China: A Documentary Collection* (New York: W.W. Norton, 1999), pp. 132–136. A thoughtful discussion is in P. Richard Bohr, "Liang Fa's Quest for Moral Power," in Suzanne Wilson Barnett, and John King Fairbank, eds, *Christianity in China: Early Protestant Missionary Writings* (Cambridge, MA: Committee on American-East Asian Relations, Dept. of History, Harvard University, 1985), pp. 35–46.

40. Many of these ideas from Ryan Dunch, *Fuzhou Protestants and the Making of a Modern China, 1857–1927* (New Haven, CT: Yale University, 2001), Ch. 1.

41. Ryan Dunch, *Fuzhou Protestants and the Making of a Modern China, 1857–1927* (New Haven, CT: Yale University, 2001), pp. 44–45, makes most of these points, with examples.

42. Robert Entenmann, "Christian Virgins in Eighteenth-century Sichuan," in Daniel H. Bays, ed., *Christianity in China: From the Eighteenth Century to the Present* (Stanford, CA: Stanford University Press, 1996), pp. 180–193.

43. Jost Oliver Zetzsche, *The Bible in China: The History of the Union Version or the Culmination of Protestant Missionary Bible Translation in China* (Sankt Augustin, Germany: Institut Monumenta Serica, 1999), pp. 260–264. Among the assistants to the missionaries whose names we do know were Zou Liwen, Zhang Xixin, Wang Yuande, Liu Dacheng, and Li Chunfan.

44. Ryan Dunch, *Fuzhou Protestants and the Making of a Modern China, 1857–1927* (New Haven, CT: Yale University, 2001), Ch. 1.

45. There are many hagiographic works on "Pastor Hsi," as he is called in that older literature. A more interesting account is the extensive coverage in Alvyn Austin, *China's Millions: The China Inland Mission and Late Qing Society, 1832–1905* (Grand Rapids, MI: Wm. B. Eerdmans, 2007).

46. Some thoughts and examples are in Daniel H. Bays, *China Enters the Twentieth Century: Chang Chih-tung and the Issues of a New Age, 1895–1909* (Ann Arbor. MI: University of Michigan Press, 1978).

47. Cohen deals with this in "Christian Missions and their Impact until 1900," in *The Cambridge History of China*, Vol. 10, *Late Qing, 1800–1911*, Part I, ed. John K. Fairbank (Cambridge, UK: Cambridge University Press, 1978) pp. 583–585, and, more extensively, in *Between Tradition and Modernity: Wang T'ao and Reform in Late Ch'ing China* (Cambridge, MA: Harvard University Press, 1974), pp. 244–278.

48. Paul A. Cohen, "Christian Missions and their Impact to 1900,"*The Cambridge History of China*, Vol. 10, *Late Ch'ing, 1800–1911*, Part I, ed. John K. Fairbank (Cambridge: Cambridge University Press, 1978), pp. 585–588.

49. Tsou Mingteh, "Christian Missionary as Confucian Intellectual: Gilbert Reid (1857–1927) and the Reform Movement in the Late Qing," in Daniel H. Bays, ed., *Christianity in China: From the Eighteenth Century to the Present* (Stanford, CA: Stanford University Press, 1996), pp. 73–90.

50. For more extensive thoughts on this, see Daniel H. Bays, "Chang Chih-tung after the '100 Days:'1898–1900 as a Transitional Period for Reform Constituencies," in Paul A. Cohen and John E. Schrecker, eds, *Reform in Nineteenth-Century China* (Cambridge, MA: Harvard University, East Asian Research Center, 1976), pp. 317–325. The social changes underlying this development are discussed in Mary Backus Rankin, *Elite Activism and Political Transformation in China: Zhejiang Province, 1865–1911* (Stanford, CA: Stanford University Press, 1986).

51. The definitive study of who the Boxers were and where they came from is Joseph Esherick, *The Origins of the Boxer Uprising* (Berkeley, CA: University of California Press, 1987).

52. A classic study here is Paul A. Cohen, *History in Three Keys: The Boxers as Event, Experience, and Myth* (New York: Columbia University Press, 1997), esp.Ch. 2.

53. Joseph Esherick, *The Origins of the Boxer Uprising* (Berkeley: University of California Press, 1987) describes these factors. There is a drawback to the main sources which Esherick used in this book, however. Much of it was transcripts of oral histories: recollections of events a half century earlier during the early years of the PRC, by which time it was obvious the direction of interpretation which the government had in mind for the Boxer events.

54. The toll could have been higher, but for some heavily Catholic villages arming themselves and fortifying their villages, and fighting off Boxer attacks.

55. Starring David Niven, Ava Gardner, Charlton Heston, and Ernest Borgnine. Running time, 150 min.

56. James L. Hevia, *English Lessons: The Pedagogy of Imperialism in Nineteenth-Century China* (Durham, NC: Duke University Press, 2003), esp. Chs. 7–8.

57. The famous pieces critical of missionaries by Mark Twain, "To the Person Sitting in Darkness," *North American Review* 172 (1901): 161–176, and "To my Missionary Critics," *North American Review* 172 (1901): 520–534. Among missionary spokesmen was Gilbert Reid, who used the unfortunate term "the ethics of loot" to justify participating in looting.

5

The "Golden Age" of Missions and the "Sino-Foreign Protestant Establishment," 1902–1927

Prologue

This period of about a quarter-century was the high point of the foreign missionary age in China (though not of the overall Christian movement). China seemed to be modernizing and Christianizing at the same time. There was rejoicing in American missions circles and in US public opinion in general when the president of the Republic of China (the Republic of China was established after the fall of the Qing Dynasty in 1912) in 1913 asked the Protestants of China to pray for him and his government on Sunday, April 27.[1] This was a public relations masterstroke by the president, Yuan Shikai. Longtime British residents in China scoffed, calling Yuan's message "arrant humbug" and "a piece of perfectly gratuitous hypocrisy." Americans, both in China and in the US, including President Wilson and his cabinet, were ecstatic, and organized their own special prayer services on April 27. Newspapers all across America had the China prayer story on the front page for a week. It seemed that China would soon become a "Christian nation," as the missionaries had long been promising. A British old China hand remarked on how this incident above all showed "the easy gullibility of pious America."[2]

A New History of Christianity in China, First Edition. Daniel H. Bays.
© 2012 Daniel H. Bays. Published 2012 by Blackwell Publishing Ltd.

For Protestants the confidence and self-assurance of the missionary vision for a "Christian China" was nowhere better shown than in the astoundingly comprehensive and detailed report titled "The Christian Occupation of China," based on a survey of 1918–1921 and published in 1922.[3] But even as this massive optimistic volume, of almost 500 pages plus more than 100 pages of appendices, appeared, the Christian movement as then constituted, especially for the Protestants, was sliding toward a precipice.

One of the many ironies of modern Chinese history is how quickly events moved, seemingly compressing processes which one might normally expect to take decades into years or months. Chen Duxiu (1879–1942), head of the literature department at Peking University, editor of *New Youth,* the most influential journal of the day, and inspiration to the nationalist youth who had been mobilized by the May Fourth Movement of 1919, penned an article for *New Youth* in February, 1920. It was entitled "Christianity and the Chinese People." In it Chen expressed great admiration for the personality and teachings of Jesus; he was especially taken with Christ's doctrine of "universal love," which he took to be the central teaching of Jesus. To be sure, in this essay he was not attracted to Christian theology or church traditions, and was critical of the "superstitious" supernatural beliefs of Christians. Yet his attitude toward Jesus is quite positive.[4] Just a year later, in 1921, Chen was one of the founders of the Chinese Communist Party and was elected the first chairman of its central committee; he had rejected the possibility that Christianity had anything positive to offer China. His intellectual odyssey during that year was emblematic of the rapid change of sympathies toward Christianity of a large portion of the intellectual elite of China.

Patterns of Protestant Growth

Ironically, the undoubted tragedy of the Boxer events in 1900 ushered in a period of more than two decades during which both the foreign mission enterprise in China and Chinese Christian communities seemed to flourish. Boxer martyrs prompted more volunteers for mission. An example was the death of Yale graduate Horace Pitkin in the Boxer Uprising of 1900. Pitkin died along with more than ten other foreign missionaries – Presbyterian, Congregational, and CIM (China Inland Mission) – in Baoding, not far from Peking. His death spurred a surge in mission applicants, many from East coast colleges, and the establishment of the Yale China Mission in the early 1900s.[5] The Qing government, abandoning the resistance to change long characteristic of it, pursued a surprisingly ambitious reform agenda during the decade after 1900, including abolition of the old examination system, promotion of modern education, and creation of a constitutional political system.[6] Many reform projects were ones where Protestant missionaries and Chinese

Christians had a long-established track record of advocacy and competence, such as a modern school system including schools for girls. North China Women's College in Beijing, Ginling College for Women in Nanjing, the McTyeire Home and School for Girls in Shanghai, and Hwa Nan college for women in Fuzhou were not rivaled by Chinese-run schools for many years. Until Chinese schools with a new curriculum could develop in sufficient numbers to meet the demand, that is, until the second decade of the century, Protestant schools, in a system now capped by post-secondary level colleges in major cities, set the standard for modern education.[7] Even after Chinese government schools multiplied rapidly, the mission schools continued to enjoy a high reputation and impressive growth. In 1915 there were almost 170,000 students in mission schools (as opposed to 17,000 in 1889). In the mid 1920s the figure reached almost a quarter million.

It should be emphasized that these mission schools, especially the colleges, were very important in raising the cross-cultural awareness of many students, and expanding the horizons of their life choices. And this would have been particularly true for the women students at girls' middle schools and the three women's colleges. Indeed, the impact of the Protestant churches and schools in showing new public roles and careers "in broadening the life possibilities for women was enormous."[8] This area is only one of several where the missions and the churches seemed to be pointing the way toward Chinese modernization.

Protestant growth between 1900 and 1915 was impressive by all indices. Foreign missionaries numbered about 3500 in 1905 and 5500 in 1915, well on the way toward their eventual high-water mark of more than 8000 in the 1920s. Chinese Protestants, about 100,000 in 1900, numbered almost 270,000 communicants (330,000 baptized) in 1915; this growth would also continue into the 1920s, reaching about 500,000 before the storms of mass nationalism hit.

The Chinese Protestant community in many ways began to come into its own as a partner with foreign missionaries in the years after 1900. Undoubtedly most Chinese Protestants were rural, and of only modest means. However, with the Christian school system having provided upward mobility for many converts, by the years after 1900 there had come into being fairly prosperous Chinese Christian communities in several coastal cities. For example, the Wenhuiguan ("Tengchow College") at Dengzhou (today's Penglai), established in 1876 by the US Northern Presbyterian Calvin Mateer, was one of the most successful Christian schools in China. After 1900 it became a core element of Shandong Union College, which in turn became Shandong Christian University and finally Cheeloo University in Ji'nan, Shandong. The Wenhuiguan's detailed list of its graduates from 1876 to 1904 shows striking upward mobility. The Wenhuiguan's graduates were all from Christian families, and almost all were from rural areas. Of the

170 graduates of the classes of 1876–1904, 156 were from rural backgrounds, representing 107 villages in 29 different *xian* (county). Most were from poor or middling families. For these rural Chinese Christian youth of the late nineteenth century, their education at Mateer's school made a dramatic difference in their lives. In 1912, not one of the 170 was listed as a farmer, and only 21 were listed as having rural addresses (including last addresses of several of the 25 deceased).[9]

The move of so many Wenhuiguan graduates up and out of the village is measurable in their subsequent careers. In 1912, of the surviving 145 graduates, the largest number by far, 87, had teaching positions. Twenty-six had posts in religious institutions, and 32 were scattered in other professions including medicine, business, the civil service, or editing (which included interpreting/translating and printing). Some had multiple careers. Of those not teaching in 1912, over half had done so at some time. More so than the later graduates of other Christian colleges, this group seems to have remained committed to a Christian identity. They willingly took up leadership roles in the Protestant Christian community, especially in Shandong, where most of them remained. At the same time, their success in various professions brought higher economic status and a broadening of the resource base of the growing Protestant communities in the cities in which the graduates settled – these were often the termini of the German railway, Qingdao and Ji'nan, and cities on the line such as Weixian (today's Weifang). A few underwrote various Christian projects, including several financially independent Shandong Protestant churches in the twentieth century. An example was Liu Shoushan (1863–1935), who came out of abject poverty, son of an opium addict, and became a real estate tycoon in Qingdao and an entrepreneur there and in other cities. At Chefoo (Yantai) in the 1890s, as his jewelry business prospered, he repaid the US Presbyterians, with interest, the full cost of his upbringing and education. Between 1911 and his death in 1935 he gave large sums of money to several churches in addition to funding other Christian institutions such as schools and hospitals and helping individual Chinese preachers, YMCA workers, and the like.[10]

Well-educated and respected Chinese Protestants were also active in social and political reform activities in cities such as Fuzhou in the period 1900–1915, founding YMCAs, leading anti-footbinding or opium suppression societies, and holding office in provincial legislatures before and after the Revolution of 1911–1912, which toppled the Qing dynasty and established a republic.[11] Sun Yat-sen, a Protestant, was the first provisional president of the Republic in 1912, and several members of the National Assembly, the national parliament, were Christians. As the Protestant communities came into their own more in producing Chinese leadership, some of them hankered after more autonomy or even independence from their missionary mentors. As early as 1903 In Shanghai, a group of Chinese Christian businessmen and professionals formed the Chinese Christian Union (*Jidutu hui*) for the purpose of encouraging more Chinese church self-support and autonomy. Soon after that, Shanghai Presbyterian Pastor Yu Guozhen (1852–1932) spearheaded a movement to create several fully independent churches in the Shanghai area. These developments were paralleled by a comparable formation of a federation of former mission-run churches in the Beijing area that in effect declared their independence in the years before and after 1910. This proclivity to take charge of their own affairs was hampered by the legal status of Christianity in the early 1900s, while the Qing dynasty was still in power.

Until the Qing abdicated in 1912, most of the legal protections for Chinese Christians actually derived from the "unequal treaties" with the foreign powers. Under the Qing legal code, Chinese Christians were called *jiaomin* (people of religion), not *pingmin* (common people or subjects), and they did not have the legal right to build and own churches under their own name. Under the Republic after 1912, Christians were simply *guomin* (citizen) like everyone else, and were perfectly free to register churches and other religious properties under their own names. All of the national constitutions adopted by the central government in the early years of the Republic also included the Western-derived concepts of freedom of religion and separation of church and state. These new religious legal provisions facilitated a larger number of churches moving towards autonomy or full independence from their missionary tutors. Chinese churches in three cities were active in taking up this pattern. Pastor Yu Guozhen of Shanghai was the first, beginning soon after 1906. He led a group of churches in and close to Shanghai into a federation called the China Jesus Independent Church (Zhongguo Yesu jiao zili hui). He drew on the circle of men he had known for years in the Chinese Christian Union, men who were prime examples of the new element of professional, white collar, or business-oriented Christians in some urban areas.

In addition to Shanghai, Tianjin and Beijing were also sites of new departures for mature Chinese congregations. In 1910 a group of influential Chinese Christians in Tianjin, including Zhang Boling, founder of the famous Nankai middle school and later Nankai University, who had become a Christian only in 1909, established a group of independent churches. Beijing soon followed. In 1912–1913 several of these churches in and near Beijing and Tianjin joined in creating the "Chinese Christian Church" (Zhonghua Jidujiaohui). A similar movement took place in Shandong Province after the 1911 Revolution. And, not surprisingly, when the first loose federation of independent churches emerged in the province, it was graduates of the Wenhuiguan who were leaders in organizing and financially supporting it. Of the nine founders of the "Shandong Independent Christian Church" (Shandong Jidujiao zilihui), seven were former students of the Wenhuiguan, graduating between 1884 and 1904. Among them was the wealthy Liu Shoushan.[12] One of the church buildings built shortly after 1920 by an independent congregation which was part of this church federation is still being used today. It is a large structure close to downtown Ji'nan, holding well over a thousand people, with a distinct Chinese flair to the roof. In three visits to this church during the period 1985–1995, in talking with the old pastors, a few of whom remembered this congregation in its early days in the 1920s, they proudly recounted the story of how the congregation at that time raised the funds and designed and built the church.[13]

On the whole, these early manifestations of independent Chinese Protestantism were not particularly anti-missionary in motive or action. Their pastors for the most part had been trained in the missionaries' own seminaries, mainly in China and after 1900 some in the West. Many of them were Presbyterian, Congregational (ABCFM or LMS), or Baptist, and these congregations often kept their denominational identification and affiliations. They invariably kept the same doctrines of belief. And there were not yet that many of such congregations – perhaps several dozen to at most something over a hundred. Thus they were not a real threat to continued foreign missionary leadership of the Protestant movement in China. Yet it must be said that for many years after 1900 foreign missionaries were largely indifferent to or actually suspicious of the desire for autonomy of some Chinese Protestants. The first few times independent churches are mentioned in the new *China Mission Year Book* it is tentatively and almost reluctantly.[14] Obviously the missionaries were uncertain of how to react. Another indication had been the almost total absence of Chinese representatives at the great centenary missions conference of 1907 in Shanghai. In honor of the one hundredth anniversary of Robert Morrison's arrival in Canton, this was an ecumenical gathering of more than 1000 missionaries from all around the country, the first such nationwide meeting since 1890, to take stock of the state of the Protestant world in China.[15] In retrospect it is striking that only about seven Chinese were invited. It is even more ironic when one notes that the program and speakers at this gathering had much to say about "the Chinese church," including issues of self-support of congregations financially, the authority of foreign missionaries vis-à-vis native pastors and other leaders, and the like.

The expanding world of Marcus Ch'eng (Chen Chonggui)

Another example of the capacity of the missionary structures embedded in Chinese society by the early 1900s to profoundly change the life courses of Chinese is the story of Chen Chonggui (Marcus Ch'eng, 1884–1964), who will also appear prominently in the next two chapters.[16] Born in Hubei Province not far from Wuhan, Chen was dirt-poor, although his father became a Christian soon after his birth. Chen was bright, and managed to study for a few years at the Covenant Mission lower middle school in Wuchang.[17] He was baptized in the Covenant Mission, then had to scramble to continue his education at the British Wesleyan Methodist senior middle school in Wuchang, called Wesley College. Still poor, it was very difficult for Chen to find the resources to continue year to year, sometimes month to month; but he persevered and graduated in 1906, partly due to the consistent generosity of foreign friends. Chen's excellent English and personal charm had already resulted in doors that appeared to be closed opening to him. At first he went into the business world, as did many with Chen's English skills, but he ended up being an evangelist and playing a major role in the establishment of a Covenant Mission Seminary in Jingzhou, Hubei Province.

This itself is revealing of some interesting aspects of the missionary scene in China at the time. A group of foreign Swedish Covenant visitors to the China mission in about 1907 became enamored of the notion of the mission having *its* own seminary in China, just as dozens of other tiny missions did. The resident Covenant Mission China missionaries hopped on the bandwagon, and then the mission executives took Chen for an extended tour of Sweden, using him very effectively, with his poignant personal story and considerable charm, to drum up support for the seminary. There is no evidence of anyone looking really closely at the question of whether and/or why a separate seminary for such a small mission was justified. At any rate, the seminary opened in 1909 in a set of fine new buildings in Jingzhou. Chen, despite his having only a higher middle school education and diploma, was on the original staff of the Jingzhou Seminary from its opening in 1909.

For more than ten years, until 1920, Chen worked long and hard at the seminary, often to the point of exhaustion and with little time off. His 1921 memoir, written when he was still on the faculty, does not allude directly to the tremendous effort Chen personally put into the seminary, but his 1947 autobiography claims that during these years he was the fulcrum of both its academics and its administration. He allegedly taught 34 hours per week, including every conceivable subject over the years. He was first to rise to muster the students for morning drill, and last to retire after locking up; he even supervised the kitchen.[18] Acutely sensitive to his lack of formal educational credentials beyond middle school, Chen put himself on a rigorous program of self-study of theology, foreign languages, and Chinese literature. His own hard work again paid off when his rising prominence in the Covenant Mission resulted in an invitation to Sweden to spend the year 1920–1921. He made the most of it; his energy, charm, and fluent Swedish made him a great hit.[19] And his first memoir, *Echoes from China* (1921) was originally written and published in Swedish. Coming home to China in 1921, Chen took advantage of stopping by the American Covenant headquarters in North Park, Chicago, to make arrangements at nearly Wheaton College to do an accelerated BA degree in one full year of course work. He received the degree in 1922, at the age of 38. What was it like when Chen returned to Jingzhou in 1922? There is evidence that after two years of relative freedom abroad, he found the seminary stifling, and especially resented the unequal pay and quality of housing between the foreign and Chinese staff.[20] At any rate, he did not stay there long. By this time the issue of the relationships between foreign missionaries and Chinese Christians was becoming a major issue of discussion. It is important to trace the development of that issue and why it appeared.

The debut of Cheng Jingyi

Before the anti-Manchu Revolution of 1911 and the establishment of the Republic and its series of national constitutions, the major stimulus to missionary recognition of the need to reassess foreign versus Chinese leadership of the Christian enterprise was probably provided by the great Edinburgh Missionary Conference of 1910. In particular, the remarks of Cheng Jingyi, a young 28-year-old LMS pastor from Beijing who was not even ordained until going home after the conference, made a large impact. Cheng had spent several years in Britain and was unusually fluent in English; indeed the eloquence of his remarks accentuated the effects of their content. Cheng's first statement, at the proceedings of Commission II, The Church in the Mission Field, emphasized the need for missions to recognize that the historical situation had changed and it was time for the missionaries, in policy and action, to give Chinese Christians, as well as national church leaders of other non-Western countries, much more responsibility for managing their own affairs and making their own decisions. Even more blunt, and to many delegates electrifying, was his contribution to Commission VIII, Cooperation and Unity. In a short presentation that many conference participants later said was the best of the entire conference, Cheng said:

> Speaking plainly we hope to see, in the near future, a united Christian church without any denominational distinctions. This may seem somewhat peculiar to you, but, friends, do not forget to view us from our standpoint, and if you fail to do that, the Chinese will remain always as a mysterious people to you." Later in his address he stated forthrightly, "denominationalism has never interested the Chinese mind. He finds no delight in it...[21]

This was sound advice; missionaries and mission boards would have occasion to recall it in the not-so distant future.

Origins and Course of the "Sino-Foreign Protestant Establishment"

What is here informally called the "Sino-Foreign Protestant Establishment" (SFPE) was not a real historical entity or a group of people who identified themselves as such. Rather it was a group of influential people who were the product of a series of processes and events of the period from soon after 1900 to about the end of World War I. But the term captures something of the sense of status, hierarchy, and sometimes contested image which surrounds the effort of any social group in a Chinese setting to accomplish anything. Certain missions in China, for example the Anglicans, American Presbyterians and Methodists, as well as the old ABCFM and the venerable British LMS and a few others, dated to well before 1900.[22] By the early twentieth century they were all long-established and reasonably well-funded. But that meant many high-budget institutions like schools, including seminaries, and hospitals to operate, as well. There were also increasing numbers of new missionaries coming on the field who were committed to those institutions and had the training and credentials to be teachers in a mission middle school or college, or a YMCA/YWCA secretary setting up a new city or school-based branch. The Student Volunteer Movement for Foreign Missions (SVM) was in its North American heyday during these pre-World War I years.[23] More young and typically idealistic SVM recruits came to China than to any other mission field. With the ambitious SVM watchword, "the evangelization of the world in this generation," there was no lack of youthful energy and confidence.

The task of operating, coordinating, and maintaining such institutions was a complex set of challenges in the early twentieth century. Certain individuals, due to factors of status, tradition, force of personality, eloquence and persuasiveness, or control of resources or access to resources, were especially influential, both in their own missions and in the wider mission community. They constituted an elite policy-setting and decision-making "establishment" among missionaries. They were the ones who gave the prime-time keynote speeches or featured presentations at the big nationwide missionary meetings of 1877, 1890, and 1907. This informal establishment created the agendas and committees of the national meetings, as well as the proceedings and priorities of smaller interest groups such as educational missions, medical missions, and so forth. This establishment had its own publications, among them *The Chinese Recorder,* published monthly in Shanghai, ably edited by Frank Rawlinson (1871–1937). The *Recorder* was joined by the annual *China Mission Year Book,* beginning in 1910, which was edited for most of the next two decades by a Canadian, Donald MacGillivray (1862–1931). Thus already before 1900, but especially by about 1910, the foreign missionary establishment was firmly in place. Making it a Sino-foreign, or joint endeavor, was not a matter of foreign and Chinese Christian leaders sitting down as equals to plan and set priorities. It was a matter of Chinese Christian leaders gradually being incorporated into the "establishment" already in existence. It was not until after 1910 that this began to happen, at first with just a handful of Chinese participants.

With plenty to do in the missionary enterprise, and with things on the whole going well for missions after 1900, there was no sense of urgency on the part of missionaries in China actively and intentionally to promote Chinese participation – that is, aggressively to seek out capable young Chinese Christian talent, and to nurture and encourage it in all ways possible, mentoring those who would then be better prepared for the uncertain future. Every mission statement of purpose mentioned the goal of turning all this responsibility over to Chinese control; and some missions even used the old slogans of the nineteenth century, including the three-self idea. But there was no sense of hurry. It is true that steadily after 1910 annually several brilliant Chinese graduates of the mission school system went abroad, mainly to the US, and gained Ph.D. or D.D. degrees, returning to prestigious positions in the Christian colleges and middle schools. And it is also true that early on in China compared to other missions, soon after 1900, the YMCA was unusually conscientious in appointing Chinese nationals to executive secretary posts (usually a full-time job) in local and national offices as well. Yet as of about 1910, there were almost no Chinese entries prominent in the galaxy of well-known names in Protestant circles nationwide. The only one who might have qualified on that score was Ding Limei, an 1892 graduate of the Wenhuiguan in Shandong, a pastor turned revivalist speaker who attracted considerable attention with his successful revivals at middle schools all over north China. In 1910 Ding was commissioned by the North China YMCA at its annual meeting to head up the newly established Chinese Student Volunteer Movement for the Ministry, established at the same meeting.[24]

However, the great Edinburgh conference in 1910 had an impact in China, as it did on many mission fields. The sharply worded presentations by Cheng Jingyi were blockbusters, especially against a backdrop of all the world's leading missions statesmen agreeing on several important initiatives, including more recognition and elevation of the "younger churches." It was clear to missionary opinion in China that change was afoot. The patriarch of cooperation and master organizer John R. Mott (1865–1955) himself, the great promoter of the SVM and the YMCA, and chairman of the 1910 Edinburgh conference, made it clear that he was not going to let the issues of the Edinburgh discussions grow stale. He had been in favor of equal Chinese representation in missions institutions since his first visit to China in 1896 as International Secretary of the YMCA; at that time he decreed that all Chinese YMCAs have a council membership at least 50 percent Chinese.[25] In practice it was almost always well over 50 percent.

In 1910, before the Edinburgh gathering dispersed, Mott won approval of the formation of a "Continuation Committee" to continue to meet and liaise with national groups. The only China representative, either Chinese or missionary, among this elite international group of 35 was Cheng Jingyi, whose performance at Edinburgh had caught Mott's attention. Moreover, just how important China was to Mott was shown by Mott's personal visit to China to preside over the 1913 organization meeting of the "China Continuation Committee." This body, like a few other national continuation committees, was to be under the umbrella of the world-wide Continuation Committee and dedicated to furthering the goals of the 1910 meeting. At this 1913 meeting Cheng Jingyi was chosen, along with a missionary colleague, to be first joint secretary of the committee. Within a short time, still barely 30 years old, he became executive secretary of the China Continuation Committee, which in 1922 became the National Christian Council of China, one of the bastions of the Sino-foreign Protestant establishment. The Chinese members of the continuation committee formed in 1913 were still a distinct minority, but the ratio of about two to one among the 120 delegates gave them much more recognition than had the centenary conference of 1907.[26] The reweighting of the representation numbers had just begun; by the next all-China national meeting in 1922, there would be parity.

Thus the roots of the SFPE partly go back to Edinburgh, and the first institutional manifestation of the SFPE was the China Continuation Committee initially formed under the personal direction of John Mott in 1913. In these years between Edinburgh and the end of the Great War, though there was some suspicion toward the small new independent Chinese congregations being formed in major cities after 1910 or 1911, a part of missionary opinion was at least somewhat more open to real partnership with a new generation of Chinese church leaders.[27] It appears that even at this early stage, missionaries and Chinese leaders were not entirely on the same page. There is no doubt that the ultimate aim of Cheng Jingyi and most of the other Chinese participants here was to move steadily toward a new church organization which would not be a super-denomination, but confessionally, ecclesiastically, and in practice a single church. That is why even at the early discussions in Edinburgh and consistently thereafter, Cheng insisted that the name of the eventual church should not be what most missionaries preferred, a Chinese church "federation", implying a combination of different denominations. The name Zhonghua Jidujiaohui was adopted, its English name The Church of Christ in China.

This new generation of Chinese who became members of the SFPE were just coming to the fore in the decade after the Revolution of 1911. Besides Cheng Jingyi, one of the most prominent was Yu Rizhang (David Z. T. Yui, 1882–1936), rising star in the fast-expanding YMCA. Another was Wang Zhengting (1882–1961), another YMCA veteran who served in Yuan Shikai's early administration as a cabinet member. Others included a few faculty at newly established (1916) Yanjing University, to be the jewel of the Christian college system, though most of these individuals became active in the early 1920s: Liu Tingfang (T.F. Liu, 1891–1947), a brilliant and prolific scholar, returned from his Ph.D. in the US to join the Yanjing faculty in

1920;[28] Zhao Zichen (1888–1979), probably modern China's foremost Christian theologian and a penetrating writer;[29] Hong Ye (William Hung, 1893–1980), a highly respected scholar with deep intellectual roots both in the West and Chinese tradition;[30] and Wu Leichuan (1870–1944), a classically trained Confucian scholar who came to Christianity in mid life, tried to reconcile Confucianism and Christianity, and in the mid 1920s became the first Chinese vice-president of Yanjing and then its chancellor for eight years.[31] These Chinese Christian intellectuals and other Chinese faculty, together with a few foreign faculty members at Yanjing, constituted the Shengming she or "Life Fellowship," which met regularly on the campus and was dedicated to a bicultural examination of issues of faith and society, especially those of reform and indigenization of the church in China. Their journal, *Shengming* (Life Journal), was widely read and influential in the intellectual world of the SFPE.[32]

The Sino-Foreign Protestant Establishment as political action committee and missionary sending agency

Members of the Sino-Foreign Protestant Establishment (SFPE) both corporately and individually were mobilized for one major politicized campaign in the "public sphere" in the middle of the second decade of the twentieth century. Not long after the establishment of the Republic of China to replace the Qing government, agitation began in some quarters of Chinese opinion to reestablish the monarchy, and/or to re-establish Confucianism as the "official" state ideology. Eventually, of course, President Yuan Shikai would attempt to do just that in 1915–1916, trying to establish a new dynasty with himself as founding emperor, causing his downfall. But reestablishment of an imperial political system realistically never had much of a chance. What seemed more feasible, however, was a campaign led by traditional scholars, but also including some prestigious political figures such as the 1898 reform leader Kang Yuwei, and others, to make "Confucianism" the official "religion" of China. A public relations campaign was carried on by this group to get a Presidential decree or National Assembly legislation to that effect. In the public debate on this issue, the China Continuation Committee, especially its Chinese members, played a significant role. After all, the Christian communities, both Protestant and Catholic, had benefitted greatly from the end of the system that before 1912 privileged Confucian learning in the examination system and dominated the rituals of the state. They valued highly the legal safeguards of the freedom of religion clauses in the Republican constitution and other documents. Both foreign missionary spokesmen and Christian Chinese intellectuals spoke out forcefully and lobbied hard – and successfully – to quash this attempt. Arguably the influence of the latter was more instrumental in the success of the movement.[33] Once again Cheng

Jingyi was at the forefront of the action, organizing a "Society for Religious Freedom" (Zongjiao ziyou hui) which was very effective in the campaign.

Another campaign was attempted by the China Continuation Committee from 1918 to 1921. This was the "China for Christ" evangelistic campaign, with the Continuation Committee sending Chinese missionaries to remote parts of the country that were basically unmissionized. This encountered all sorts of obstacles from denominationalism, budgetary woes, and poor coordination, and it was quietly dropped after 1920.

Diversification of the Christian Scene

The well-educated, well-connected, and articulate Western and Chinese members of the SFPE were not the only players in the game by the end of the second decade of the twentieth century. The worlds of both missionaries and Chinese Christians were changing, qualitatively as well as quantitatively, and had been doing so for some time. One factor was the rise of revivalism after 1900, first among established missions and then among new ones.

Revivalism

The first missionary to be extensively involved in revivalism was Jonathan Goforth (1859–1936), an unprepossessing Canadian Presbyterian stationed in the North Henan mission who followed closely the events of the "great Wales revival" of 1903, and developed an "expect a revival and it will happen" syndrome.[34] Hearing of large emotional revival meetings sweeping Korea, Goforth, accompanied by the visiting Canadian Presbyterian missions home secretary, who was then touring Asia, went and spent some time observing Korean events in 1907. En route back to China, the two stopped and enthusiastically shared their findings with the Scots–Irish Presbyterian missionaries in Manchuria. The latter invited Goforth to return for evangelistic meetings in 1908, and the result was the "Manchurian revival" of that year.[35]

Directly on the heels of Goforth came Ding Limei, the mild-mannered evangelist from Shandong who headed the Chinese Student Volunteer Movement for the Ministry. Big-name Western evangelists followed, including John R. Mott, who after his initial YMCA visit of 1896 found an enthusiastic mass response on a return visit in 1907 and again in 1913 when he came to set up the China Continuation Committee. Another top name in international evangelism was Sherwood Eddy, longtime Asia secretary of the international YMCA, who first came to China in 1911, accompanied Mott in 1913, and then returned in 1914, 1918, and several more times into the 1930s.

Revivalism, with its accompanying characteristic of a certain degree of emotionalism, has been present throughout church history, for example in the US and North Atlantic we have the Anglo-American revivals of George Whitefield, Jonathan Edwards, Charles Finney, and D.L. Moody, among others. In China the development of revivalism went well beyond the segment of the Protestant community that was represented by the SFPE. In fact revivalism came more naturally to other parts of the spectrum of Protestants. Essentially, the rapid increase in the size of the foreign missionary community in China augmented the numbers of both "liberal" elements such as the SVM volunteers, who tended to accept the higher criticism approach to the Bible and the primacy of social action over preaching, and on the other side the conservative groups who were by about 1920 being called "fundamentalists," and who on the whole were very different from the SFPE. As the number of "missions" in China increased from a few dozen to well over one hundred between the late nineteenth and the early twentieth century, a significant number of those new arrivals were very conservative theologically, fundamentalists or Pentecostals.[36] Many of the new arrivals came with one of the established conservative evangelical missions such as the US Southern Baptists, the Christian and Missionary Alliance, or especially the CIM, which continued to be, overwhelmingly, the largest Protestant mission.[37] A number were sent by new denominational agencies established only in the early twentieth century, such as various Scandinavian groups, some of them Free Church and some of them Lutheran; the Seventh Day Adventists; the Christian Reformed Church, etc. But a large number also came to China as tiny bands of "faith Missionaries" or even just as lone individuals. These had no institutional support, no salary, had to raise funds somehow, and in all this simply trusted the Holy Spirit to learn the language and be able to preach. Understandably, the attrition rate was high in this category. Some Pentecostals believed that the "gift of tongues" meant that they would supernaturally be given fluent Chinese language skills as they stepped off the boat.[38].

This proliferation of new missions, most of them small and sectarian, meant an infusion of eager (though often ill – prepared and naïve) missionaries unencumbered by institutional preoccupations and intensely concentrated upon spiritual regeneration for themselves and for Chinese Christian converts, all in a context of strong pre-millennialist expectations. This meant, among other things, much less structure; more fire, brimstone, and second coming; and a fair dose of adventuresome creativity on the China mission scene by the 1920s, along with a high dropout rate among the enthusiastic newcomers. There was also a distinct new ingredient of Holiness/Pentecostal emphasis on the Holy Spirit and the gifts of the Spirit in some quarters, and a generally high stress on the importance of revivalism. And revivalism as a missions strategy after about 1920 was more likely to be used by conservative evangelical groups and independent traveling evangelists than by the SFPE.

By the late 1920s, for example, Ding Limei was no longer much in demand; he was obsolete after only 20 years. All in all, the menu for a potential Chinese Christian convert seems to have become far more varied, and perhaps more interesting, than it had been only a few years before.

Pentecostalism in particular has proven to be a significant attraction to twentieth century Chinese, with its radical egalitarianism and provision for direct revelation from God, not just guidelines from the Bible or the words of a pastor. It can be readily seen that both of these characteristics could facilitate the emergence of independent churches. Historically elsewhere Pentecostalism was nothing if not a revolt against hierarchy in the Church. And on the practical level Pentecostalism not only provided all believers with the capacity for spiritual enlightenment and knowledge of God's will through revelation; it also provided for self-interpretation of this revelation via the gifts of prophecy and tongues. Any common believer could be chosen to receive God's revelation; one did not have to be a missionary, or ordained, or even a deacon.[39]

The end of consensus

What might be called the "nineteenth-century evangelical missionary consensus" among missionaries, which enabled the three great national conferences of 1877, 1890, and 1907, in which all groups were represented despite doctrinal differences, did not survive much past World War I.[40] The broadened spectrum of Christianities now available could not easily co-exist. The old consensus was already disintegrating even as preparations were being made by the China Continuation Committee for the National Christian Conference of 1922. Already in the summer and fall of 1920 some China missionaries who disliked the direction of theological education as being too "modernist" formed the Bible Union of China, which became a magnet for fundamentalists among missionaries for the next several years.[41] In some ways the world-wide "Fundamentalist-Modernist Controversy" began in China in the summer of 1920, with acrimonious disputes over Biblical authority, higher criticism, evolution, and the like breaking out in some of the mountain summer retreats that provided relief from the summer heat for many missionaries. Some visiting theologians from the US were appalled by the prevalence of "modernist" views of the Bible which they encountered, and complained bitterly and publicly. Obviously the Sino-foreign Protestant Establishment could no longer speak for the entire missions community, if it ever could. World War I itself took a toll on the SFPE. The SVM and its idealism survived the war but in a crippled state, never regaining its old vigor.[42] Likewise the campus YMCAs and YWCAs noticed a drop-off in student interest in programs and accessibility to the local Y secretary whether foreign or Chinese. And the bloody debacle of internecine warfare in Europe was costly to the image and credibility of Christianity insofar as the prospect of becoming as progressive or as "civilized" as the West was a frequent apologetic for Christianity.

Aftermath of the May Fourth Movement and the Christian Movement in China (I)

For the first several weeks, even months after the May 1919 student demonstrations and arrests at Tiananmen Square (the square was tiny then, a small fraction of the size of today's), there was little or no indication that the rippling effects of those precipitating events would soon constitute a mortal challenge for the Protestant movement in China. The immediate issues of May Fourth – mainly for China to refuse to sign the Treaty of Versailles of 1919, which transferred much of the heartland province of Shandong from German to Japanese control instead of giving it back to China – had given occasion for Chinese nationalism to vent itself more forcefully than anyone had ever seen. The urban mass protests and demonstrations, going far beyond the student class to include urban merchants, white collar and factory workers, revealed a simmering resentment of foreigners' privileged status and power, and an equally deep animus toward the dozens of warlords who ruled China in independent fiefdoms and pillaged the land and the people. The intense nationalism expressed in these developments was fully shared and supported by students and faculty at Christian schools and colleges all across China, who joined the demonstrations in some cities. Moreover, concerning the cultural iconoclasm and the severe critique of traditional Confucian social structure and social values that had been circulating in the politicized intellectual circles of the "New Culture movement," statements of support from Christian intellectual leaders were frequent in 1919 and 1920. Indeed, Christian leaders (that is, those who were members of the SFPE) shared many of the same diagnoses of China's ills, for example the dead hand of Confucius and tradition, a patriarchal social structure that was obsolete, and a venal and corrupt politics.[43]

All in all, there was scant inkling that within a year the ire of an aroused Chinese nationalism, which at first was directed at the foreign governments who had wronged China at Versailles and Chinese warlord "traitors", would take dead aim at Christianity – its institutions, its believers, and especially the missionary movement. By 1921, China's non-Christian intellectuals were discovering two reasons for intensely disliking Christianity. One, it was crass superstition, with outlandish beliefs in a virgin birth, rising from the dead, and the like; the educated Chinese elite had always had disdain for the superstitions of the common people. As the May Fourth Movement proceeded in the early 1920s, all religions came under indictment by the movement's reification of "Science." Two, it came to be an article of faith that China's weakness and pitiful condition were not due solely to foreigners' bad intentions or wicked actions, but to a deeply rooted system of socioeconomic relationships that operated worldwide (capitalism), and involved colonial empires which were exploited and kept servile by those countries with more advanced economic and social class systems (imperialism).

With these concepts (or "theory," some might call it) digested, from this point in the analysis it was easy for excited students and intellectuals to identify the alleged true nature of the missionary movement – it was a case of "cultural imperialism" or "cultural aggression," with foreign missionaries working hand in hand with foreign governments and corporations, to make the Chinese docile and compliant, accepting semi-colonial status. That indictment of missionaries and Christianity as agents of imperialism was not an instantly arrived at conclusion, but developed steadily between 1921 and 1925. As young Chinese looked around in the early 1920s, they could see evidence what seemed to be proof of that accusation. Missionaries themselves, after several decades of the unequal treaties, still had an obviously privileged position. As subjects of countries with continuing treaties with China, missionaries still had extraterritorial legal status.[44] And the view of many Chinese was that missionaries were religious leaders of the Chinese churches not because they were best "qualified" (i.e. ordained), but as a historical holdover from the nineteenth century. Likewise also their special legal status underlay their monopolizing the management of the Christian schools, hospitals, and all the other institutions and structures of the SFPE. To many Chinese and to a few foreigners as well, that seemed a historical anomaly, entirely inappropriate in an age of nationalism and national sensitivities. In fact on this issue, as well as the issue of formal foreign or Chinese leadership of Christian institutions such as schools, Chinese members of the SFPE tended actually to share some of the secular criticism levied at the monopoly on leadership status held by the foreign missionaries, and here agreed with the critique of Cheng Jingyi in Edinburgh already in 1910.

Thus missions-centered Christianity turned out to be extremely vulnerable to the fallout from the May Fourth Movement on two scores. The New Culture movement, an integral part of May Fourth, was quite anti-religious in general, and anti-Christian in particular. However, it should be remembered that Chen Duxiu as late as February 1920 wrote his article praising Jesus, described in the Prologue to this chapter. It would still be over a year after that article before the anti-Christian movement would really blossom. The other score on which Christianity was vulnerable was the charge of cultural imperialism or cultural aggression. Like the "religion is superstition" issue, the danger to Christianity was readily apparent. Yet even as the forces which would try to demolish Christianity were gathering in the early 1920s, the momentum of the now two decades-long success story of Protestant influence continued. Total numbers of missionaries and of converts continued to mount, and the Christian movement as a whole seemed to move from success to success.

The Great Effort, 1922–1927: National Christian Conference, National Christian Council, Church of Christ in China

During these five years occurred the events that Cheng Jingyi and his Chinese colleagues in the China Continuation Commitee had been hoping for since 1913. The first was the National Christian Conference of 1922, held in Shanghai in the spring of 1922. However, in preparation for that conference the continuation committee wished to conduct a remarkably thorough survey of the entire Protestant edifice in China, province by province and even district by district. A "Special Committee on Survey and Occupation" was formed in 1918, with 35 members (12 Chinese) who worked hard for three years and then on the eve of the conference published a large volume of statistics and analysis. It was nearly 500 pages with well over 100 pages of appendices. Its Chinese title was fine: *Zhongguo gui zhu* (China for Christ). The English title was a public relations disaster: *The Christian Occupation of China, a general survey of the numerical strength and geographical distribution of the Christian forces in China made by the Special Committee on Survey and Occupation, China Continuation Committee.*[45] There was an immediate uproar of protest. As fate would have it, a separate special foreign commission (not of the continuation committee), the Burton Commission, had also just finished up its assigned task of evaluating and making recommendations for the 13 Protestant colleges and universities.[46] The report of this body, *Christian Education in China*, published in the first part of 1922, and which recommended expansion of Christian higher education, already had aroused the ire of many Chinese students and intellectuals. Now came the "Occupation" volume.

Then occurred yet another provocation to Chinese sensibilities, the third within a few weeks. This was the news that Tsinghwa (Qinghua) University in Beijing was to host the international meeting of the World Student Christian Federation in early April. In response, anti-Christian and anti-religion associations took largely uncoordinated action in many cities and on many campuses. Some of these reactions, such as those of the campus branches of the Anti-Christian Student Federation, though local, were assisted by organizations with connections to the small Chinese Communist Party such as the Socialist Youth League and The Young China Association; but there was no national-level campaign such as there was three years later. The spring of 1922 saw many demonstrations and denunciations, issuing of manifestoes, rallies, flyers, handbills, and harsh rhetoric directed at Christianity, missionaries, and Chinese Christians. These protest activities were carried out with some enthusiasm, though without much central coordination, and also without the sharp anti-imperialist edge of the demonstrations to come three years later. Moreover, for all the rhetoric, this 1922 campaign had very little effect; the April meeting at Tsinghwa was not delayed or disrupted, and the National Christian Conference went ahead as scheduled in Shanghai.[47] When summer came, many of the student participants went home, and that was the end of it – for now. These events in the spring of 1922 should have constituted a shot across the bow for the leaders of the SFPE, Chinese and foreign alike. They did not.

Cheng Jingyi was chairman of the National Christian Conference held in spring 1922; he must have been gratified by seeing his long-held dream take shape. In sharp contrast to 1907, Chinese delegates outnumbered the foreign ones. Moreover, the theme of the conference was "The Chinese Church," and the thrust of all the preparatory papers and of the reports adopted by the plenary sessions was to stress how much divisive denominationalism was disliked, and the great desire for unity in the church. The conference provided legitimization of the two major organizational steps yet to be taken, creation of the National Christian Council (hereafter NCC) and the unified Chinese church, the Church of Christ in China (hereafter CCC).[48]

The NCC was appointed by the 1922 conference; it held its first meeting May 10–16, 1923, over a year after the appointment of its members. 38 of 64 delegates were Chinese; several were women. David Z. T. Yui of the YMCA was elected chair, Cheng Jingyi and E. C. Lobenstine general secretaries. In retrospect, it appears that the NCC was a prestigious but basically powerless body which, its supporters hoped, would be effective doing informal or semiformal brokering between various constituencies of the Chinese Protestant world. It would function as a roundtable, a venue where the voices of the entire Christian community could be heard. But, hoped many like Cheng, it would also accrue prestige and power over time, and eventually have more than token powers, perhaps even the leverage to require compliance of its members. In the meantime, the NCC would investigate problems, discuss all kinds of social as well as church developments, make reports and recommendations, and function something like an executive committee.

It was not until 1927 that the Church of Christ in China was formally created. The delay was due partly to the national political turmoil. But there were also unresolved issues of concern especially to missionaries, including criteria of membership, authority of bodies in the new church, ecclesiastical issues, budgetary matters, and so forth. Another reason was the constant sniping of the conservatives from the Bible Union of China and other theological critics. A distressingly large percentage of conservative evangelicals such as the Christian and Missionary Alliance, the CIM, even the major Lutheran bodies and the Southern Baptists, refused to join, or dropped out of the National Christian Council before the CCC was established.

Fundamentalist criticism was unrelenting that the NCC, and inevitably its creature, the CCC, were allegedly so shot through with modernist theology that they were to be avoided at all costs.[49] There had already been a defection from the Presbyterian move towards the NCC and CCC when a group of Presbyterian conservatives led by Watson Hayes "seceded" from the main seminary at Shandong Christian University and set up a new fundamentalist one, North China Theological Seminary, elsewhere in Shandong Province, at Tengxian. Within a few years, by the mid 1920s, the NCTS had more students than any other seminary, and remained throughout its life as the most important conservative or evangelical theological institution in the country.[50] When the CCC was finally formed, the great majority of the approximately 120,000 Chinese Christians represented by delegates at its first General Assembly, held in early October, 1927, were Presbyterian (US North) or Congregationalist (mostly from the ABCFM); 16 mission boards joined, containing about 30 percent of the Protestant community. That minority representation of the CCC was a matter of disappointment and concern to many, especially the SFPE. We will return to the CCC in later chapters. For now it suffices to note that as they emerged in the mid 1920s, both the NCC and CCC fell short of the size, unity, and agreement on basics that Cheng Jingyi and several other Chinese church leaders had hoped for.

In the meantime, much had happened on the larger scene in China.

Aftermath of the May Fourth Movement and the Christian Movement in China (II)

In 1924–1925, a cataclysm much more powerful than the relatively unco-ordinated anti-Christian propaganda of 1922 engulfed a substantial part of the Protestant world in China. Several forces were at work:

- The national political arena was much more highly charged, with the Guomindang and the Chinese Communist parties in a united front and both parties starting to use the issue of imperialism and the unequal treaties still in effect to demonize the Western presence and privileges for purposes of political mobilization.[51] This was not good for missionary-run schools, for example.
- The focus of Chinese attack included not only demands for tariff autonomy and an end to extraterritoriality, but "educational rights", that is, Chinese control of mission schools, or at least the registration of schools with the government and making religious instruction elective. This became, in the mid 1920s, a huge issue in many mission schools, including upper and even lower middle schools.[52]

The explosion of the May 30 (1925) movement in every major Chinese city from late spring through early 1927 created a deadly situation for Christians, especially foreign ones.[53] The two political parties, still tenuously collaborating in the "united front" (with one eye on the succession to Guomindang leader Sun Yat-sen, who had died in March 1925), continued their political action and intense propaganda for the "nationalist revolution" and its aim of destroying the warlords and expelling foreign privilege and the treaty system. When the parties sent their military forces northwards from Canton in the summer of 1926, Christian venues, including churches and landmarks, were harassed or disrupted or damaged, and some casualties were suffered. After J. E. Williams, the vice president of Nanking University, was shot and killed on campus by revolutionary troops in early 1927, and several other foreigners were killed, the foreign consuls ordered evacuation by their citizens. All but a handful of foreign missionaries fled to the coast, mainly to Shanghai. Over two thousand returned home, some taking early furlough; some decided never to return. Of those who did return to their posts, they did so only in late 1927 or 1928, though many who worked in major cities returned earlier.

Thus there was a definite hiatus in the Christian movement in 1926–1927, and a profound loss of confidence, at least in the missionary sector. The entire Protestant missionary world in China was traumatized, much as in the immediate aftermath of the Boxer Uprising. In fact those who had experienced the Boxers did make that comparison. Much of Christianity's future in China would depend on what political elements achieved ascendancy, whether the "left wing" of the Guomindang party allied with the communists, or its "right wing," already coalescing around Chiang Kai-shek and anti-Communist elements. In fact, the Christian movement was about to become a factor in high-level political circles, as will be recounted in the next chapter.

It seems almost certain that the political uncertainties of the times contributed to the delay from 1923 to1927 of the formation of the CCC. Other uncertainties of the mid 1920s included the future of the Christian schools. Would the new government being brought together in Nanjing require registration for Christian schools or permit any religious instruction? Yet other questions: Would foreigners retain their habitual rights under the treaty system? What is the missionary's proper role – preacher, educator, social engineer, informal adviser, dispenser of resources? One missionary educator who in the end grappled honestly with these issues was Edward Hume, president of Yale-in-China in Changsha, Hunan Province, from its founding in 1909 to Hume's departure in 1926. Hume was sensitive and not unsympathetic to students' political activism in the 1920s, but found himself in an impossible position between demands of the students, local Chinese political forces, and the refusal of the trustees back in New Haven to grant Hume's urgent requests for changes in policies and practices. Having lost the confidence of the board of trustees, Hume had little choice other than to resign in frustration.[54]

If there were questions about the foreign missionaries' role, there may have been even more about the Chinese Christian leaders who had in effect thrown in their lot with the foreigners as partners by becoming active in the SFPE. They were as patriotic as any other Chinese, but it was easy for critics of Christianity to tar them with the brush of disloyalty and untrustworthiness because they were part of a "foreign religion." Due to the unwillingness of the foreign mission boards, and for that matter the unwillingness of most of the missionaries in China, to alter significantly their policies and actions to meet Chinese concerns halfway, SFPE stalwarts like Cheng Jingyi and David Yui were never able fully to shake off the label "foreign toady" or "running dog."

Roman Catholics: momentum and inertia

The first quarter of the twentieth century did not bring a great deal of actual change to the Roman church in China, but it brought considerable movement toward eventual change and a willingness of the Papacy to begin to press for more sharing of power with Chinese priests and bishops.[55]

The twentieth century began for Catholics as it had for Protestants, with the mayhem of the Boxers. Perhaps as many as 30,000 Catholics were killed by Boxers, and only formation of effective armed self-defense forces enabled many Catholic villages to fortify and defend themselves.

Not many Catholics were participants in the late Qing reform movement after 1902, nor in the new intellectual currents of the post-World War I years. Yet a few were involved. The most outstanding intellect among Chinese Catholics in these decades was Ma Xiangbo (1840–1939), the former Jesuit, who was already 60 years old at the turn of the century. Ma was also an excellent organizer and advocate especially for educational improvement for Catholics at the higher levels. Ma, together with Vincent Ying Lianzhi (1867–1926) of Tianjin, a very capable lay leader, were major figures in the establishment of two excellent universities: Aurora (Zhendan) University in Shanghai, whose campus is now part of Fudan University; and Furen University in Beijing, whose campus is now part of Beijing Normal University. Ying Lianzhi also in 1906 single-handedly established and edited for many years the respected Tianjin newspaper *Dagongbao* ("the Impartial").

Meanwhile, the French government was tiring of its policy of more than a half-century of being the "protector" of all Catholic missions in China. Cleaning up after the Boxer mess in 1900–1901 was a huge task for French diplomats. And violent incidents involving Catholic clergy and converts continued even after 1900. There was a violent outbreak in Nanchang, Jiangxi Province, in 1906. The headaches resulting from trying to settle this case strengthened the resolve of the Quai d'Orsay to lessen its involvement in such incidents.[56] The Holy See, which had been frustrated for decades by the adamant French insistence on her right of protection, was delighted at the opportunity perhaps to play a more direct role in China. But there was still resistance within the Roman church to the Vatican's desires, especially from the well-entrenched Missions Etrangères de Paris as well as other European clergy. The Pope's solution was to dilute that Paris Mission resistance and did so by several means. One was to send other nationalities; the first American Catholic missionary priests sent overseas were the Maryknollers, who were assigned to China, where they might be a non-French voice.[57] Vincentians and Passionists were among others sent to China.

However, much of the credit for any twentieth century changes Roman Catholic reformers were able to make must go to Fr. Frederic Vincent Lebbe (1877–1940), a Belgian who, just out of training as a Vincentian priest, at age 18 was sent to China in 1901. He spent time in Tianjin and made friends with Vincent Ying Lianzhi and Ma Xiangbo. Soon he was a tireless advocate for better and more effective sharing of duties with Chinese priests and also for there to be some Chinese bishops, of whom there had been exactly none, for more than 200 years. Lebbe angered the church hierarchy in China, which resulted in his being transferred several times to still his voice, but through various connections he got the ear of the pope on this issue, and the pope, Benedict XV, responded favorably. The Holy Father issued an apostolic letter in November 1919 entitled *Maximum illud*, which proclaimed the urgency of letting native priests and bishops have real control over territorial jurisdictions. This encyclical was not well received by the European bishops who controlled the church. The very next month the Pope appointed an Apostolic visitor, the Bishop of Guangzhou, Jean-Baptiste Budes de Guebriant (1860–1935), to visit all the China missions, then report back to the Vatican. Guebriant's report more than a year later confirmed Lebbe's analysis of the situation. After a transition in the Holy See, the new pope (Pius XI) renewed the initiative of the Vatican in 1922, by appointing Bishop Celso Benigno Luigi Constantini to be apostolic delegate to the China missions; the Holy Father also consecrated him as archbishop, to boost his status in China. Constantini engineered the appointment to important posts of two very capable Chinese priests, making sure they were receiving due respect from the European clergy in China. In 1923 Constantini convened the first council of the Catholic Church in China. This was a meeting for bishops and those of equivalent rank. Then in 1926 came a pivotal event – the consecration of six Chinese bishops at St. Peter's Basilica in Rome with Pius XI himself presiding. Fr. Lebbe's dream, and that of countless Chinese Catholic believers for more than 200 years, had seemingly been realized.[58]

Catholic and Protestant worlds did not overlap much during these decades. Catholics remained basically rural, focused on internal ecclesiastical issues and barely edging into higher education, whereas Protestants were increasingly urban, and were putting huge resources into higher education. And while the number of Catholics remained much higher in absolute terms, in the 1902–1927 period the rate of Protestant growth was significantly higher. The Protestants were also diversifying rapidly. Liberals and conservatives, modernists and fundamentalists, Pentecostals almost in a category of their own – these labels cannot be used blithely, but they do denote some discernible differing emphases in theology, education level, social class, and so forth. As the scene shifts to the period about 1927–1950, it should be noted that there is one category of the Protestant world that actually stems from the pre-1927 world but has not yet been discussed. This is the emergence of sectarian independent Chinese church bodies, which grew not out of the missionary sector or the missionary consciousness, but out of a combination of, on the one hand, the world of orthodox Christian belief and practice, and, on the other hand, features which seem to originate in Chinese popular religion and the world of popular sects with a millenarian cast. In the 1920s we can see the embryonic shape of homegrown Christian groups that proved to be able to survive down to the present. At the time of establishment of the new government in 1949, it is likely that fully 25 percent of Protestants were in these independent churches. They constitute a surprisingly little-known story, with some fascinating personalities. The next chapter will include among other things a brief history of the most important of these wholly independent Chinese-led movements and their leaders. For example, Paul Wei, the Peking cloth dealer who founded the True Jesus Church; Jing Dianying, who developed and ruled rural Christian communities of the Jesus Family on the principles of common ownership and group-directed life; Ni Tosheng (Watchman Nee), creator of the "Little Flock;" John Sung (Song Shangjie) and other talented members of the "Bethel Band" of zealous young musician-evangelists who spread revival all over China. Some women were important leaders, as well, for example Mary Stone (Shi Meiyu), first Chinese woman to receive a US MD degree, whose Bethel Seminary in Shanghai produced the "Bethel Band."

We now turn to the next crucial period of Christian history in China, from the turmoil of the mid 1920s until the Chinese communists' victory in the civil war in 1949.

Notes

1. James Reed, *The Missionary Mind and American East Asia Policy, 1911–1915* (Cambridge, MA: Council on east Asian Studies, Harvard University, 1983), pp. 35–39.
2. James Reed, *The Missionary Mind and American East Asia Policy, 1911–1915* (Cambridge, MA: Council on east Asian Studies, Harvard University, 1983), p. 36.

3. The full title is quite revealing of assumptions. *The Christian Occupation of China: a general survey of the Numerical Strength and Geographical Distribution of the Christian Forces in China made by the Special Committee on Survey and Occupation, China Continuation Committee, 1918–1921*, ed. Milton T. Stauffer (Shanghai: China Continuation Committee, 1922).

4. Parts of Chen's essay are in Jessie G. Lutz, ed., *Christian Missions in China: Evangelists of What?* (Lexington, MA: D.C. Heath, 1965), pp. 47–50.

5. Jonathan D. Spence, *To Change China: Western Advisers in China 1620–1960* (New York: Penguin, 1980), Ch. 6,"Edward Hume: Yale for China."

6. Douglas Reynolds, *China, 1898–1912: The Xinzheng Revolution and Japan* (Cambridge, MA: Harvard, c1993. Also Daniel H. Bays, *Christianity in China: From the Eighteenth Century to the Present* (Stanford, CA: Stanford University Press, 1996).

7. One of the most impressive Protestant achievements was the creation of 13 colleges and universities in these decades. The classic source here is Jessie G. Lutz, *China and the Christian Colleges, 1850–1950* (Ithaca, NY: Cornell University Press, 1971). Also Daniel H. Bays and Ellen Widmer, eds, *China's Christian Colleges: Cross-Cultural Connections, 1900–1950* (Stanford, CA: Stanford University Press, 2009).

8. Quotation from Ryan Dunch, *Fuzhou Protestants and the Making of a Modern China, 1867–1927* (New Haven, CT: Yale University Press), p. 44. Also see the personal life trajectories in Daniel H. Bays, *Christianity in China: From the Eighteenth Century to the Present* (Stanford, CA: Stanford University Press, 1996), essays by Heidi Ross, Judith Liu, and Emily Honig. Two volumes of biographical sketches of Chinese Christians include several women. Carol Lee Hamrin, with Stacey Bieler, *Salt and Light: Lives of Faith that Shaped Modern China*, 2 vols (Eugene, OR: Pickwick Publications, 2008, 2010). An important collection entirely on Christian women is Jessie G. Lutz, ed., *Pioneer Christian Women: Gender, Christianity, and Social Mobility* (Bethlehem, PA: Lehigh University Press, 2010.

9. The point here is that while the data do not show it, it seems likely that some alumni who had been urbanites all their adult lives went home to the countryside to die. This material on the Wenhuiguan is from Daniel H. Bays, "A Chinese Christian 'Public Sphere'?: Socioeconomic Mobility and the Formation of Urban Middle Class Protestant Communities in the Early Twentieth Century," in Kenneth Lieberthal, Shuen-fu Lin, and Ernest P. Young, eds, *Constructing China: the Interaction of Culture and Economics* (Ann Arbor, MI: Center for Chinese Studies, the University of Michigan, 1997), pp. 101–117. Irwin T. Hyatt, Jr. kindly supplied some key data on the Wenhuiguan.

10. Daniel H. Bays, "A Chinese Christian 'Public Sphere'", p. 109.

11. See Ryan Dunch, *Fuzhou Protestants and the Making of a Modern China, 1857–1927* (New Haven, CT: Yale University Press, 2001).

12. There is a fair amount of documentation on these movements, which is brought together nicely by Jonathan T'ien-en Chao, "The Chinese Indigenous Church Movement, 1919–1927: A Protestant Response to the Anti-Christian Movements in Modern China," Ph.D. dissertation, University of Pennsylvania, 1986.

13. This could be discounted as what one would expect pastors at a registered church to say; but there was no other ideological jargon or criticism of the missionaries or mission churches in these conversations.

14. *China Missions Year Book*, published in Shanghai by the Christian literature Society of China, volumes for 1912–1914, *passim*, 1912, ed. G. H. Bondfield, "The Chinese Christian Church," pp. 216–221. 1913, D. MacGillivray, ed., "Independence of the Church in China," pp. 182–191, and J. Rawlinson, "Problems faced by the church," mentioning the desire of the Chinese for more church unity, pp. 193–195. 1914, ed. MacGillivray, "The Independence of the Chinese church," pp. 255–271, esp. pp. 261–267 on Pingyuan, Shandong Province, where the contributor, A.R. DeHaan, mentions, in regard to independence, the "troubles of last year" and the "storms of last year. "

15. The first such meeting was in Shanghai for two weeks in May, 1877. The second, also in Shanghai, was likewise for two weeks in May, 1890. This one, the third, the Morrison centenary conference, was from April 5 to May 9, 1907, more than twice as long as the previous two. For the records of 1877 and 1890, one volume sufficed for each. For 1907, there were two volumes, a "historical volume," and a post-conference volume of records and proceedings. D. MacGillivray, *A Century of Protestant Missions in China (1807–1907), being the Centenary Conference Historical Volume* (Shanghai: American Presbyterian Mission Press, 1907; and *China Centenary Missionary Conference Records: Report of the Great Conference* (New York: American Tract Society, 1907),

16. The most detailed source for Chen's early life is his own *Echoes from China, the Story of my Life and Lectures* (Chicago, 1921). The best recent treatment of him is Xing Fuzeng (Ying Fuk-tsang), *Zhongguo jiyao zhuyizhe de shijian yu kunjing: Chen Chonggui de shenxue sixiang yu shidai* (the Praxis and predicament of a Chinese fundamentalist: Chen Chonggui [Marcus Cheng], his theological thought and his times) (Hong Kong: Alliance Press, 2001).

17. The Mission Covenant's history is complex. Begun as pietist dissenters from the state Lutheran church in Sweden, the Swedish Mission Covenant which they formed became the Swedish Evangelical Mission Covenant of America, made up of immigrants; later it took the name Evangelical Covenant Church of America. The Chinese name for all these is the Xingdaohui., As was the case with other immigrant groups in the late nineteenth century, some immigrants were hardly off the boat to America when they were on another one for an Asian mission field.

18. Marcus Ch'eng [Chen Chonggui], *After Forty Years* (London, 1947), p. 12.

19. The Covenanters portrayed Chen as a "model" native convert,

20. Oral recollections of Chen's son, Chen Renbing, in Shanghai, 1986, indicated Chen's resentment over this disparity of pay and living quarters.

21. Brian Stanley, *The World Missionary Conference Edinburgh 1910* (Grand Rapids, MI: Wm. B. Eerdmans, 2009), pp. 107–111.

22. American Board of Commissioners for Foreign Missions, the oldest American mission in China; by the early 1900s it was mainly Congregationalist. The London Missionary Society, the oldest British mission in China, like the ABCFM, was a multidenominational organization.

23. Terrill E. Lautz, "The SVM and the Transformation of the Protestant Mission to China," in Daniel H. Bays and Ellen Widmer, eds, *China's Christian Colleges: Cross-Cultural Connections, 1900–1950* (Stanford, CA: Stanford University Press, 2009), pp. 3–22.

24. Daniel H. Bays, "Christian Revival in China, 1900–1937," in Edith L. Blumhofer and Randall Balmer, eds., *Modern Christian Revivals* (Urbana IL: University of Illinois Press, 1993). The Chinese student volunteer movement for the ministry program was clearly modeled on the successful North American SVM.

25. Shirley Garrett, *Social Reformers in Urban China: The Chinese Y.M.C.A. 1895–1926* (Cambridge, MA: Harvard University Press, 1979), pp. 65–66.

26. The 120 delegates making up the China Continuation Committee were chosen from five regional meetings all across China earlier in 1913, with John Mott personally chairing all five of those meetings. Wallace C. Merwin, *Adventure in Unity: The Church of Christ in China* (Grand Rapids, MI: Wm. B. Eerdmans, 1974), p. 26.

27. The same articles cited in the references in note 14 of this chapter contain much seemingly sincere encouragement of the independence of the Chinese church.

28. Philip West, *Yenching University and Sino-Western Relations, 1916–1952* (Cambridge, MA: Harvard University Press, 1976), pp. 59–62.

29. Philip West, *Yenching University and Sino-Western Relations, 1916–1952* (Cambridge, MA: Harvard University Press, 1976), pp. 70–74.

30. Philip West, *Yenching University and Sino-Western Relations, 1916–1952* (Cambridge, MA: Harvard University Press, 1976), pp. 74–76.

31. Philip West, *Yenching University and Sino-Western Relations, 1916–1952* (Cambridge, MA: Harvard University Press, 1976), pp. 62–66. It should be noted, however, that John Leighton Stuart remained president the whole time of Wu's chancellorship, as he did for the entire period 1919–1946.

32. The Life Fellowship was first established in 1919 under a different name; its journal began in 1920. There were other intellectual Christian journals, for example *Zhenli* (Truth), but not so long-lived.

33. Charles Keller, "Nationalism and Chinese Christians: The Religious Freedom Campaign and Movement for Independent Chinese Churches, 1911–1917," *Republican China* 12.2 (April 1992), 30–51.

34. Rosalind Goforth, *Goforth of China* (Grand Rapids, MI: Zondervan, 1937).

35. Jonathan Goforth, *By my Spirit* (London: Marshall, Morgan, and Scott, n.d.), and *When the Spirit's Fire Swept Korea* (Grand Rapids, MI: Zondervan, 1943). For Manchuria there are marvelous first-hand accounts in Rev. James Webster,. *Times of Blessing in Manchuria*, 4th edn (Shanghai: Methodist Publishing House, 1909).

36. I do not wish to delve into these two terms at length. By fundamentalist I mean the position which emerged in the 1920s in the "fundamentalist-modernist controversy", with the former stressing the literal truth of the Bible, including the virgin birth, all the miracles, the second coming, anti-Darwinist, and not prepared to be "tolerant" of the truths in other faiths. "Modernists" would be more or less the opposite on all these issues. Pentecostalism is a radical form of fundamentalism which to all or most of the above characteristics adds the "gifts of the Holy

Spirit," such as speaking in tongues, healing, prophecy, and a strong dose of millenarianism. Pentecostalism emerged historically very early in the twentieth century.

37. Well over 900 members in China in the early 1920s.

38. Daniel H. Bays, "The Protestant Missionary Establishment and the Pentecostal Movement," in Edith Blumhofer, Russell Spittler, and Grant Wacker, eds., *Pentecostal Currents in American Protestantism* (Urbana, IL: University of Illinois Press, 1999), pp. 50–67.

39. Daniel H. Bays, "The Protestant Missionary Establishment and the Pentecostal Movement," in Edith Blumhofer, Russell Spittler, and Grant Wacker, eds., *Pentecostal Currents in American Protestantism* (Urbana, IL: University of Illinois Press, 1999), pp. 62–63, has a more extensive discussion.

40. This is persuasively argued in James Alan Patterson, "The Loss of a Protestant Missionary Consensus: Foreign Missions and the Fundamentalist-Modernist Conflict," in Joel A. Carpenter and Wilbert R. Shenk, eds, *Earthen Vessels: American Evangelicals and Foreign Missions, 1880–1980* (Grand Rapids, MI: Wm. B. Eerdmans, 1990), pp. 73–91. Patterson argues that the consensus had rested on agreement on four basics: to make known Jesus and to encourage churches to form; the uniquely divine character of Christ; recognition of the social dimension of the Gospel; a pragmatic ecumenism.

41. Kevin Xiyi Yao, *The Fundamentalist Movement among Protestant Missionaries in China, 1920–1937* (Lanham, MD: University Press of America, 2003).

42. Nathan D. Showalter, *The End of a Crusade: The Student Volunteer Movement for Foreign Missions and the Great War* (Lanham, MD: the Scarecrow Press, 1998).

43. Samuel Ling, "The Christian May Fourth Movement," (Th.D. dissertation Westminster Seminary, Phil., 1980).

44. Actually, a few foreign nationals lost extraterritorial rights as a result of World War I: Germany, Austria-Hungary, and Russia.

45. Milton T. Stauffer, ed. (Shanghai: China Continuation Committee, 1922).

46. Ernest D. Burton was the chair.

47. Ka-che Yip, *Religion, Nationalism, and Chinese Students: the Anti-Christian Movement of 1922–1927* (Bellingham, WA: Western Washington University, 1980), pp, 22–30.

48. Wallace C. Merwin, *Adventure in Unity: The Church of Christ in China* (Grand Rapids, MI: Wm. B. Eerdmans, 1974), pp. 26–29.

49. Kevin Xiyi Yao, *The Fundamentalist Movement among Protestant Missionaries in China, 1920–1937* (Lanham, MD: University Press of America, 2003), esp. pp. 183–230.

50. Kevin Xiyi Yao, "The North China Theological Seminary: Evangelical theological education in China in the Early 1900s," in Ogbu U. Kalu, ed., *Interpreting Contemporary Christianity: Global Processes and Local Identities* (Grand Rapids, MI: Wm. B. Eerdmans, 2008), pp. 187–206.

51. The unequal treaties, *bupingdeng tiaoyue*, only about this time became a major political slogan. See Dong Wang, *China's Unequal Treaties, Narrating National History* (Lanham, MD: Lexington Books, 2005).

52. The extremely effective way in which the educational rights issue, the treaties, and other issues were orchestrated by the two political parties in this period is fascinating. The story is very well told in Jessie G. Lutz, *Chinese Politics and Christian Missions: The Anti-Christian Movements of 1920–1928* (Notre Dame, IN: Cross-Cultural Publications, 1988).

53. The May 30 Movement was mass demonstrations in response to foreign troops shooting Chinese demonstrators in May–June 1925.

54. Jonathan Spence, *To Change China: Western Advisors in China 1620–1960* (New York: Penguin, 1980), pp. 161–183. Another portrait of Hume is in Lian Xi, *The Conversion of Missionaries: Liberalism in American Protestant Missions in China, 1907–1932* (University Park, PA: Penn State Press, 1997), pp. 25–58.

55. In contrast to the seventeenth and eighteenth centuries, where there are probably close to a dozen fine works of scholarship, major secondary works covering catholic history in the first half of the twentieth century are very rare, and more general works have little to offer. A partial exception ("partial" because no focus on the Europeans) is Jean-Paul Wiest, *Maryknoll in China, a History, 1918–1955* (Armonk, NY: M.E. Sharpe, 1988). Other marginally useful works are Thomas A Breslin, *China, American Catholicism, and the Missionary* (University Park, PA: Pennsylvania State University Press, 1980), and Jean-Pierre Charbonnier, *Christians in China: A.D. 600 to 2000*, trans. M.N.L. Couve de Murville. Original French edition, Paris, 2002 (San Francisco, CA: Ignatius Press, 2007).

56. Ernest P. Young, "The Politics of Evangelism at the end of the Qing: Nanchang 1906," in Daniel H. Bays, ed., *Christianity in China: From the Eighteenth Century to the Present* (Stanford, CA: Stanford University Press, 1996), pp. 91–114.

57. Jean-Paul Wiest, *Maryknoll in China: A History, 1918–1955* (Armonk, NY: M. E. Sharpe, Inc., 1988).

58. This section largely adapted from Jean-Pierre Charbonnier, *Christians in China: A.D. 600 to 2000* trans. M.N.L. Couve de Murville. Original French edition, Paris, 2002. (San Francisco, CA: Ignatius Press, 2007), pp. 387–398.

6

The Multiple Crises of Chinese Christianity, 1927–1950

Prologue

In the first half of the twentieth century, the foreign missionary movement in China matured, flourished, declined, and died. In these same decades, a Chinese church was born, a church which today is growing very rapidly. In effect, in the 50 years from 1900 to 1950, Christianity in China forsook its foreign origins and put on Chinese dress. It was not an easy process. The turbulent forces of history, which shaped all aspects of China's politics, economy, and culture, also burst upon foreign missionaries and Chinese Christians in the mid 1920s, as the last chapter has described. Both missionaries and Chinese Christians discovered their continued vulnerability to these historical forces in the decades from the 1920s to 1950. This also affected the new autonomous Chinese parts of the Protestant world in China; but it began with the transformation of the missionary endeavor itself. The missionary community in China remained split between liberals or modernists on one side, and conservatives or fundamentalists on the other. These divisions only worsened in the 1930s. Several issues and events were responsible. If we first take a historical telescope and focus just on two years, 1932–1934, we can see the transformation of Christianity in China in mid process.

On an autumn day in 1932, Pearl Sydenstricker Buck, born in China of missionary parents and herself a Presbyterian China missionary, strode to the

A New History of Christianity in China, First Edition. Daniel H. Bays.
© 2012 Daniel H. Bays. Published 2012 by Blackwell Publishing Ltd.

podium in the ballroom of New York City's Hotel Astor, to address 2000 Presbyterian women. Perhaps the most famous missionary of the day, Buck had just received the Pulitzer Prize for her novel *The Good Earth*. Now she addressed the topic, "Is There a Case for Foreign Missions?" While her answer at the end of the speech was technically a tepid "yes," this affirmative was so qualified and so unenthusiastic, and her criticisms of missionaries for being arrogant, ignorant, and narrow-minded so trenchant, that at the end the audience was stunned. They did not even applaud until Buck was almost off the stage. This event ignited a firestorm of agitated comment, pro and con, by critics and defenders of foreign missions, in almost all quarters of American Protestantism, and of course especially in China, where conservatives demanded that Buck resign from the Southern Presbyterian Mission Board.[1] It was a sign of the times for China missions.

Another sign of the times was the publication just a few months earlier of a seven-volume study which had been commissioned by John D. Rockefeller, Jr., the foremost individual American financial supporter of foreign missions. This project, entitled "Rethinking Missions," was conducted by a commission of appraisal chaired by William Ernest Hocking (1873–1966), of Harvard University. The subject was missions world-wide, but the main single focus was China. The resulting seven volumes were condensed into a single volume and published by Hocking under the title *Rethinking Missions: A Laymen's Inquiry After One Hundred Years*. Widely circulated and read, the Laymen's Report forthrightly advocated an overhaul of missionary thinking, especially on such questions as the exclusivity of Christianity. On the whole, it was shot through with "modernist" theology, and although it greatly offended evangelical mission supporters, and stimulated a floodtide of controversy and criticism from fundamentalists, the report was very influential. It influenced other aspects of missionary discourse for several years.[2] The Laymen's Report in conjunction with the attack on missions by Pearl Buck constituted formidable factors in causing all but the most firm fundamentalists among American Christians to have second thoughts about the legitimacy of foreign missions.[3]

Yet another indication of trends was that some familiar parts of the Sino-Foreign Protestant Establishment came upon hard times in 1932–1933. Robert Service, former college track star at UC-Berkeley, who went to China in 1905 under the auspices of the Student Volunteer Movement (SVM) for Foreign Missions with his wife Grace, and who pioneered the establishment of YMCAs in West China, was faced with an unexpected early retirement. Having poured out his life in service to the Chinese people and in loyal commitment to the "Y" and its mission, he was summarily sacked by International YMCA headquarters in New York. Service was one of hundreds thus cut loose or given involuntary retirement. In the midst of the Great Depression and dwindling contributions, the YMCA and other well-established missions in China had a massive financial crunch in the early 1930s. Their expensive institution-heavy facilities, especially hospitals, schools and colleges, swamped the mission budgets. Many missionaries headed home in the 1930s.[4]

Continued Forward Movement

Although it is clear that speaking broadly, most missions were on the defensive by the early 1930s, not all were, especially not the evangelical ones. There were still enthusiastic young people answering the "call" to China. The China Inland Mission (CIM), that remarkable international creation of J. Hudson Taylor, continued the dramatic growth it had enjoyed since the late 1800s. Its "faith mission" principles (that is, accepting no denominational or other regular financial support) managed to adapt relatively well to the new climate of scarcity. Even as other missions were shrinking in the early 1930s because of discouragement or budgets, the nondenominational CIM launched a successful campaign to add 200 new missionaries. Learning of this campaign for "the Two Hundred," the late David Adeney (1911–1994), a young British college student at Cambridge, felt a strong call to China. He came to north central China with the CIM in 1934, and found his niche working with students, which he did until leaving China in 1950. He established personal ties which remained intact though dormant for more than 30 years, and which were renewed in heartwarming fashion in the 1980s when Adeney returned to China.[5] In these years it could still be dangerous to be a Christian in China, whether foreign or Chinese. But even tragic martyrdoms could be transformed into effective recruiting opportunities, as we saw in the last chapter in Yale graduate Horace Pitkin's death at the hands of the Boxers in 1900. A few months after David Adeney's arrival in 1934, one of the most dramatic incidents of martyrdom in China missions history occurred. An attractive young couple who were products of Moody Bible Institute in Chicago and had come to China a couple of years before, John and Betty Stam, of the CIM, were stationed in a small city in Anhui Province (central China). When Communist troops captured the city in late 1934, they beheaded the Stams, and killed some local Christians who pleaded for the foreigners' lives, but spared their three-month-old child, who was safely spirited to a nearby mission station. This story gained much publicity, and motivated many young people to go to the mission field.[6]

In addition to continuing signs of life in the CIM and some other theologically conservative missions, a wave of Pentecostal revivalism was sweeping some parts of China in the early 1930s. Its stress on the "gifts of the spirit," including prophecy, divine healing, and speaking in tongues, had a huge impact on some missions. A steady stream of new missionaries from small new missions or as individuals, almost all of them faith missionaries, arrived in China every year, answering their "call." Many of these were Pentecostals.[7] These new Pentecostal ideas and claims also fed the growth of most of the Chinese independent churches that were organizing by the 1920s, as we will see later in this chapter.

What was going on in the early 1930s among Chinese Christians? Those in the young union Church of Christ in China (CCC), organized in 1927, were feeling their way forward in an organization that had a shared but not equal division of power between foreign and Chinese elements in the Sino-Foreign Protestant Establishment (SFPE). The CCC grew very little in the 1930s, and remained perpetually short of resources because of the Great Depression-induced slashes in missions budgets. However, not all Chinese Christians were in partnership with foreign missionaries. A portent of life and growth in the church was John Sung, a fiery independent evangelist/revival leader, traveling the country and drawing huge crowds as part of an evangelistic "Bethel Band" sent out by the Bible school and mission run by two women, Dr. Shi Meiyu and Ms. Jennie Hughes, a Chinese and an American, in Shanghai. We can also see the Peking Fundamentalist pastor Wang Mingdao (who would have a fateful clash with the new regime in the 1950s) building his own "tabernacle" for services in Peking, in addition to doing speaking engagements all over China. Other independent Chinese Christian groups and leaders were leaving their mark on these years as well: Watchman Nee, largely based in Shanghai, was working out his Holy Spirit-centered theology of body, soul, and spirit; the Jesus Family was learning how to live communally in rural Shandong province, under the firm leadership of its founder Jing Dianying; and the True Jesus Church, based on the visions received by Peking cloth dealer Paul Wei, comparable to the visions of Taiping founder Hong Xiuquan in the 1840s, had grown explosively for more than a decade. All these were home-grown Christian movements, although all their founders came out of missionary-run churches. Their histories are one of the foci of this chapter. But first we must review the national scene.

Protestant Christianity in the "Nanjing Decade," 1927–1937

After the Guomindang purged the Communists in 1927 and set up their new national government in Nanjing, 200 miles up the Yangzi River from Shanghai, the Nanjing government proved much less radical in its attitude toward foreigners and Christianity than had been feared by many. Conditions were not onerous for missionaries to operate quite freely. And the fact that the political group that was most intolerant of Christianity, the CCP, was out of the field of vision and almost without influence during these years, was helpful. Most of the foreign missionaries who had fled in 1926–1927 returned in 1928–1929, though only about 6000 rather than the former more than 8000. They did have to abide by the new Guomindang (or "Nationalist") government requirement that the chief officer of every Christian school must be Chinese, that religious instruction be optional for students, and that there be Chinese patriotic political instruction under the banner of Sun Yat-sen's "three people's principles" (*sanmin zhuyi*). But missionaries themselves still had extraterritorial privileges, and many government officials were Christians, which facilitated the work of both missionaries and Chinese.

Moreover, missionaries and most Chinese Christians were greatly encouraged by the fact that Chiang Kai-shek was baptized a Christian in 1930. His marriage to Song Meiling (Soong Mei-ling) in late 1927 was also in effect a marriage to one of the most prominent families in the SFPE, that of Charles Soong (1866–1918), who had been a pillar of the Shanghai Christian community for many years. Soong's widow Ni Guizeng, also from a prominent Christian family, became matriarch of the family after Soong's death in 1918, presiding over the final stages of the overseas education of the six children, and their marriages. The oldest daughter, Soong Ching-ling, married Sun Yat-sen, and did not remarry after Sun's death in 1925; the second, Ai-ling, married H. H. Kung, well-connected and a future political power player. All three sons were later important officials in Nationalist China.[8] Chiang Kai-shek, after 1928 the ruler of a more or less unified China, courted Meiling in 1926–1927, but Mother Ni refused to agree to a marriage unless Chiang promised seriously to investigate Christianity and consider being baptized. Chiang agreed, the two were married in December 1927, and about two years later Chiang did in fact convert to Christianity. He was baptized in 1930. This was naturally immensely gratifying to the Christian community, and it did open doors of access for Christian spokespersons, both foreign and Chinese, to get the ear of the President in coming years. In some cases missionaries or leading Chinese Christians were turned to as advisers or as direct administrators of government programs. In his last book, a general history of China, the late John King Fairbank, the dean of American China scholars, speaks briefly of the "limits of Christian reformism" in China during these years.[9] The leaders of the National Christian Council wanted the Christian movement in China to do something tangible to contribute to national development and amelioration of the wretched material circumstances of peasants and urban factory workers alike, which had been aggravated even more by effects of the world-wide depression. Several reformist projects were attempted in this decade which involved Christian inspiration or participation. "Rural reconstruction" was a term in common usage in the 1930s. Under this rubric came several local programs. One very important one was Y. C. James Yen, who was a Christian, and his decade-long experiment in rural socio-economic improvement in health, including village doctors; in village schools; and in farming techniques and credit cooperatives for farmers. This effort centered in Ting Hsien (Ding xian), a county in Hebei Province, and became an admired model for rural reconstruction.

Another attempt at rural reconstruction, one directly implemented by the National Christian Council (NCC), involved the Nanjing Theological Seminary, which was part of the (Christian) University of Nanjing, in setting up a Rural Training Institute in Shunhuazhen, a village close to Nanjing. Professor Frank W. Price took seminary students out to this site to make them more aware of rural problems. This project began quite early, in 1930, several years before the Guomindang government evinced a serious interest in rural reconstruction. But it remained small and unable to contemplate any large programs.[10] Yet another program, partially initiated by the Rural committee of the NCC, was in the years after 1934, when the Communists were routed from their base in Jiangxi Province. The initial NCC-connected effort was taken over by the Guomindang government, although the respected ABCFM missionary George Shepherd was appointed to do rural reconstruction work in Lichuan in Jiangxi, which became the site of a comparable multifaceted effort at rural reform, including education, health measures, technology transfer, rural industries, and credit cooperatives.[11]

The basic problem encountered by these reformist, partly Christian-inspired efforts was twofold: one, these were very limited model programs, designed to show the possibilities of what might be done. To play their desired role as catalysts for change, it would have been necessary to reproduce them several hundred times all across China. That was not going to happen without the elite class of China being willing to go "to the People," and China's elite, small and urban-bound, and preoccupied with their lives there, were not willing to do that. The small number of Chinese trained and experienced in rural work were not nearly sufficient to staff more than these models.

The second problem encountered by would-be reformers was the sheer size and intractability of some of the rural realities that Christian reformers faced. The respected British scholar R. H. Tawney published a comprehensive objective study of rural society and economy in 1932, making clear the amount of effort and resources it would take to impact significantly rural society.[12] Moreover, in the countryside, social activism to better the lives of the common people, while commendable in Christian terms, was in fact often threatening to the local rural elite or "gentry," and resulted in local elite opposition. Patterns of ownership and tenancy, buildup of landed estates, technology used, credit for small farmers at manageable rates of interest, education, even health care – changes in these things had a potential impact on power and political relationships in the countryside. As a result, the Christian efforts at rural reconstruction in the 1930s, like the entirely secular efforts, "barely scratched the surface of the Chinese people's problems."[13] And the reformers often ended up frustrated and disillusioned. For example, both Zhang Fuliang and ABCFM missionary George Shepherd were among the most knowledgeable and dedicated Chinese and foreign missionary experts, respectively, on rural reconstruction. They both were discouraged by the difficulties encountered in Lichuan, Jiangxi Province, in their attempts in the mid 1930s to implement a program there after the communists were expelled. Nationwide, no rural reform program in non-Communist areas could be called a "success."

Urban social problems also attracted the attention of Christian reformers. The YWCA of China was from almost its inception very socially aware, and beginning in the years of and after the Great War was particularly conscious of the deplorable working conditions of the women and child workers in the textile mills of Shanghai. This was the purview of the industrial department of the YWCA, which in Shanghai, at least, had some radical and only tenuously "Christian" staff members, both American and Chinese, such as Ida Pruitt (1888–1985) and Cora Deng (Deng Yuzhi, 1900–1996).[14] Despite the suspicion with which any initiative to work with factory laborers was viewed in the capitalist center of Shanghai, the YWCA managed to implement a women's three-year literacy program in night schools. This program, while not directly encouraging strikes or other work actions, gave the worker–students not only the ability to read and write, but also resources for managing groups of people, communication skills, and for seeing themselves as able to attempt such a thing as a strike. And they did organize some strikes.[15] Nevertheless, despite giving women factory workers some self–confidence and organizing tools, this approach did not call into question the legitimacy of the entire system.

Thus the Christian reformist efforts of the "Nanjing decade" came to naught or very little, stymied by the old rural elite and its prerogatives in the countryside and by the urban business and industrial power structures in cities like Shanghai. Their recalcitrance made impossible a successful reformist approach to China's problems. What China desperately needed, it could be argued, was revolutionary land reform and firm direction of the modern sector of the economy toward effective state-imposed goals and behaviors. And Christian reformism of the NCC or other parts of the SFPE could not go so far.

Foreign and Chinese Christian leaders, however, engaged in one more episode of involvement with the Guomindang regime of Chiang Kai-shek after 1934. In that year the Generalissimo, in cooperation with the infamous "Blue Shirts," a fascist organization of military officers intensely loyal to him and modeled on Hitler's and Mussolini's examples from Europe, launched the "New Life Movement." Extremely authoritarian, focused on loyalty to the leader, the New Life Movement (NLM) was a mixture of traditional Confucian virtues, exhortations to patriotism, and a ban on uncivic behavior such as spitting on the street. Its Puritanical moral punc-tilios were derided by intellectuals, but in fact the NLM made a big, and partly successful, bid for Christian support and participation[16] The Chinese YMCA and the NCC were both repelled and attracted to the NLM, while most foreign missionaries responded somewhat favorably to the overtures for Christian support made by the government. After Chiang's kidnapping by some of his disgruntled generals in late 1936, and then his dramatic release, he stressed how his Christianity pulled him through the ordeal. That brought on board the previously skeptical parts of the Sino-foreign Prot-estant establishment to support the NLM. And even more missionaries became active supporters. Growing Christian support for the NLM was also enhanced by government and Guomindang party pressures on the Christian community, for example to make registration of schools an easy, or a difficult, process, depending on the response to the NLM. In the end, the NLM did not turn out to be an extremely useful tool of statebuilding, however. Rigidly authoritarian and first loyal to Chiang above all, it was of no use in promoting needed social and economic reforms, and faded from the scene in the late 1930s, with its Christian supporters losing face among liberals and progressives.[17]

Statebuilding, Social Reform, and Soul-Saving: The Rise of Independent Chinese Christianity

In the mid 1930s, foreign and Chinese Christians were arrayed along a spectrum of missions, churches, and Christian organizations and move-ments. The remnants of the Sino-foreign Protestant established were still very much in evidence in the Church of Christ in China and the National Christian Council, where they dominated discussion and decision-making. Both nationalism and social conscience motivated this end of the spectrum. Further along the spectrum were mission groups and churches of a more distinctively "conservative" cast, who had left or had never joined the NCC because of its liberal theology and pursuit of social reform, and who were more likely to be members of the Bible Union of China. This included, first and foremost, the CIM, but also the Christian and Missionary Alliance, the US Southern Presbyterians, the Anglican communion,[18] several ethnic Lutheran groups, the American Free Methodists and the Church of the Nazarene, the Assemblies of God and a few smaller Pentecostal missions, and finally literally dozens of tiny, sometimes one-person, faith missions. These all put relatively more stress on the conversion and regeneration of the individual than of society, and most of them did so partly because of a strong Christian millenarian belief that Christ was not long in coming again. With that would come the Last Judgment, as described in the book of Revelations in the New Testament; therefore time was short to reach the unsaved with the Gospel. They were not without patriotism, but they did not rank statebuilding or improvement of society as high a priority as preaching the Gospel and winning souls. Yet further along the spectrum of Christian groups were the new churches of the Republican period (post-1912), wholly independent and without any foreign leadership whatsoever, although each of the founders of these movements was influenced by foreign Christians at times early in his development. These churches have become an important subject of research and writing in the field of "Sino-Christian studies" or the "History of Christianity in China" in recent years. Here we will look at three of them: The True Jesus Church (Zhen Yesu Jiaohui), The Jesus Family (Yesu Jiating), and the movement centered around Ni Tosheng in Fuzhou and Shanghai which is variously called "The Assembly Hall (Juhuichu)," "The Little Flock (Xiaoqun)," even simply "the Local Church (Difang jiaohui)."[19]

The True Jesus Church[20]

The TJC had its earliest roots in a newspaper published by the small Sino-foreign Pentecostal community in Hong Kong, which was formed there in 1907 and in early 1908 put out the first issue of *Pentecostal Truths* (*Wuxunjie zhenlibao*).[21] It was edited by one of the early Hong Kong Chinese converts to Pentecostalism. Copies of this paper were seen in North China by a group of Swedish faith missionaries based in Zhengding, Hebei Province. One of those missionaries, named Peterson, laid hands on a certain Wei Enbo in Beijing in 1916 to heal his tuberculosis. The movement which became the TJC was mainly the product of the fertile mind of this same Mr. Wei Enbo (1876–1919), a Beijing cloth dealer and former LMS member who had been plagued by tuberculosis for some time. Healed, as he thought, Wei himself now became a Pentecostal, and received the gift of the Holy Spirit and "tongues."[22] Then a few months later he was "led by the Holy Spirit" to a river outside Beijing, where the voice of God spoke to him directly from heaven. God's voice told Wei to receive "face-down" baptism by immersion, which he did in the river immediately, unassisted by clergy. The voice then declared that Wei would receive "a wholesale armor . . . and the sword of the Holy Spirit to kill the demons" – which he then proceeded to do, chasing them with gusto somewhere in space. At this point, the student of modern Chinese history cannot help being aware of the remarkable similarity of Wei's experiences to those of the Taiping founder, Hong Xiuquan, in the mid nineteenth century. After this Wei went on a 39-day fast (just shy of the 40 days in the wilderness of Jesus), during which time he saw Jesus, the patriarchs, and the 12 disciples. He was given his new name, Paul (Baoluo), and commissioned by God to "correct" (*gengzheng*) the church, meaning (as Paul Wei interpreted it) all Christian churches. The name True Jesus Church was already in use by Wei and his first followers in 1917, when they began visiting mission churches in and near Beijing and Tianjin prophesying Christ's soon return and denouncing Western Christianity, calling for parishioners to leave the foreign churches. The doctrines of the church were refined by Wei's contact with some individuals from Shandong, especially Zhang Lingsheng of Weixian (today's Weifang), who had been a Pentecostal for some years, having picked it up on a trip to Shanghai. It also may have been this Zhang who contributed the practice of worship on the Sabbath.[23] By 1919 the new church started its first publication, which recorded its doctrines in the first issue. Interestingly these are very little changed today. TJC doctrines and practices are a unique eclectic combination of sabbatarianism (only Saturday worship), Pentecostalism (all should seek baptism of the Holy Spirit, tongues, prophecy and healing), and a kind of "Jesus only" Unitarianism (baptize only in the name of Jesus, not Father/Son/Holy Spirit; shun the doctrine of the Trinity [*sanwei yiti*] and teach the unitary and undivided [*shu'yi wu'er*] true God). All this is packaged in a radical egalitarianism, with directives not to have the office of pastor, only elders and deacons; church workers are not to receive a salary; worship services may not have set time limits, and all must be given the chance to speak and pray.

Paul Wei's tuberculosis had not been permanently healed, and he died in October 1919. The first General Assembly of the TJC was held in 1920. Two delegates from the TJC attended the National Christian Conference in Shanghai in 1922, though that was its last venture into ecumenism. The church grew exuberantly in the 1920s, as it split into two headquarters, one headed by Barnabas Zhang (Zhang Dianju) of Weixian and the other by Paul Wei's son Isaac (Wei Yisa). In 1930 a national conference expelled Barnabas Zhang and reunited the movement under Isaac Wei. The TJC grew rapidly in the early 1930s, especially in rural areas in central China. It was always troubled by splinter groups that hived off, at least 15 of them by 1937. One, "The Church of the Heavenly Mother" (*Tianmuhui*), was very reminiscent of late imperial millenarian sects such as the White Lotus, that centered on the "unborn mother" (*Wusheng laomu*) of the Western paradise. There seems to have been a large potential rural audience for an end-times message carrying over from the late imperial decades of the nineteenth century and the early twentieth century, which the TJC somehow tapped. By the time of the war with Japan the TJC was already very likely the second largest Protestant church in China, second only to the union CCC. And it is still thriving in China today.

The Jesus Family[24]

The Jesus Family was a product of the North China Plain in Shandong Province and its alternating cycle of flood and drought. Shandong peasants were rooted in their ancestral villages, yet the inhabitants were accustomed to being on the road, away from the old family locale. Roving bands of rootless young peasants fed the ranks of the Boxer movement in 1900. At the end of the Qing, after longstanding Manchu prohibition of Han Chinese migration to Manchuria was permitted to lapse, there was massive immigration from Shandong to the northeast provinces, including more than four million during the 1920s, but population pressure in Shandong still remained high. And because Shandong was strategic and relatively flat, in the warlord years (1916–1927) Shandong was the key to north China warlord coalitions. The constant fighting accentuated the misery of the people, who suffered at the hands of bandits (of which there were tens of thousands) as well as from soldiers. A partial remedy in the eyes of many was the formation of mutual-aid societies for extending credit to farmers, marketing crops or local products, and generally filling in the gaps or weaknesses in the community's solidarity. It was in this milieu that the Jesus Family was formed. The Jesus Family, in the words of Lian Xi, was "a sectarian mutual-aid community independent of mission Christianity and bound together by Pentecostalism and an ascetic pursuit of end-time Salvationism."[25]

The founder of the Jesus family was Jing Dianying (1890–1957), from an educated, well-off family in Mazhuang village, Tai'an County (Xian). While still in his 20s, Jing patched together an eclectic miscellany of religious connections, including his baptism in the Methodist church in Tai'an city in 1914, but also including sects that merged Confucian ethics, Daoist mysticism, and a dash of millenarianism from Maitreyan Buddhist sources. Starting in 1921 he organized in succession a business cooperative for credit and savings and a Christian silkmaking cooperative. At the same time during the early 1920s Jing was frequenting the American Assemblies of God mission in Tai'an city and becoming a Pentecostal.[26] In 1927 he combined and renamed the cooperatives the Jesus Family. From this time on, the major center of the Jesus Family nationwide was in Mazhuang, where Jing ruled in an authoritative, if not authoritarian, manner. Early on the first members built a palisade of cypress trees around the "family's" land, which grew to be 15 feet high. Inside, all who joined had to give up all their property to the communal group, and were assigned to productive work, whether agricultural or light industrial or manufacturing. The JF aimed to be entirely self-sufficient. Families were separated into men's and women's dormitories, children were shared by all, and all ate common meals. The real glue holding it all together, however, was a strong Christian faith. Several hours a day were spent in prayer and worship. Individual religious experiences of several kinds were not unusual in the Jesus Family. Being "born again" (*chongsheng*) or being "filled with the Holy Spirit" (*Shengling chongman*), with the latter accompanied by dancing, for example, were common. Most prized and prestigious was what the JF called "testimony" (*jianzheng*) which involved first being caught up to heaven in a kind of vision, and there receiving special words to the faithful from God. Coming back to earth (or out of a trance), the individual then reported to the community, giving voice to what he or she had been vouchsafed by God. Many of the family members, and most of the leaders, experienced this phenomenon.[27] A ritual practice associated with the Boxers of three decades earlier seems linked to this "testimony" behavior of the Jesus Family, and may indicate a common origin in the popular culture of the north China plain. This was the phenomenon of *beiti*, being elevated or lifted up to the presence of God to hear direct revelations from God, which would be reported via "testimony" to the entire community. This ritual is very reminiscent of one of the key Boxer practices in 1899–1900, the possession ritual called *jiangshen futi*.[28] Yet another similarity between Shandong popular culture and the Jesus Family was the latter's strong millenarianism, looking for the end times, which were imminent.

From its founding in 1927 through the 1930s, with Shandong and most of north China continuing to suffer from disasters and many people looking for a way simply to survive, the egalitarian Jesus Family looked attractive. It grew and spread to all the neighboring provinces. Several dozen more Jesus Family locations were formed over the next few years, into the 1940s. For each, a "family head" (*jiazhang*) was appointed by Jing. These family heads had the same extensive control over the lives of the members as Jing had in the original family at Mazhuang. Contact was maintained to some extent by establishing the practice of once every year the scattered Jesus Family communities sending their heads and other responsible persons to a two-week meeting at Mazhuang. Thus the Jesus Family was growing steadily by the time of the Sino-Japanese war, having nowhere the numbers of the TJC but providing a simple subsistence life along with intense religious experience for its members.

Ni Tosheng (Watchman Nee) and his Movement[29]

Watchman Nee (name at birth Ni Shuzu; 1903–1972) grew up in Fuzhou, where his grandfather had been the second native Chinese minister in the ABCFM. Converted in 1920 at an evangelistic meeting of Dora Yu (Yu Cidu), the earliest Chinese woman evangelist, Nee developed his ideas in the height of the nationalistic movement of the 1920s, in the company of several other Fuzhou students of the Anglican Trinity school.[30] In 1926–1927, at the height of national political drama in the "Nationalist revolution", Nee barely paid attention. He was busy refining some of his basic ideas, applying the fruits of extended reading in works of the mystic Jessie Penn-Lewis and, holed up in Shanghai, writing the longest book he ever wrote, *The Spiritual Man (Shuling de ren)*, which he published in three volumes in 1928 (English translation, 1968). Just as most other independent Christian leaders were adopting Pentecostalism, likewise in the late 1920s and early 1930s Nee, whose own thinking so much stressed the Holy Spirit, flirted with Pentecostalism, but chose a different path to spiritual transcendence. This was the concept of distinguishing body, soul, and spirit, as well as the insight into the "mystery of the cross" or the "truth of the cross" – that is, the realization for the Christian that "I am dead with Christ," enabling the believer to live in victory over the world's evils. Moreover, Nee elaborated, all of history was moving toward the "Age of the Kingdom," when those who had been victorious would "sit with Christ on his throne" at the end of the age and death itself would be vanquished. This basic millenarian vision of an imminent "end of time" cataclysm characterized most other Protestant groups as well, but Nee made the most detailed elaboration of it.

By about 1930, Nee was rapidly gathering followers, more from urban than from rural areas, and many of them from the urban middle and professional classes. He also addressed the issue of denominationalism, which had bothered him for some time, and which he decried as pernicious, refusing to let his followers call themselves by any particular name. To some degree this anti-denominationalism easily overflowed into anti-foreignism and suspicion of foreign churches and pastors. Ironically, Nee's experience with the Plymouth Brethren in the UK in the 1930s made him wary of foreign entanglements and foreigners using him for purposes of mission or for any other reason. Yet he also made use of his two trips to England to deepen his familiarity with the "dispensationalist" writings and interpretations of the major Plymouth Brethren thinkers, especially those of John Nelson Darby (1800–1882).[31] His Brethren-influenced ecclesiological views grew more complex, but the essence of his teaching remained the millenarian vision of the spiritual victory over the evils and trials of the world through identification with Christ's death and, for those who thereby are the victors or "overcomers," to be with God and Christ in the timeless New Jerusalem. Nee's elaborate theology and strongly opinionated ecclesiology are apparent in the work he wrote in 1938, *Concerning our Missions* (English translation, 1939).[32] Most of what have been published as his writings are actually transcriptions of notes taken at lectures or teaching sessions for "co-workers." Nee did very little traveling and revivalist preaching, preferring to let his message be disseminated via his writings and publications, as well as the evangelistic work of the co-workers. His emphasis on the "local church" or only one church in each city, and not using trained and ordained pastors but simply "co-workers" for local church leadership, were among other practices setting Nee and his group apart. Several of the "co-workers" who rose to prominence in the movement's leadership (for example, Li Chang-shou, "Witness Lee") were from Shandong province, an area which we have seen also contributed substantially to the origins and growth of the True Jesus Church and the Jesus Family. At any rate Nee's movement grew steadily throughout the 1930s.

The Spiritual Gifts Society (Ling'en hui)

The Spiritual Gifts Society was not a church or an organization, but simply a minimally organized movement of revivalist enthusiasm which began in Shandong and swept across north and central China in the early 1930s. It apparently began in the county of Feixian in southern Shandong, then spread North and East over the next two or three years. It is said to have been started by some Pentecostal missionaries, but it is not entirely clear whether these were foreign or Chinese missionaries.[33] What is more clear is that the meetings held under the auspices of the "society" were highly emotional and raucous, indeed so much so that the behaviors they entailed were appalling to observers, especially missionary observers. After attending some Spiritual Gifts Society meetings, Paul Abbot, the chairman of the Shandong Presbyterian Mission, as well as other missionaries, reported that the meetings were pandemonium, with messages in tongues ubiquitous, swoons and trances (called "raptures") frequent.[34] As the movement spread, it attracted many adherents who were members of US Presbyterian (North) Chinese congregations. The missionaries responsible for these congregations were suspicious if not outright hostile. In writing about the Ling'en hui in the Shanghai missions press, they used terms such as "primitive psychology," "misuse of the Bible," "vagaries of the leaders," their meetings a "liturgy of disorder," and more.[35] In some cases, if foreign opposition was too great, a Chinese pastor with his congregation would leave the local presbytery and the mission to join the Spiritual Gifts Society, perhaps to return later, or perhaps not. In the end, the Ling'en hui did not develop any sort of ecclesiastical identity or institutional staying power. No records or information has appeared indicating that it ever went beyond this stage of development, or survived even as late as 1940.

The missionary hesitation or criticism of the Ling'en hui was ironic, because at the same time that the Ling'en hui was flourishing in the early 1930s, a movement called the "Shandong revival" was sweeping through the missionary ranks of the province. It was set off by the extended visit to Shandong of Ms. Marie Monsen, a freelance Norwegian missionary who had a Pentecostal experience which transformed her missionary work into revivalism among missionaries. Monsen had already visited the US Southern Baptists in Shandong in the late 1920s. Now in 1930 she returned, and got a huge response from Southern Baptists and US Presbyterians as well. During the next two years many missionaries and Chinese as well were not only "born again" for the first time, but large numbers had, in the words of participant Mary Crawford, "a definite experience of the baptism of the Holy Spirit."[36] It seems manifestly clear that the revival meetings were substantially Pentecostal. Crawford's account describes people being hurled to the ground unable to rise, "holy laughter and praise," all-night meetings, "the Holy Spirit moving as an audible wind," involuntary sounds in prayer, and many miraculous healings. Of course by this time the Southern Baptists had rejected the practice of speaking in tongues or anything else labeled "Pentecostal," so Crawford never mentions the words "Pentecostal" or "tongues" in her 1933 book. But the contents make it clear what was going on. Crawford's account was so transparent that when C. L. Culpepper, a participant in the events as a young missionary, wrote about it in his memoirs in 1968 he used Crawford's book extensively, but rewrote parts to make the account less obviously Pentecostal.[37]

An age of individual evangelists

Until about 1920, foreign evangelists like Sherwood Eddy of the YMCA frequently came to China for revival meetings, and a few resident missionaries, such as the Canadian Presbyterian Jonathan Goforth (1859–1936), were also on the revival circuit. Moreover, a few Chinese revivalists began to attract a following. We have encountered Ding Limei, associated with the YMCA and the SVM for the ministry, who continued his work well into the 1920s but not beyond; Ding died in 1936. Likewise Dora Yu (Yu Cidu, 1873–1931), who began her evangelistic career after 1903 in the Methodist Episcopal churches around Shanghai, then in 1908 stepped onto a wider national stage to become the first woman revival speaker in China. It was Dora Yu's revival ministry coming to Fuzhou in the early 1920s that made such an impact on Watchman Nee and his early followers.[38] There was a handful of other Chinese revivalists who operated regionally in the first two decades of the century. For example, one, a medical doctor turned evangelist, Li Shuqing, influenced Marcus Ch'eng deeply about 1906, and a Lutheran missionary described in 1936 several revivalists who were popular in the Yangzi Valley in the 1930s.[39] But in the 1920s and 1930s, an entire new generation of independent Chinese revivalists, born just before or just after 1900, came to dominate the ranks of Chinese revival ministry.

Wang Mingdao

Among the first to emerge was Wang Mingdao (1900–1991).[40] He is also perhaps the best known of this group in the West, because of his public resistance to the Communist authorities in the 1950s and his subsequent long imprisonment before his release in 1979. Wang had a salvation experience and then a Pentecostal experience about 1920, but later rejected Pentecostalism. A stern and rather dogmatic man, often critical of foreign missionaries and vociferously opposed to "liberal" theology, he was a powerful, effective speaker and teacher. Ignoring the anti-Christian uproar of the early 1920s, he preached in the environs of Beijing and by 1925 had a sufficient following to set up his own independent church in Beijing, later called the "Christian Tabernacle" (Jidutu Huitang).

From the late 1920s on, he spent about half of each year on the road, conducting revivals and evangelistic meetings at evangelical or fundamentalist churches. He did not create new churches, but worked with established ones, whether denominational or not. He also edited and published for more than two decades a popular quarterly Christian magazine, *The Spiritual Food Quarterly (Lingshi jikan)*, in which appeared some of his most trenchant criticisms of the social Gospel, liberal Christianity, the SFPE, NCC and CCC and their world. He called the true Church to come out of this corrupted one and prepare for the fast-approaching time of Judgment.[41] As we will see, Wang's stance did not change from political regime to regime; warlords, Guomindang, Japanese, finally Communists, they were all the same to him in that he paid no attention to any restrictions they may have wanted to impose on him.

Dora Yu and Women's Evangelism

Dora Yu's career is very difficult to track because of the scarcity of documentation, but it seems clear that she was instrumental in the conversion of several individuals who were important in the group gathered around Watchman Nee in the 1920s. Some of these were women. Ruth Lee (Li Yuanru) and Peace Wang (Wang Peizhen), from Nanjing, soon affiliated with Watchman Nee and Leland Wang (Wang Zai) in Fuzhou. Other important participants in this revivalist group were Wilson Wang (Wang Shi), Faithful Luke (Lu Zhongxin), Simon Meek (Miao Shaoxun), and John Wang (Wang Lianjun), all in their 20s during these years in Fuzhou.[42] Most of them remained visible figures on the Chinese Christian scene for decades, some of them in cooperation with Nee's movement, others as independent forces. Dora Yu was also one of the backers of the summer 1925 Shanghai revival, which took place in the immediate aftermath of the explosive hyper-nationalistic May 30 movement. Considering the anti-Christian and anti-foreign currents in the air, it is remarkable that a combined revival sponsored mainly by missionaries with some role played by Dora Yu, Leland Wang, and Mary Stone (Shi Meiyu), co-director of the local Bethel Mission, could still be held – especially when the featured speaker, Paget Wilkes, was a British missionary from Japan, and the British were the main targets of the volatile May 30 protest movement.[43]

After the mid 1920s the days of foreign-led revival meetings were over in China. That became the bailiwick of the "second generation" of Chinese evangelists. By 1930, both of the stalwarts of the first generation, Dora Yu and Ding Limei, were long retired; she would live until 1931, he until 1936. But now, partly because of the impact of the 1925 revival on the Bethel Mission, a whole new generation of young revival speakers entered the fray.

The Bethel Band and the paradoxical John Sung (Song Shangjie)

In 1920, an American Methodist-Episcopal educational missionary, Jennie Hughes, joined Mary Stone (Shi Meiyu, 1873–1954), an MD from the University of Michigan (1896), in creating the "Bethel Mission" in Shanghai.[44] In the next several years Bethel developed a remarkably comprehensive approach to mission. It created primary and secondary schools, a chapel, a hospital, a nursing school, and an orphanage. Inspired by the Paget Wilkes revival in 1925, some students, among them Ji Zhiwen (Andrew Gee, 1901–1985), organized what were called "evangelistic bands" to spread the Gospel. These, probably modeled after the evangelistic bands used for decades in Japan, were small teams of students or alumni who would conduct revival meetings in churches. The student bands were almost always appealing in having musical talent. Plus they were of neat and tidy appearance, articulate of speech and in preaching, indeed altogether winsome. They were quite popular in churches of all theological orientations. Then, in 1931, Andrew Gih assembled what would become the most famous group of all, the Bethel Worldwide Evangelistic Band. This group also added a new member, an evangelistic tornado named John Sung (Song Shangjie). For the next several years, practically no one would dispute that Sung was the most dynamic, even if not the most beloved, evangelist in China. With Sung on board for most of the time the Bethel Band between 1931 and 1935 traveled over 50,000 miles, visited 133 cities, and held almost 3400 revival meetings in all kinds of congregations.

Sung's life story was as exciting as his preaching style. Sung, son of a Fujian pastor, studied in the US from 1919 to 1927, receiving a Ph.D. in Chemistry at Ohio State University in 1926. He then went to Union Theological Seminary in New York, where he had a religious and psychological crisis due to the clash between his traditional Christian beliefs and the higher Biblical criticism and liberal theology that surrounded him at Union. After denouncing his professors publicly, he spent some months in a sanatorium in 192, then returned to China reconverted to the very conservative tenets of his childhood. He became an independent evangelist, and had already developed a reputation for flamboyance when he joined the Bethel Band in 1931.

Sung had an imaginative but abrasive style, using all kinds of props to illustrate his points (his favorite was a coffin), but being ruthlessly direct and acerbic in his denunciations of those with whom he disagreed, especially liberal theologians and pastors. He called Christians to be truly born again, to confess old sins, make restitution, and be cleansed. His meetings were very intense, and many wept during them. He also stressed healing and many claimed to have been healed at his hands. But he also did not hesitate to denounce pastors and leaders of denominational churches even in their own buildings, in their presence. His extremism led to his leaving the group in 1934, after which he operated as a lone evangelist. Not surprisingly he alienated many and was barred from some churches, but others loved him, and he must be considered probably the single most powerful figure in Chinese revivalism in the mid 1930s.[45] Unfortunately he had only a few more years to live.

Marcus Ch'eng (Chen Chonggui): a peripatetic life[46]

In the previous chapter we followed Chen's rise in stature through his years at the Swedish Covenant Mission and seminary. It appears that Chen was frustrated by his inability to achieve both financial security and personal autonomy at the seminary. He left in 1925, and later that year ended up being chaplain to the troops of the warlord "Christian general," Feng Yuxiang, for two years. In 1927 he moved to Shanghai, which was much safer, and became editor and proprietor of a Christian magazine, *Evangelism (Budao zazhi)*, which became quite popular under his editorship (in the 1930s, it had a circulation of 4500–5000 copies per issue). In 1928 Chen accepted a speaking tour in Sweden for the Covenant Mission headquarters, indicating the lessening of any hurt feelings over Chen's leaving the seminary. En route, he attended the Jerusalem meeting of the International Missionary Council, its first meeting since Edinburgh in 1910. There despite his lack of an advanced academic degree he received some recognition as a peer by fellow attendees and SFPE magnates Zhao Zichen of Yanjing University and Yu Richang, head of the Chinese YMCA. After a successful tour of Sweden he returned to China via the U.S., where again he visited several Covenant churches.

Upon his return to China in late 1928, Chen joined the faculty of the Hunan Bible Institute in Changsha, Hunan Province. He took his magazine with him. Chen's experience there is indicative of the sensitivity of Sino-foreign relations in the Christian realm. This seminary had been founded several years before by Frank Keller, who had been a member of the CIM but who had established a private link with the wealthy Stewart family of Los Angeles, who funded the Bible Institute of Los Angeles (BIOLA). Stewart resources also enabled Keller to create the Bible Institute in Changsha (which was sometimes called "BIOLA in China"). The relationship between the two institutions was ambiguous. Keller raised some funds for operations in China, whereas other funds were raised by BIOLA and sent to Keller and the school in Changsha. Keller had a local Changsha board of directors, but the BIOLA board also had some authority. Besides Keller, the entire academic staff was Chinese; Charles Roberts, the accountant and liaison with BIOLA, was not an academic. Keller was quite autonomous, but as his retirement approached in the mid 1930s the uncertainty of the Los Angeles–Changsha relationship became problematical.

Chen was on the faculty of the Hunan Bible Institute from early 1929 until 1937. He was one of only three teachers appointed as full "professor." Clearly Chen took a leading role in the instructional program, and evidently was popular with the students. He also continued his successful editorship of *Evangelism*, which reached the height of its national circulation and reputation in the mid 1930s. The institute subsidized the magazine, to the extent of perhaps $2000 per year, and this subsidy was probably crucial in making its publication viable.[47] Finally, Chen also continued his guest evangelistic and revival appearances and speaking tours, including nearly all of the Covenant Mission churches of central China. Changsha seemed to be a perfect answer to Chen's quest for security as well as a degree of autonomy.

Between 1935 and 1937, there occurred a protracted crisis over the succession to Keller as president of the institute, a crisis in which Chen played a central role. The story is complex, though it is well documented in letters and telegrams still preserved in the archives of Biola University in Los Angeles. The roots of the controversy were twofold. One factor was the strong current of Chinese nationalism of the times, to which many allude in the record. Chinese staff and students, and even local officials, expected that leadership should devolve to Chinese nationals once Keller retired.

The other factor was intense dislike and distrust on the part of some staff and students towards Charles Roberts, the business manager, who was rumored as early as 1935 to be slated to succeed Keller. Chen Chonggui and other staff wrote back to the BIOLA board that Roberts was unfit, but nevertheless Roberts won the power struggle and eventually succeeded Keller as president.[48]

Chen's position at the Hunan Bible Institute was now untenable. He maintained a pro forma affiliation with the institute into 1937, and then had to seek another base of operations and income. His task was complicated by the need also to find support for his magazine, which left Changsha with him. And in mid 1937 life was of course further complicated by the beginning of full-scale war between China and Japan, the precursor of World War II in the Pacific.

Chen now went back to his heritage and earlier roots, perhaps swallowing his pride in so doing. In December 1937 he proposed to the combined American and Swedish Covenant Mission bodies in central China that he reaffiliate with them on a half-time basis, spending three months annually with the churches of each. The mission would also provide some support for his magazine. He could thus support his magazine and retain his standing and activities as an autonomous figure during part of each year. But Chen received a humiliating rebuff in this attempt to rejoin his old mission. Despite the willingness of mission headquarters in North Park, the American Covenant Mission group in China voted 7 to 6 to reject Chen's offer. The reasons for this were complex, but it seems to me that the basic issue was that of Chen's independence – he would be largely beyond the mission's control.[49] And of course autonomy was precisely one of the major issues to Chen himself.

Undoubtedly stung by such an egregious insult, Chen had to turn elsewhere. With the Japanese advancing westward in late 1938, Chen accepted the invitation of Bishop Frank Houghton, General Director of the China Inland Mission (CIM), to come to the far West: the inland province of Sichuan, which was the wartime base area of Chiang Kai-shek's Nationalist government. Chen was close theologically to the CIM. Yet he must have had mixed feelings about once again serving under a foreign director. Houghton wisely gave Chen considerable slack, helping him continue to publish "Evangelism" and sending him on evangelistic and revival meeting tours of several provinces in Free China.[50] Five years later, in 1943, Houghton urged him to establish an independent evangelical seminary not under the control of any mission organization, with Chen himself as president. Chen responded with enthusiasm. Although Bishop Houghton stroked Chen's ego by emphasizing the independence of the new seminary, Houghton and the CIM actually were extensively involved in the creation and initial operation of Chungking [Chongqing] Theological Seminary (CTS). Chen was clearly identified as president, but in 1944 he was the only Chinese on the staff. In the late 1940s the staff, as well as having several Chinese members by this time, still included some missionaries "loaned" by the CIM.[51] This CIM continued role seems not to have bothered Chen, because the missionaries didn't have the job of disbursing the funds (even though they provided the funds). He enjoyed his years in Chongqing, and was much appreciated by the students.

The Chongqing seminary was Chen's home and base of operations for almost a decade; in 1953 he retired to Dalian in the Northeast. By that time he was an officer in the Christian Three-Self Patriotic Movement (TSPM). We will conclude his story in Chapter 7.

Roman Catholics from the mid 1920s until War with Japan

As the twentieth century progressed into its third decade, one can see ever-widening differences between Protestants and Catholics. Besides the difference between the urban orientation and emphasis on education of the former and the rural orientation of the latter, there were other differences which were important. First, although there were several segments to the whole (for example, a miscellany of vicariates apostolic and other ecclesiastical jurisdictions), the Catholic presence was more or less unified and all parts of it were supposed to be under the authority of the Pope and the Vatican, or of individual orders. Individual priests and bishops were usually not free to choose their stations and come and go as they pleased, but went where directed by their superiors. Second, although the number of Chinese priests was steadily increasing, they were still far fewer than the number of Western clergy. And there was no option among Catholics to leave the church and create a Catholic equivalent of the True Jesus Church or the Jesus Family. So the church remained very heavily missionary-dominated, as it had been for a century. Despite the consecration of the six Chinese bishops by Pius XI in 1926, the new bishops were not assigned to very meaningful posts, and the stranglehold of the European clergy on the church in China remained firm. Even the American Maryknollers, perhaps at first seen as a counterweight to the power of the French clergy, could not easily break down the rigidities of the old power structure. In fact they became as adept as the Europeans in excluding Chinese from a decision-making role.[52]

Meanwhile, Father Vincent Lebbe, by now well known for his championing the native Chinese clergy in the issue of the bishops, was successfully excluded from China by the hierarchy there, even before the pivotal encyclical of 1919, *Maximum illud*. He was exiled to Europe, where for most of the 1920s he worked with the Chinese students, especially those in France. There he gained the enmity of Zhou Enlai, who was working with those same students to recruit them for the Communist movement. He finally gained reassignment to China in the late 1920s, where he served under one of the newly consecrated Chinese bishops, and he became a Chinese citizen in 1928. Lebbe founded at least two religious orders, one of them the Little Brothers of St. John the Baptist, who worked with the poor in rural areas, and with whom he would spend the rest of his life.

Chinese Protestantism during the War of Resistance against Japan, 1937–1945

The full-scale warfare between China and Japan that was set off by the incident at the Marco Polo Bridge outside Beijing (it was called Peiping at the time) in early July 1937 led to eight years of disaster for China. It also gave Chinese Christians an opportunity to demonstrate their loyalty and patriotism. The main danger to China's unity and development was no longer Western imperialism, but Japanese imperialism. This fact enabled Chinese Christians to shed some of the stigma of foreignness, which had plagued them for more than a decade and which had not been eliminated yet.

There has been almost no substantive research done on the church or the Christian movement during the wartime period, with the single exception of a 1996 essay by Timothy Brook.[53] A conference in June 2009 at Hong Kong Baptist University was devoted to the church in wartime, and resulted in some fresh reflections. There seems to be wide agreement that the wartime period lends itself to breakdown as follows:

1. The impact of the war on Chinese Christianity during the period 1937–1941, when the Allied Powers were not yet at war with Japan. This includes in particular the Chinese churches in Japanese-occupied parts of China, where in most cases at least some of the Western missionaries remained at their stations for some or all of the time between July 1937 and December 1941. This situation meant that Chinese pastors, elders, and other church leaders were still substantially under the authority of their Western missionary colleagues and the mission boards that had sent them, that is, *if* the missionaries had not left. But even when the missionaries remained, their scope of action and authority were usually circumscribed by the Japanese occupation authorities; in almost all cases the Japanese military commanders did not welcome the continued presence of the Westerners, although the Japanese authorities had no choice but formally to recognize their right to remain.

2. In cases where missionaries returned home or went to a different part of China for safety's sake during 1937–1941, the indigenous leadership of the local Chinese churches there was faced with a sudden increase in their responsibilities. Chinese church leadership was on its own for as long as eight years (1937–1945) in these cases. Typically, administration of schools or medical facilities, and the handling of mission/church finances in general were often functions still performed by Western missionaries. Now Chinese had to take over.

3. After the Japanese attack on Pearl Harbor, December 7, 1941, and declarations of war between Japan and the US-led Allies, almost all the remaining Protestant missionaries in Japanese-occupied China now were considered enemy nationals. Their movements were restricted almost immediately, and within several months, during 1942, the majority of them were put into internment camps, most in Shandong or the suburbs of Shanghai, and some in the Philippines. There already exists a modest

literature on them.[54] The issue that needs work is the historical experience of the Chinese Christians left behind.

It seems evident that, even though we do not have many case studies yet, both the Western missionaries and the Chinese Christians who were in Japanese-occupied territory for 1937–1945 were part of a process of realignment of roles in the Protestant community. The Chinese Christians in these areas, forced to live under the strictures of an often arbitrary Japanese occupation, had in addition to that burden to step forward and take much more practical and formal responsibilities for church life if the churches were to continue to exist and function at all. This gave them a very different historical experience and perspective in comparison with those Christians who had fled to the interior with the Chinese government. This fact gave rise to several issues, perhaps foremost among them that of alleged "collaboration" with the Japanese. There is also the issue to consider of how wartime events changed the power relationships between Christians and missionaries when the latter returned after the war.

On the issue of collaboration, Timothy Brook's recent book on it offers many insights, even though Christians do not constitute one of his case studies. As Brook has argued very convincingly, the simple polarity of resistance and collaboration is not helpful in understanding this wartime experience. In fact as soon as the term "collaboration" or "collaborator" is used, even by a careful scholar, the historian's ability to analyze objectively what was going on is significantly diminished, and the reader's potential for understanding almost disappears.[55] The national myths centered on the moral norms of (commendable) "resistance" and (reviled) "collaboration" take hold, and the possibility of dispassionately analyzing a case study is virtually gone.

What issues appear in relationship to "collaboration?" A study could be made of the church leaders of north China who had to deal with demands of the Japanese concerning the Christian churches and Christian organizations like the YMCA. It was impossible for Christian leaders not to accommodate Japanese demands to accept Japanese pastors and YMCA workers, even though it was well known that they functioned as watchdogs. Some were kinder than others, and tried to help the Chinese, while others were viewed by the Chinese with suspicion as simply being intelligence agents. In the months after the Pearl Harbor attack and the beginning of the Pacific war, the Japanese made a concerted effort to create an umbrella structure to contain all the Chinese churches of whatever Protestant denomination. Obviously this was for control purposes. The Protestant churches of north China were represented on October 15, 1942, at the founding meeting at Huairen Church, Peking, which established the North China Church of Christ League (Huabei Zhonghua Jidujiao tuan).[56]

The new organization oversaw the Protestant church affairs of four provinces (Hebei, Shandong, Henan, and Shaanxi), and that of three "special cities" (*tebie shi*—Beijing, Tianjin, and Qingdao). Jiang Changchuan (Z. T. Kaung), a respected bishop in the Methodist Church, who had married Chiang Kai-shek and his wife in 1927 and had baptized Chiang in 1930, was director (*zhuli*) of the administrative committee (*zhixing weiyuanhui*) and Zhou Guanqing was vice-director. There were 13 other members, including a secretary, financial officer, seven regular members, three "specially invited members," and an "executive secretary" (*Zong ganshi*), who was Kang Deqi. Kang was probably the day-to-day manager. One of the "specially invited members" was a Japanese.

The "standing committee" of the 15-member administrative committee included 10 people: all the officers and, of course, the Japanese "specially invited member." There was a subordinate church (*fenhui*) organization for each province, down to the circuit (*dao*) level. Each subprovincial unit had at least two representatives on the provincial assembly. Questions abound in the mind of the historian. What role did Z. T. Kaung play as buffer between the Japanese authorities and Chinese Christians? Did he or other church officials secretly foment resistance? How many of these churchmen were accused of collaboration after the war?[57]

Other material available on local pastors, elders, and lay leaders across Shandong Province, for example, may be complementary to the contents of this "handbook".[58] This remains to be investigated, along with other local issues relating to collaboration. For example, did local church leaders who seemed too close to the Japanese receive punishment or ostracism after the war?

Another issue is what the wartime years meant for Chinese-foreign relations in the church. Is the experience in north China comparable to that of central China? There Timothy Brook suggests a dual legacy of the occupation with regard to foreign missions – that is, on the one hand was emphasis that there was much devastation and human damage to repair in the churches, and the quick return of the foreign missionaries and their resources was essential. On the other hand was emphasis that though there was indeed much to repair, there was also much to celebrate because of the strong steps the Chinese churches had taken toward dealing with their own problems with their own resources.[59]

I believe it is probable that some of the movement toward unity pushed by the Japanese during the wartime years was actually welcomed by those Chinese Christian leaders who had long rued the denominational fissures in Chinese Protestantism. Beginning with Cheng Jingyi's electrifying denunciation of denominationalism as an unwanted legacy of missions at the Edinburgh Missionary Conference in 1910, there had regularly been heartfelt regrets expressed by Chinese Christian leaders over the bad effects of too many divisions in the churches.[60] In this regard we have perhaps been led astray by the oft-told story of Beijing Pastor Wang Mingdao, who in the 1940s stubbornly withstood Japanese pressure to take his independent Christian Tabernacle in Beijing into the new union North China Church of Christ.[61] This story, which makes Wang's recalcitrance look virtuous, implies that others, who joined, were doing so for unworthy reasons – such as lack of faith or lack of courage. But some of those undoubtedly approved of merger on principle, despite its Japanese sponsorship.

This question of Sino-foreign church relations is illuminated by two other sources. One is the study of the CCC by Merwin, in which (writing in the early 1970s) he assumes that it was crucial for the missionaries to return to China after 1945, and also assumes that they would quite reasonably take up their old leadership role and near-monopoly of decision-making.[62] The second is a recent study by Professor Liu Jiafeng of Huazhong Normal University in Wuhan, which shows how the boards of the Christian colleges, meeting in the US during the wartime years to plan for the postwar period, produced proposals that did not take into account the wishes of the Chinese school leaders, and continued the old and rather condescending assumptions that the foreigners were indispensible.[63]

Impact of the war

The offices of the CCC moved west with the Nationalist Government in 1938, and spent the wartime years operating from Chongqing (Chungking) or Chengdu in Sichuan Province. In November 1939, Cheng Jingyi, the secretary-general of the CCC, died, and the CCC mourned the man who for almost 30 years, since his dramatic appearance in Edinburgh in 1910, had personified the quest for a unified Chinese Protestant church. Cheng was replaced by the capable but less well known Cui Xianxiang. Yu Rizhang, head of the YMCA, had died not long before, so the SFPE had lost two respected seasoned leaders just as wartime pressures were building. The NCC and the CCC were not terribly effective during the anti-Japan War. The skeleton of a church bureaucracy continued to function, but some new tasks addressed by them – the West China Border Mission on the edge of Tibet, and the Guizhou Mission to the minority tribes of that province – do not seem to have made much progress by 1945. Most of the Christian Colleges also moved to the west early in the war, as did many government colleges, and conscientiously tried to carry on the educational enterprise as best they could.[64]

The tone of NCC/CCC programs and activities was subdued during the war. The CCC did not grow very much in membership, and still had fewer than half of all Protestants. But on the contrary, the endtimes preaching and the rampant millenarianism of the independent churches, calling people not to works of mercy like tending wounded soldiers or easing the ravages of famine or disease, but to repent of their sins and be regenerated before God through Jesus Christ, seems to have been well received by many. All of the groups we have mentioned – the TJC, the Jesus Family, Watchman Nee's movement, had significant growth during the wartime years. The Jesus Family probably had the greatest percentage growth because of its ability, due to its communal egalitarian structure, to keep people from starving and to provide shelter. New Jesus Family outposts were established in several provinces of north and central China during the wartime years. In fact for the Jesus Family, the growth continued throughout the late 1940s, the civil war years, as well. The TJC and Watchman Nee's movement also grew steadily during the wartime years, as far as we can tell, both in occupied and unoccupied China.

A final effect of the wartime circumstances for Protestants was the scattering of some Christian elements across a wider geographical tableau than ever before, including the margins of the former empire in the southwest up to the edge of Tibet, into Mongolia and the steppe lands, and the far west of Xinjiang Province. Some of these Christian "seeds" were intentionally sent by, for example, the Jesus Family; others were more serendipitous, with sometimes rapidly changing circumstances in the wartime situation resulting in unforeseen population movements and resettlement. The CIM helped establish the Northwest Bible Institute in Shaanxi Province, and one of the visions developed by a group of people there was to go further west to Xinjiang to spread the gospel. Beginning with a revelation received by Mark Ma on Easter, 1943, and subsequently confirmed by others, they formed a "Chinese Back-to-Jerusalem Evangelistic Band", dedicated to evangelizing the vast reaches of Xinjiang and the far west. The Sino-foreign organization (it included several CIM missionaries as well) was still functioning and providing newsletters as late as mid 1950. A few of them did go west and established churches in the late 1940s.[65] Likewise in the southwest, with refugee Christians temporarily in Sichuan, some of them ended up creating ministries to the minority peoples neighboring them to the west, in Guizhou and Yunnan.

End Game: Christianity and the Civil War, 1946–1950

The moribund political structure of the Guomindang state collapsed in the late 1940s before the onslaught of its dynastic successor-to-be, the CCP. Similarly, in these same years the fading energy of the older parts of the Sino-foreign Protestant establishment slowed its progress. The dynamism of initiative of action and growth passed to an increasingly politicized younger sector of the SFPE and even more to the independent churches. These churches, and some of the individual evangelists, had some distinct advantages over the Sino-foreign churches: they had relatively low visibility, flying under the radar screen of the casual observer; they were quite decentralized in terms of ecclesiology; and they had been practicing self-support for many years. They knew how to survive on very few resources. At any rate, of the three major independents (TJC, Jesus Family, and Nee's followers) all continued the momentum of wartime growth into the late 1940s. By 1950, the total number of independent church adherents must have been at least 200,000, perhaps more; that would be at least 20 percent of the total number of Protestants, which was probably 900,000 to one million.[66]

The Return of the National Christian Council (NCC) and the Church of Christ in China (CCC), and the Missionary Role

It took several months from the time of Japan's surrender in August 1945 to get much of the personnel of the NCC and the CCC back into the former Japanese-occupied territories.[67] When the Christians from "free China" returned, they had to deal with those Christians who had remained under Japanese rule, some of whom were suspected of "collaboration" with the enemy. Libraries and equipment of the wartime Christian universities also had to be shipped back to their old campuses, a major task. And those facilities, not just of schools but of hospitals as well, had many ruined or badly damaged buildings. At this point the resources made available by the returning foreign missionaries played a key role. Relief supplies and materials, large amounts of medical supplies bought from the military by the missions, and help in repairing buildings, all came from the missionary groups returning in a flood in early 1946. Mission–church relations were sensitive regarding missionary re-establishment in places where they had been absent for up to eight years, and many missions tried to avoid running roughshod over their Chinese colleagues; but others, including some new missionaries who were coming to China for the first time, were oblivious to the patterns of past inequity and assumed that they should be in charge. So inevitably there was some tension in mission–church relations. One contested issue was the nature of the postwar Christian colleges. The US-based Associated Boards for Christian Colleges in China wanted to merge and/or downsize some colleges, and the Chinese leadership of those colleges resisted strenuously.[68]

The NCC, which had not met since 1937, finally met in December 1946. Dr. Wu Yifang, President of Ginling Colllege for Women in Nanjing, was able to step down as chair of the NCC, having served 11 years. She was replaced by Dr. S. C. Leung, General Secretary of the National Committee of the YMCA. The CCC was unable to have its general assembly meeting until 1948; the standing committee of the general assembly met in February 1946 and a couple of times more before the entire general assembly met in 1948. The delays in convening the CCC were probably due both to the chaos of the times and to its own institutional decrepitude.

Student work

In 1946 the NCC set up a Committee on Student Evangelism, which reported in 1947 that it had established seven university centers in cooperation with the YMCA and YWCA. In these centers there were sixteen secretaries working, eleven Chinese and five foreign. The YMCA/YWCA became the main base for "The Chinese Christian Movement," or "The Student Christian Movement" (SCM), a group of intellectuals and students who were liberal and leftist in politics, somewhat sympathetic to the Communist side in the civil war, loosely identified as Christian, but not organized as a church.[69] Kiang Wenhan (Jiang Wenhan) and Y. T. Wu (Wu Yaozong), both of the YMCA, were two of the main activists shaping whatever influence the movement had. Some of that influence was evident after "Liberation," in the creation of the Three-Self movement in the early 1950s.

However, this liberal beachhead in student evangelism established by the SCM appears to have been outdone by the achievements of the more conservative evangelical student groups affiliated with China Inter-Varsity, the latter linked to the international Inter -Varsity Christian Fellowship.[70] This evangelical student movement began in July 1945 in Chongqing, the wartime capital of Chiang Kai-shek's government. There Pastor Calvin Chao (Zhao Junying) gathered together for a conference representatives of the evangelical student organizations which had sprung up on almost all of China's college and university campuses since 1942 or 1943. This launched China Inter-Varsity on a very fast growth trajectory, which was hard for Zhao to coordinate when the students began to move back to their campuses all over China. In late 1945 Zhao appealed to the CIM for help, and the CIM sent David Adeney, who had been waiting impatiently to return since 1941and who was able to get to China in February 1946, by aircraft. Adeney made a good teammate for Zhao, who did most of the preaching. Chao and his China Inter-Varsity team, of which Adeney was the only non-Chinese, followed the students back to their old campuses in the east, and they set up China Inter-Varsity headquarters in Nanjing. In spring 1946 Adeney went to Beijing and met with Wang Mingdao for the first time. Many evangelical students attended Wang's church, The Christian Tabernacle. Adeney spent three months in Beijing, then settled in Nanjing. The largest and most ambitious conference that he and China Inter-Varsity did was in Nanjing in July 1947, with 350 students attending. This was the high point of China Inter-Varsity's postwar record. Adeney moved to Shanghai, working openly with student groups there until 1949, privately for a few months after the new regime established control, and left China in 1950. He was able to return only in 1978, then returned frequently until his death in 1994.[71]

Politics and the churches

As national political events in late 1945 and early 1946 drifted unmistakably toward civil war, some church leaders spoke out, denouncing both Guomindang and the CCP for the growing tension. But civil war did come, and China went through another three and a half years of turmoil before the Communists emerged victorious in the summer of 1949. It was difficult for the Christian churches to avoid lining up behind Chiang Kai-shek's government. After all, he was a baptized Christian. There was, however, more than a handful of church and institutional Christian leaders who were so disgusted with the proven incompetence and venality of the Guomindang government that they were willing to live under a new communist regime. Two publications of the liberal and even radical wing of Christian opinion were *Xie Jin* (Progress), the organ of the NCC, and the independent *Tianfeng* (Heavenly wind), the latter of which in the 1950s became the official voice of the Three Self Movement. A few of those Christian leaders of the late 1940s who wrote frequently for these publications, including Y. T. Wu and Kiang Wenhan of the YMCA, seemed not only to be reconciled to a Communist victory but even to welcome it.

As the civil war ground inexorably toward the victory of the CCP, and this was clear in the first weeks of 1949, stark choices presented themselves. It remained for individuals among the Protestants, missionaries and Chinese Christian leaders alike, to make the decision about whether to go (to Hong Kong, Taiwan, Southeast Asia, North America, or Europe) or to stay. Although a few left China during 1949, not many did so, and most of the Chinese churchmen who were still abroad in 1949 returned home to China by mid 1950. Their apprehension at living under communism was outweighed by their patriotism and desire to make a contribution to the Chinese church.

Thus on the eve of "Liberation," while many Protestants, missionaries and Chinese alike, were uneasy about the future, many others were hopeful that some kind of Sino-foreign Protestant community could continue to exist under communism, and make a Christian contribution to the "new China." Catholics were not so sanguine.

Roman Catholics 1937–1949: Vulnerabilities

Chinese Catholics, being as patriotic as non-Catholics, nevertheless were caught on the horns of a dilemma when full-scale war with Japan came in 1937. The Catholic Church in China, European-run, inevitably to some extent reflected the intense anti-Communist attitudes of Pope Pius XI and the Vatican. Rome was not as condemning of Japanese aggression in China as were some other Western nations. Moreover, the Vatican or Catholic orders or provinces owned many properties in China, those of which in Japanese-occupied territory would be threatened by a serious rift between the Vatican and the Japanese government. And of course the Italian missionaries, with their country being one of the Axis powers, had an especially sensitive relationship with the Japanese.

This meant that there was not a rush of Catholic missionary clergy in China to help China resist. That is, except for Father Vincent Lebbe and a few others. Father Lebbe and his Little Brothers order, already present in north China, took on the task of mobilizing hundreds of Catholic peasants to assist the Chinese Nationalist armies as they retreated from the north by forming stretcher bearer teams to evacuate wounded soldiers from the battlefields. The determined fortitude and indefatigable dedication of Lebbe and his Catholics received much commendation, including from Chiang Kai-shek himself. Lebbe burned himself out physically, and also became embroiled in intramural Chinese politics between Dai Li (1895–1946), Chiang Kai-shek's spymaster, and the Chinese communists, who were suspicious of Lebbe (as Zhou Enlai had been since 1920 or 1921, when he and Lebbe had competed for the allegiance of Chinese students in France). In late 1939 or early 1940 nearby Communist forces captured and tortured Lebbe, and the abuse was too much for his fragile body. He was released after several weeks, but never recovered, and died in the spring of 1940 in Chongqing, the Guomindang government's wartime capital, after being evacuated there.

As the tension rose between Japan and the US, General William Donovan and his just-formed Office of Strategic Services, better known by its acronym OSS, the precursor of the Central Intelligence Agency, already set up shop in China even while the US was officially neutral in the China–Japan conflict. Donovan and his people worked with Dai Li, the Nationalist intelligence chief, who had worked with Father Lebbe to facilitate the work of the Little Brothers since 1938. After Lebbe's death the OSS recruited the American priest Father Thomas Megan, Lebbe's successor as head of the Little Brothers. Megan for some years, until the end of the war, worked closely with the OSS and with Dai Li, who had a reputation for ruthlessness rare even in Guomindang circles. When the Chinese communists later insisted that missionaries were spies, they certainly had in mind both Lebbe and Megan, and their murky relationships with both Guomindang and US wartime intelligence.[72]

We have noted that one of the features of the Catholic church in China was its domination by Europeans. There was very little further progress toward native agency in the church after the initial consecration of the six bishops in 1926. Only belatedly, in 1946, were the first Chinese bishops given actual territorial jurisdictions. In 1948, very late in the game, out of 139 key ecclesiastical posts in China, Chinese clergy were at the head of 26 of them (18.7%).[73] Another political and public relations factor by the late 1940s was that the church was thoroughly entrenched in a visceral anti-Communism, best represented by the views of the Pontiff himself, Pius XII.

With ideological antagonism and tension, if not conflict, between Catholics and Communists in China almost guaranteed, socio-economic issues also contributed as well. In many village communities, north and south, a longterm Catholic strategy of growth was for the church to buy up land, and then lease it to those peasants who agreed to join the church with their families. This had succeeded spectacularly. Land surveys done in the 1940s in preparation for land reform often confirmed that in fact the Catholic church was the biggest landlord in the area. And those families closest to the church and its resources were often, in effect, elites by dint of that alone.[74] Other, non-Catholic families resented this, their rancor sometimes brewing for years or even decades. Now it appeared that under the communists, "accounts would be settled" with the church and the missionaries. The communists also saw clearly that it was in their interest to switch from a moderate to a radical and violent confiscatory land policy; they made the change in the summer if 1946. So the new and harsher land reform process, attacking the landlords and killing some of them, by 1947–1948 was already well underway in the provinces of the north and the northeast, which were under communist military control. A few foreign Catholics had in fact been killed.

Thus the political, socio-economic, and ideological arenas were all predictable areas of friction between the new rulers and the Catholic church. When one adds into the mix the militant, hardline anti-communist stance of the Holy See, for example in ordering Chinese Catholics in 1949 not to cooperate with the new Chinese government on pain of excommunication, all the ingredients were present for a massive showdown. Antonio Riberi, the papal nuncio, implemented the Vatican's policy zealously; he was actively hostile to the new authorities from 1949 on, and incited Catholics to use all kinds of methods, including devotional sodalities such as the Legion of Mary, to thwart the goals of the new state. As a result, many Catholics faced the advent of the "new China" with apprehension, even fear.

Notes

1. Grant Wacker, "The Waning of the Missionary Impulse: The Case of Pearl S. Buck," in Daniel H. Bays and Grant Wacker, eds, *The Foreign Missionary Enterprise at Home* (Tuscaloosa, AL: The University of Alabama Press, 2003), pp. 191–205. Lian Xi also has a fine chapter on Buck in his *The Conversion of Missionaries: Liberalism in American Protestant Missions in China, 1907–1932* (University Park, PA: Penn State Press, 1997), pp. 95–128.

2. Lian Xi, *The Conversion of Missionaries: Liberalism in American Protestant Missions in China, 1907–1932* (University Park, PA: Penn State Press, 1997), pp. 191–199.

3. Buck's speech and the *Laymen's Report* were the two biggest flashpoints, but other issues were also irritating. The China Sunday School Union had a bitter dispute with the World Sunday School Association, accusing the latter of plotting to infuse the materials used by the former with modernist biblical contamination. The two organizations ended their relationship in 1930. Kevin Xiyi Yao, *The Fundamentalist Movement among Protestant Missionaries in China, 1920–1937* (Lanham, MD: University Press of America, 2003), pp. 231–239.

4. Grace Service, *Golden Inches: The China Memoir of Grace Service*, ed. John Service (Berkeley, CA: University of California Press, 1989).

5. Carolyn Armitage, *Reaching for the Goal: The Life Story of David Adeney* (Wheaton, IL: OMF, 1993), pp. 1–40; David H. Adeney, *China: The Church's Long March* (Ventura, CA: Regal Books, 1985), pp. 17–28.

6. The classic hagiography is Mrs. Howard Taylor, *The Triumph of John and Betty Stam* (London: The China Inland Mission, 1935).

7. Marie Monsen, *The Awakening: Revival in China, a Work of the Holy Spirit*, trans. Joy Guiness (London: China Inland Mission, 1961). Mary Crawford, *The Shantung Revival* (Shanghai: China Baptist Publication Society, 1933).

8. A sensationalist yet useful account of the family is Sterling Seagrave, *The Soong Dynasty* (New York: Harper and Row, 1985). A more sober treatment is Daniel H. Bays, "The Soong Family and the Chinese Protestant Christian Community," in Samuel C. Chu, ed., *Madame Chiang Kaishek and her China* (Norwalk, CT: Eastbridge, 2005), pp. 22–32.

9. John King Fairbank, with Merle Goldman, *China: A New History*, enlarged edition (Cambridge, MA: Harvard University Press, 1998), pp. 260–262.

10. William A. Brown, "The Missionary and China's Rural Problems: The Protestant Rural Movement in China (1920–1937)," in Kwang-Ching Liu, ed., *American Missionaries in China: Papers from Harvard Seminars* (Cambridge, MA: Harvard East Asian Research Center, 1966), pp. 217–248. Also Price's own account, Frank Wilson Price, *The Rural Church in China* (New York: Agricultural Missions, 1948).

11. James C. Thomson Jr., *While China Faced West: American Reformers in Nationalist China 1928–1937* (Cambridge, MA: Harvard University Press, 1969).

12. R. H. Tawney, *Land and Labor in China* (New York: Harcourt, Brace and Co., 1932.

13. John King Fairbank, with Merle Goldman, *China: A New History*, enlarged edition (Cambridge, MA: Harvard University Press, 1998) p. 261.

14. Both were remarkable women. Pruitt grew up in a S. Baptist missionary family in rural Shandong. Marjorie King, *China's American Daughter, Ida Pruitt (1888–1985)* (Hong Kong: The Chinese University Press, 2006). Cora Deng identified herself as a Christian at various seasons of her life. Emily Honig, "Christianity, Feminism, and Communism: The life and times of Deng Yuzhi," in Daniel H. Bays, ed., *Christianity in China: From the Eighteenth Century to the Present* (Stanford, CA: Stanford University Press, 1996), pp. 243–262.

15. Emily Honig, *Sisters and Strangers: Women in the Shanghai Cotton Mills, 1919–1949* (Stanford, CA: Stanford University Press, 1986), esp. pp. 217–224.

16. For concise accurate discussion of both the Blue Shirts and the NLM, see Lloyd E. Eastman, *The Abortive Revolution: China under Nationalist Rule, 1927–1937* (Cambridge, MA: Harvard University Press, 1971), pp. 66–70.

17. *While China Faced West: American Reformers in Nationalist China 1928–1937* (Cambridge, MA: Harvard University Press, 1969), Chs. 7–8, has a long discussion of foreign and Chinese Christians and their conflicted dealings with the NLM.

18. Anglicans failed to join the CCC not because it was theologically too liberal, but because of ecclesiastical concerns such as the role of bishops, priests, and the House of Delegates, plus the fact that Anglicans had done their own unification in 1912, creating the Shenggonghui, the Anglican Church of China.

19. There is accumulating a body of scholarship on these groups. Sources dealing with all three include Daniel H. Bays, "The Growth of Independent Christianity in China, 1900–1937," in Daniel H. Bays, ed., *Christianity in China: From the Eighteenth Century to the Present* (Stanford, CA: Stanford University Press, 1996), pp. 307–316; and especially a major work by Lian Xi, *Redeemed by Fire: Popular Chinese Christianity in the Twentieth Century* (New Haven, CT: Yale University Press, 2010). A shorter version was in Lian Xi, "The Search for Chinese Christianity in the Republican Period (1912–1949)," *Modern Asian Studies,* 38.4 (2004), pp. 851–898. The multiplicity of names for Ni Tosheng's movement is due to Ni's refusal to adopt a name because it might turn into a denomination-like label.

20. Material on the True Jesus Church is from Daniel H. Bays, "Indigenous Protestant Churches in China, 1900–1937," in Steven Kaplan, ed., *Indigenous Responses to Western Christianity* (New York: New York University Press, 1995), pp. 124–143. Also Lian Xi, "The Search for Chinese Christianity in the Republican Period (1912–1949)." *Modern Asian Studies,* 38.4 (2004), pp. 859–862.

21. Actually one can trace this Hong Kong group, led by A. G. Garr, back across the Pacific to the great 1906 Azusa Street Revival in Los Angeles.

22. To this point, the story is from Daniel H. Bays, "Indigenous Protestant Churches," in Steven Kaplan, ed., *Indigenous Responses to Western Christianity* (New York: New York University Press, 1995), pp. 127–131.

23. The American Seventh Day Adventists came to China before 1910, and almost immediately began an extensive publication and distribution program.

24. A fine Chinese language study and interpretation of the Jesus Family is Tao Feiya, *Zhongguo de Jidujiao wutobang: Yesu Jiating, 1921–1952* (A Chinese Christian Utopia: The Jesus Family, 1921–1952) (Hong Kong: Chinese University Press, 2004).

25. The quotation is from Lian Xi, *The Conversion of Missionaries: Liberalism in American Protestant Missions in China, 1907–1932* (University Park, PA: Penn State Press, 1997), p. 863. This part of the present chapter agrees with Lian Xi's book at pp. 862–867, also Tao Feiya, "Pentecostalism and Christian Utopia in China: Jing Dianying and the Jesus Family Movement, 1921–1952," in Ogbu U. Kalu, ed., *Interpreting Contemporary Christianity: Global Processes and Local Identities* (Grand Rapids, MI: William B. Eerdmans, 2008), pp 38–252.

26. L. M. Anglin, a former Baptist, turned Pentetcostal about 1910 and affiliated with the A of G. His mission was called the Home of Onesiphorus.

27. It reminds one of the way in which the Taiping leadership competed for influence by transmitting direct messages from, variously, God, Jesus, and the Holy Spirit.

28. I discuss this in a Chinese article, "*Ihetuan zongjiao tiyan yu 20 shiji 20 niandai Shandong Jidujiao 'Yesu Jiating' de bijiao*" (Comparison of the religious expeience of the Boxers with the Christian Jesus Family in 1920s Shandong), in Chinese Society for Boxer Studies, ed., *Ihotuan yundong yu jindai Zhongguo shehui guoji xueshu yantaohui lunwenji* (Papers of the international academic symposium on the Boxer movement and modern Chineses society) (Jinan: Jilu shushe, 1992), pp. 521–525.

29. Sources dealing with most or all of his career include Lian Xi, "The Search for Chinese Christianity in the Republican Period (1912–1949)," *Modern Asian Studies*, 38.4 (2004), pp. 881–890, *passim*; Angus Kinnear, *The Story of Watchman Nee: Against the Tide* (Wheaton, IL: Tyndale House, 1973); Leslie T. Lyall, *Three of China's Mighty Men* (London: Overseas Missionary Fellowship, 1973); there are many works in Chinese, including a collection of his complete works, published in 33 volumes in Hong Kong in 1995, as well as dozens of shorter items in English which are of uncertain provenance but are apparently transcriptions of talks.

30. One of Nee's early colleagues was Wang Zai (Leland Wang, 1898–1975), who himself went on to become a popular evangelist and traveling revival meeting speaker.

31. Dispensationalism is an arcane practice of divining the "ages" (dispensations) of human and cosmic history and sometimes predicting when will occur the second coming of Christ, the New Jerusalem and the end of time.

32. Actually the Chinese title was different; it was *Womende gongzuo zaisi,* which would be something like "Rethinking our Work."

33. Lian Xi, "The Search for Chinese Christianity in the Republican Period (1912–1949)," *Modern Asian Studies*, 38.4 (2004), pp. 868–869.

34. The process of being "raptured" seems very similar to the *beiti* experience of the Jesus Family. As Lian Xi points out, what is often reported is that the person being raptured sees marvelous sights, great cities, beautiful clothes and music, wonderful food, and more. A half-century before, observers had reported an almost identical repertoire of visionary sightings of native religious sects in rural Shandong.

35. "Indigenous Revival in Shantung," *Chinese Recorder* (1934), pp. 768–772.

36. Mary Crawford, *The Shantung Revival* (Shanghai: China Baptist Publication Society, 1933), p. 40. Marie Monsen, *The Awakening: Revival in China, the Work of the Holy Spirit,* trans. Joy Guiness (London; China Inland Mission, 1961).

37. C. L. Culpepper, *The Shantung Revival* (Dallas: Baptist General Convention of Texas, 1968).

38. Silas H. Wu, *Dora Yu and Christian Revival in 20th-Century China* (Boston, MA: Pishon River Publications, 2002), is a very interesting account of a little-known figure.

39. Marcus Ch'eng (Chen Chonggui), *Echoes from China: The Story of my Life and Lectures* (Chicago, IL: Covenant Book Concern 1921); Gustav Carlberg, *China in Revival* (Rock Island, IL: Augustana Book Concern, 1936), pp. 84–103.

40. Lian Xi, *Redeemed by Fire: Popular Chinese Christianity in the Twentieth Century* (New Haven, CT: Yale University Press, 2010), pp. 111–118.

41. Lian Xi, "the Search for Chinese Christianity in the Republican Period (1912–1949)," *Modern Asian Studies*, 38.4 (2004), pp. 870–874. Wang's own story is told in his *Wushi nianlai (These Fifty years)* (Hong Kong: Bellman House, 1950), which has been haphazardly translated in Wong Ming-Dao, *A Stone Made Smooth* (Southampton, UK: Mayflower Christian Books, 1981).

42. Silas H. Wu, *Dora Yu and Christian Revival in 20th-Century China* (Boston: Pishon River Publications, 2002), pp. 189–199.

43. The leading organizational role was played by Mrs. Henry Woods, who created the World-Wide Prayer Revival Movement as the main support for it. Several other top Shanghai figures from the CIM, US Presbyterians, and Southern Baptists were co-sponsors.

44. Shi Meiyu is well worth a study in her own right. For work thus far, see Connie Shemo, "Shi Meiyu, an 'Amy of Women' in Medicine, " in Carol Lee Hamrin, with Stacey Bieler, *Salt and Light: Lives of Faith that Shaped Modern China*, 2 vols. (Eugene, OR: Pickwick Publications, 2008, 2010), pp. 50–63.

45. A condensation of my treatment of Sung in Daniel H. Bays, "Christian Revival in China, 1900–1937," in *Modern Christian Revivals*, ed. Edith L. Blumhofer and Randall Balmer (Urbana, IL: University of Illinois Press, 1993), pp. 172–173. Good detail is in Lian Xi's discussion of Sung in "The Search for Chinese Christianity," pp. 876–881. A unique observer's first-hand account of the intensity of Sung's meetings is a a contribution to a collection of essays on events of a single day sent in by people from all over China. Chen Rongzhan, "Notes on Dr. Song's Preaching," in Sherman Cochran *et al.*, ed. and trans., *One Day in China: May 21, 1936* (New Haven, CT: Yale University Press, 1983), pp. 186–188. The observer's comment was that 'Dr. Song spoke like a traveling medicine peddler, and his style appealed only to the lowbrow taste of ignorant women."

46. Much of this section is condensed from Daniel H. Bays, "Foreign Missions and Indigenous Protestant Leaders," pp. 152–157. An especially heavily used source for this period is O. Theodore Roberg, "Marcus Cheng (c. 1883–1963): Apostle or Apostate? Relations with the Covenant Mission in China" (M.A. thesis, North Park Theological Seminary, Chicago, 1982).

47. Chen himself used the $2000 figure in a two-part letter to the US denominational newspaper, *The Covenant Weekly*, issues of 27 July and 3 August 1937.

48. Interestingly, Keller's personal inclination seems to have been to pass power to the Chinese nationalistic group. But by 1936 he was desperate to retire, and was happy to accept either group.

49. O. Theodore Roberg, "Marcus Cheng (c. 1883–1963): Apostle or Apostate? Relations with the Covenant Mission in China" (M.A. thesis, North Park Theological Seminary, Chicago, 1982), pp. 52–57, discusses this.

50. Marcus Ch'eng (Chen Chonggui), *After Forty Years* (London: n.p.), p. 13. Apparently the magazine had to cease publication in late 1939 or 1940. But it resumed again sometime after Chen's return from Singapore in 1943.

51. Marcus Ch'eng (Chen Chonggui), *After Forty Years* (London: n.p.), pp. 69–71, 113.

52. This is my reading of Jean-Paul Wiest, *Maryknoll in China: A History, 1918–1955* (Armonk, NY: M. E. Sharpe, 1988), Ch. 5.

53. Timothy Brook, "Toward Independence: Christianity in China under the Japanese Occupation," in Daniel H. Bays, *Christianity in China: From the Eighteenth Century to the Present* (Stanford, CA: Stanford University Press, 1996), pp. 317–337.

54. To mention just a few: Langdon Gilkey, *Shantung Compound* (New York: Harper & Row, 1966). David Michell, *A Boy's War* (n.p.: OMF Books, 1988); Norman Cliff, *Courtyard of the Happy Way* (Evesham, UK: Arthur James Ltd., 1977); and at least one novel, J. G. Ballard, *Empire of the Sun* (London: Grafton, 1985).

55. Timothy Brook, *Collaboration: Japanese Agents and Local Elites in Wartime China* (Cambridge, MA: Harvard University Press, 2005), Ch. 1, pp. 1–31.

56. *Huabei Zhonghua Jidujiao tuan chengli zhounian jiniance* (Commemorative handbook [register?] of the establishment of the North China Church of Christ League), n.p., 1943. This name was very similar to that of the first association of N. China independent churches, in the Beijing-Tianjin-Shandong area about 1910, and also to that of the union Church of Christ in China (Zhonghua Jidujiaohui) established in the 1920s and which had about thirty percent of the Protestant population enrolled. As Tim Brook points out, this October meeting was a follow up to an earlier unsuccessful meeting that revealed a lot of Chinese Protestant resistance to the idea.

57. Unfortunately, the portrait of Jiang Changchuan in his entry in Howard L. Boorman, ed., *Biographical Dictionary of Republican China*, 4 vols. (New York: Columbia University Press, 1967) seems too adulatory, and perhaps undependable. See Vol. 1, pp. 305–306.

58. I am in possession of three or four listings of place/name information on the wartime church in Shandong, but none of them has a title, issuing entity, or date of publication.

59. "Toward Independence: Christianity in China under the Japanese Occupation," in *Christianity in China: From the Eighteenth Century to the Present*, ed. Daniel H. Bays (Stanford, CA: Stanford University Press, 1996), pp. 334–337.

60. Brian Stanley, *The World Missionary Conference, Edinburgh 1910* (Grand Rapids, MI: Wm. Eerdmans, 2009), pp.107–109.

61. For example, Thomas Alan Harvey, *Acquainted with Grief: Wang Mingdao's Stand for the Persecuted Church in China* (Grand Rapids, MI: Brazos Press, 2002).

62. Wallace C. Merwin, *Adventure in Unity: The Church of Christ in China* (Grand Rapids, MI: Wm. B. Eerdmans, 1974).

63. Liu Jiafeng, "Same Bed, Different Dreams: The American Postwar Plan for China's Christian Colleges, 1943–1946," in *China's Christian Colleges: Cross-Cultural Connections, 1900–1950*, ed. Daniel H. Bays and Ellen Widmer (Stanford, CA: Stanford University Press, 2009), pp. 218–240. For an example of one wartime refugee university in exile, see John Israel, *Lianda: a Chinese University in War and Revolution* (Stanford, CA: Stanford University Press, 1998).

64. Sources on the wartime years for the NCC and CCC are few. Chs. 7–8 in Wallace C. Merwin, *Adventure in Unity: The Church of Christ in China* (Grand Rapids,

MI: Wm. B. Eerdmans, 1974). Archie R. Crouch, *Rising through the Dust: The Story of the Christian Church in China* (New York: Friendship Press, 1947), has several parts that are relevant.

65. James H. Taylor III kindly gave me copies of the following: The Chinese Back-to-Jerusalem Evangelistic Band, *A Prayer Call to Christian friends of the Chinese Church* (n.p., n.d.); also *Newsletter*, no. 10 (Dec., 1949, and no. 11 (April, 1950). The relationship between this "Back-to-Jerusalem" movement of the 1940s and the purported one since 2000 which has excited some circles, is problematic. Claims for the latter are in Paul Hattaway, *Back to Jerusalem* (Carlisle, UK: Piquant, 2003).

66. However, there is no way to determine exact figures.

67. This section is also treated by Wallace C. Merwin, *Adventure in Unity: The Church of Christ in China* (Grand Rapids, MI: Wm. B. Eerdmans, 1974), pp. 154–164.

68. Liu Jiafeng, "Same Bed, Different Dreams: The American Postwar Plan for China's Christian Colleges, 1943–1946," in *China's Christian Colleges: Cross-Cultural Connections, 1900–1950*, ed. Daniel H. Bays and Ellen Widmer (Stanford, CA: Stanford University Press, 2009), pp. 218–240.

69. The only thing written on this as far as I know is Philip L. Wickeri, "The Chinese Christian Movement on the Eve of Liberation," unpublished, written for a symposium on the History of Christianity in China, the University of Kansas, June 17–23, 1990.

70. China Inter-Varsity was the short form of China Inter-Varsity Evangelical Christian Students Fellowship, the name adopted by Calvin Chao in July 1945. The remainder of this paragraph is partially based on Lian Xi, *Redeemed by Fire: Popular Chinese Christianity in the Twentieth Century* (New Haven, CT: Yale University Press, 2010), pp. 190–194.

71. Adeney's own account of this period is in his *China: Christian Students Face the Revolution* (Downers Grove, IL: InterVarsity Press, 1973). Also Carolyn Armitage, *Reaching for the Goal: the Life Story of David Adeney* (Wheaton, IL: Harold Shaw, 1993), pp. 101–116.

72. Maochun Yu, *OSS in China: Prelude to Cold War* (New Haven, CT: Yale University Press, 1996), pp. 216–219.

73. The 139 included 20 archbishoprics (one for each of the 20 ecclesiastical provinces); 84 bishoprics (one for each diocese); and 35 prefectures apostolic.

74. A detailed recounting of a village Catholic community undergoing radical land reform and expropriation in the late 1940s is the description by William Hinton, *Fanshen: A Documentary of Revolution in a Chinese Village* (NY: Alfred A. Knopf, 1966).

7

Christianity and the New China, 1950–1966

Prologue

We Christians in China feel the urgent necessity of re-examining our work and our relationship with the older churches abroad in the light of this historical change....The Christian movement will have its due place in the future Chinese society and will have a genuine contribution to make. Its future road will not be a bed of roses.... The Chinese church will not emerge through this historical change unaffected. It will suffer a purge, and many of the withered branches will be amputated.

"Message from Chinese Christians to Mission Boards Abroad," Dec. 1949[1]

Recognize clearly the evils that have been wrought in China by imperialism; recognize the fact that in the past imperialism has made use of Christianity; purge imperialistic influences from within Christianity itself; and be vigilant against imperialism, especially American imperialism, in its plot to use religion in fostering the growth of reactionary forces.

"The Christian Manifesto," May 1950[2]

Communism is intrinsically wrong, and no one who wishes to defend Christian civilization against extinction may collaborate with it in any way whatsoever.

Pius XI, "Divini Redemptoris," March 19, 1937[3]

A New History of Christianity in China, First Edition. Daniel H. Bays.
© 2012 Daniel H. Bays. Published 2012 by Blackwell Publishing Ltd.

Both Protestant and Roman Catholic missionaries and Chinese Christians in 1949 faced something they had never encountered in their lifetimes: a powerful central state that was capable of demanding their compliance, if not their allegiance. It had been over a century since Christians in China had to deal with a secular regime that had both the capability and the inclination to intervene in mission and church affairs. It should not have been surprising that this new government, like the emperors of several dynasties of the last millennium, evinced an insistence on monitoring religious life and requiring all religions, for example, to register their venues and leadership personnel with a government office. The repeated historical experience of sectarian popular religious movements (such as the White Lotus, the Eight Trigrams, among many) turning into anti-dynastic rebellions was sufficient to make all central governments instinctively vigilant of religion.[4] The new government of the People's Republic of China (PRC) inherited this default attitude from the imperial past, and added to it another level of animus deriving from its Marxist ideology. That is, the new leaders assumed that because Marxist dogma taught that religion was socially retrograde, doomed to eventual extinction, the mechanisms of control devised for all religions were not only to register and monitor religious believers, but also systematically to reduce the influence of religion in society. At times this resulted in harsh policies trying to eradicate religion, especially in the late 1950s and during the Cultural Revolution (1966–1976). However, priorities for the new government in the early 1950s did not include destruction of religion, only getting a secure grip of control on it. Moreover, there were several higher priorities on the new leaders' agenda, such as rehabilitation of transport and communications after the civil war, controlling the rampant inflation, reviving agriculture, and dealing with active armed opposition of Guomindang diehards or criminal gangs. Scholars have recently been taking a fresh look at the multiple and complex challenges faced by the new regime.[5]

The course of future religious policy was unclear in the first several months of the PRC; still the regime was particularly observant of the two Christian communities, Protestant and Catholic, because of their extensive foreign ties – that is, their "imperialist connections." The centerpiece of the policy agenda of the new government for both Protestants and Catholics was simple: cutting all ties with their foreign former associates and foreign institutions, putting them under the jurisdiction of state and party bodies assigned to monitor them. The regime used the "Three-Self" concept for both. In the first years of the decade of the 1950s the Protestants, on the whole, responded favorably to the new framework; the new system for them was operating before 1954. The Catholics, however, especially those of Shanghai, mounted a prolonged resistance and were not brought to heel until 1957 or later.

The communists found the three-self idea convenient to use for purposes of eliminating foreign influences; they did not invent it. The three "selfs" were self-support, self-government, and self-propagation; the ideas had first been used by the heads of the American Board of Commissioners for Foreign Missions, Rufus Anderson, and the [British] Church Missionary Society, Henry Venn, in the mid nineteenth century. The Sino-Foreign Protestant Establishment in the first half of the twentieth century talked frequently of the three-self principles, but did not move very far toward actually implementing them in their Chinese congregations. The three-self idea was actually best seen in the various independent movements of the 1910s–1940s, such as the True Jesus Church and Watchman Nee's followers (Chapter 6). Three-Self ideas did not fit easily with Catholic structure and practice, especially the idea of self-governance, considering that built in to the Catholic system was an important role for the Vatican, for example in Papal consecration of bishops, and issuance of bulls and other documents that were binding in ecclesiastical law.

Thus it should not be surprising that patterns of compliance and resistance for Protestants and Catholics in the years after 1949 differed considerably.

Protestants 1949–1954: Compliance

Though almost all foreign missionaries and many Chinese Protestants were suspicious of if not hostile to communism at the time of regime change in 1949, a number of urban Christians were hopeful of decent relations with the new government. Some of these were Christian intellectuals who by the late 1940s had established themselves as openly sympathetic to the communist movement and its victory.[6] Among this group, which might be called the "left wing" of the liberal National Christian Council and the Church of Christ in China, was Y. T. Wu (Wu Yaozong, 1895–1979), a national YMCA secretary and editor of the foremost Protestant publication, *Tianfeng* (Heavenly Wind).[7] In 1948 Wu wrote a scathing indictment of the Protestant establishment in Marxist terms, decrying the hand of imperialism on China.[8] This caused an uproar in Christian circles, and may have brought Wu to the notice of the communist party.[9] At any rate When Wu went to Beijing in spring 1950 with a small group of Chinese Christian "progressives," it was Wu's reputation and connections that opened doors for them to see some top leaders, including Zhou Enlai.

The "Christian Manifesto" and Growth of the Three Self

By early 1950, there were in effect two groups of Chinese church leaders with potential influence in the new political situation. First there were those who were distinguished longtime leaders and church bureaucrats, veterans of the

NCC and of the CCC. These central pillars of the Sino-Foreign Protestant Establishment had for the most part been relatively inactive in recent years. To me, it seems likely that the NCC sorely missed the leadership of Cheng Jingyi and Yu Rizhang, who had both died in the 1930s. The NCC did rouse itself to send three letters of hope and encouragement in the uncertain times to Chinese Christians nationwide in 1948–1949. Many of this group would have liked the new government to deal with the NCC and large established church bodies like the CCC. Then there was a group of Christians, several of them from YMCA/YWCA background, which in early 1950 became loosely gathered around Y. T. Wu, and which eventually became the launching pad for the Three-Self movement. Some among this group first came together in December 1949, when they sent a long open letter to the West, especially to Western mission boards, entitled simply "Message from Chinese Christians to Mission Boards Abroad."[10] This "message" was signed by 19 Protestant leaders, interestingly not including Y. T. Wu. Anyone reading it carefully (see quotation at beginning of this chapter) could see that the missionary era in China was over, and that its legacy would be contested; it was clear that the historical record of imperialism would be a major item of discussion between foreign missions and Chinese Christians, at least for the near future.

Some of the Y. T. Wu group, including Wu, had attended the first meeting of the Chinese People's Political Consultative Conference (CPPCC) in Beijing in the early fall of 1949.[11] The "Common Program" approved by the CPPCC was in effect China's constitution until 1954, when the NPC approved the first formal constitution. The Common Program, which was the foundation enabling establishment of the PRC on October 1, 1949, contained provision for the "freedom of religious belief'" for all religious believers. Several Shanghai Christian leaders who attended the CPPCC upon return to Shanghai in late 1949 formed teams to travel around the region and other parts of China to see if the Common Program's legal provision for the right to religious belief was being respected and to investigate the general situation of Christians across China. In May 1950 Y.T. Wu and 18 other Protestant leaders returned to Beijing, intending to report to the highest authorities their findings on the state of Protestantism, local problems of adaptation between Christians and local officials, and other matters. In several discussions with Premier Zhou Enlai, they dropped the idea of the report to the party and decided to write a statement to address directly the issue of the churches' political standpoint, that is, attitudes toward their own missionary past, especially complicity in imperialism. It was this document that was reworked through several drafts, coordinated by Y. T. Wu, who remained in contact with Zhou Enlai during the process. It has been asserted that Zhou Enlai just wrote the document and imposed it on the Christian leaders, but it seems clear that they did it themselves.[12] The content was concise and clear: it called upon Christians and churches to recognize the reality of the record of imperialism in China and to pledge to eliminate its remnants and lingering attitudes. By summer 1950 the document was starting to circulate and collect signatures of Chinese Christians; it was simply called the "Christian Manifesto" (full title, "Direction of Endeavor for Chinese Christianity in the Construction of New China").[13] The manifesto was issued with the signatures of 40 Christian leaders. In August 1950 about 1500 had signed; by May 1951 there were 180,000; eventually 400,000 (allegedly) did so.[14]

By late summer 1950 the manifesto signature campaign had become combined with creation of a new entity to tend to Protestant affairs. This was called the Three Self Reform Movement. The basic outline of the new structure indicated that it would manage the affairs of Chinese Protestants under communism; it was also clear that it would be under the leadership of Y. T. Wu. In October 1950, the NCC met for its national meeting for the first time since 1946. After first not even having the Three Self on the agenda, the meeting ended up with all 140 delegates voting to sign the manifesto and embrace the Three-Self movement. The NCC in effect ceased to exist after this event, although several of its leaders continued to be active in the Three Self. The swell of compliance in signing the manifesto was not unanimous. Some conservative groups and leaders such as Wang Mingdao ignored it. The House of Bishops of the Sheng gonghui (Anglican Church) declined to sign, and issued their own pastoral letter (later all the Anglican bishops did sign).

We can only speculate how deeply the campaign to sign the manifesto would have affected the churches had it not been for the impact of some extraneous events. There certainly would have been pressure on church bodies and congregations to cut ties with foreigners with concrete actions, and generally to comply with the government and the emerging Three Self body. But then in October and November 1950 the process going on among Protestants intersected with the trajectory of the rapidly escalating Korean War, and everything changed. The war, which had begun as the Korean civil war in late June, 1950, in November–December became a direct and bloody contest between the US/UN forces and the Chinese People's Liberation Army (sent to Korea as "volunteers"). For the next nearly three years the conflict in Korea greatly increased the tension and pressures of the domestic campaigns being pushed by the CCP: Land reform, the campaign to root out "counter-revolutionaries" (that is, active Chiang Kai-shek or Guomintang supporters, prostitutes, gangsters and drug traffickers), later campaigns such as the 'Three anti" campaign against corruption in the party and the "Five anti" campaign against the business class. In this more highly charged political atmosphere, the "Christian Manifesto" campaign to secure Christian renunciation of foreign ties and a commitment to the new regime took on a much sharper edge. In early 1951 the movement to sign the document overlapped with the campaign against counter-revolutionaries, and leaders in the Protestant churches, both missionaries and Chinese, were subjected to denunciation meetings or "struggle sessions" in their workplace or in public venues. Although the Christian denunciation meetings resulted in few imprisonments and only a handful of executions, those chosen for attack suffered intense humiliation and trauma, as their co-workers and even family members were pressured to denounce them. This was a nasty business, continuing for months and held in all sorts of Christian institutions – denominations, YMCAs, the Christian Literature Society, the NCC itself. Some who had signed the letter to mission boards in December 1949 were denounced in 1951 as lackeys of imperialism. Most ironically of all, at least three members of the 25-person "preparatory council"' for the national organization of the Three Self, appointed in May 1951, had been denounced and purged later in 1951 and 1952. One of them, the Jesus Family founder Jing Dianying, was in prison, where he died about 1957.[15] All this was certainly aggravated by the Korean War.[16] Yet another result of the war was that the departure of foreign missionaries was abruptly accelerated. In retrospect it was not realistic to expect that more than a handful of foreign missionaries would be permitted to stay in the new China. However, without the war the exodus of the foreigners might well have been considerably less unpleasant.

The war produced a flush of zealous patriotism which occasioned the final and rapid takeover by the government of the major institutions of the old Sino-Foreign Protestant Establishment. Missionary-supported hospitals and clinics, schools from elementary to college levels, all had been continuing to receive operating funds from abroad and a large number of them still had foreign missionary personnel as of the fall of 1950. That changed rapidly in late 1950. In mid December, the US government froze all Chinese assets in the US, which made it nearly impossible to send remittances to China from the US and for those in China to receive them. The Chinese government retaliated by freezing all US assets in China, compounding the near-impossibility of transferring funds.[17] There was no solution to this impasse other than the foreign institutions being taken over by a Chinese body or institution, unless they were terminated.[18]

While the manifesto was adding signatures and denunciation meetings were still going on around the country, in early May 1951 in Beijing Y. T. Wu convened a conference of Protestant activists. Its purpose was formally to launch the Three Self as an institution-in-creation through a "preparatory council". Wu and other Three Self proponents, with Zhou Enlai's blessing, had been working for months to broaden the base of support for the new organization among Christians. He was more successful than some expected, perhaps. At this still-preliminary stage, he had recruited Marcus Ch'eng (Chen Chonggui), a well-known evangelical, indeed a Fundamentalist, as one of the four vice-chairmen.[19] And one of the 20 regular members was Jing Dianying, founder and still leader of the communal and Pentecostal Jesus Family. Other members included Christian college presidents (Wei Zhuomin [Central China

University in Wuhan], Wu Yifang [Ginling College for Women in Nanjing], other respected academics like Zhao Zichen [Yanjing University, Beijing]), and representatives of the YMCA and YWCA. Wu, of course, was chairman. The title of the organization as a work in progress became a bit awkward at this point. It threw into the mix every conceivable function. It was called the "Preparatory Council of the China Christian Resist-America Help-Korea Three-Self Reform Movement."

With the successor organization to the NCC now in place, there remained two further tasks: the first was to clarify the channels of interaction between the unwieldy-sounding Three Self entity and the government and party structures; the second was to persuade all Chinese Protestants to affiliate with the Three Self. It is important to remember that the three-self organization was not itself a church, just as the old NCC dating back to the 1920s had not been a church. The first task was accomplished by 1954, in parallel with the development of the overall government structure, which after a national census in 1953 had its first National People's Congress in 1954, with "elected" delegates from every province. The 1954 meeting to launch the Protestant organization formally was called the First National Christian Conference. The Three Self had been operating for three years already, since the 1951 meeting, but 1954 was the first national-level ratification of its legitimacy. Nothing of major importance changed at the 1954 meeting. In order to meet the concerns of some, mostly conservative, Protestant groups that they would be forced to undergo "reforms" against their will, the word "reform" was dropped from the title, which now became the (China Christian) "Three Self Patriotic Movement" (TSPM). The place of the TSPM in the overall state and party setup was also clarified by 1954. It was placed under the direct supervision of the Religious Affairs Bureau (RAB), a state agency under the State Council which was responsible for the affairs of all five of the officially sanctioned religions (Protestant Christianity, Catholic Christianity, Buddhism, Daoism, Islam). The RAB in turn came under the authority of the party's United Front Work Department (UFWD), which supervised and directed relationships with all non-party groups. This is the institutional structure that lasted until the turmoil of the Cultural Revolution 1966–1976, when it was dismantled, and then was reestablished in the late 1970s and continues down to the present. All three of these bodies (TSPM, RAB, UFWD) have national, provincial, county and municipal offices or committees. The TSPM personnel are normally all Christian pastors or laymen; the government and party officials are decidedly not religious believers (there are a few exceptions)

The second task in the regime's Protestant agenda was to bring all Protestants under the purview of the TSPM. This has never been achieved – neither in the 1950s nor from 1980 to the present. But it was certainly attempted in the 1950s. There were many important targets in the hundreds of Protestant mass denunciation rallies held in 1951–1952. Some of the original preparatory council of the TSPM were put through this ordeal and a few were purged. Other important figures who were condemned and incarcerated included Watchman Nee, who was a target of the "Five anti" movement against the business class. Nee had been president of a family pharmaceutical company in the 1940s and still had connections with it. He was sent to prison in 1952 on charges of malfeasance and economic crimes. His movement, the "Little Flock," did not come under pressure until later in the decade; several of its local leaders cooperated with the TSPM in the early 1950s and most of its local assemblies affiliated with the TSPM. At the same time several of Nee's associates, notably his longtime lieutenant Witness Li (Li Changshou), went to Taiwan and continued the movement there. As for Nee, he was reviled in 1952 as a corrupt capitalist and imprisoned, then reviled again in 1956 as a religious charlatan and swindler, which apparently in effect lengthened his sentence. He died in a labor camp in 1972. Despite Nee's fate, the "Little Flock" has proven very resilient and is a major presence in Chinese Christianity in the twenty-first century, as I will discuss in the next chapter. In addition to Jing and Nee, leaders of two of the three most important of the pre-1949 independent non-missionary churches, the third, the True Jesus Church, could not avoid a similar fate. Wei Yisa (Isaac Wei), son of the founder Paul Wei, who had died in 1919, and who himself had taken the leadership of the rapidly growing church in about 1930, was also purged in 1952, despite an abject letter of self-criticism that appeared in *Tianfeng* in February 1952.[20]

Thus all three of the independent church movements which had compelling grounds for claiming that they were already examples of "three self" – the Jesus Family, the True Jesus Church, and the "Little Flock"--were decapitated by removal of their longtime leadership in the mid 1950s. The lay believers of these independent churches were taken care of by breakup and scattering of the communities for the Jesus Family and by absorption into other churches for the True Jesus and the "Little Flock." Both of these latter traditions are still distinctly visible in the Chinese church of the twenty-first century. In the mid 1950s, however, clearly there was intended to be only one competitor on the Protestant playing field. As of about 1955, almost all the well-known Protestant leaders were in prison, or under indictment for spying or serving the imperialists, or were the recent target of a denunciation campaign; several had left the country, gone to Hong Kong or the West. The regime had been relatively successful in discrediting and toppling from power those Protestant leaders who might be hard to control. It was important to tag these targets as disloyal to China, or swindlers using religion as a cover, or self-serving "fleecers" of the people. Then the party and state could claim that it was not their faith that was being prosecuted (after all, freedom of religious belief was in the constitution), but criminal behavior. Then they could not easily become religious martyrs, an outcome which the party wanted by all means to avoid, since it would create more problems in the future.

In the mid 1950s, probably the biggest single remaining obstacle to TSPM Protestant hegemony was Wang Mingdao, the old warhorse independent evangelist and preacher, and his Beijing Christian Tabernacle. We last saw Wang in the early 1940s as he was successfully defying the pressures of the Japanese occupation authorities to join the union North China church federation being promoted by the Japanese. That success may have led him to believe that he could do the same now, and simply stubbornly resist first the blandishments, then the threats, of the authorities and the TSPM leaders. In June 1955, Wang published a long, blistering printed attack on not the politics, but the modernist theology of the TSPM leaders, in which he categorically stated that they were not Christian believers. At this point apparently both the authorities and the TSPM leaders lost patience and had Wang arrested.[21] This was a risky strategy: there was every chance that he could be seen as a martyr, with protests from his followers, among whom were a large number of zealous believers, many of them young people. The drama of Wang's case continued well after his arrest. After about a year in jail, constantly under intense psychological pressure, Wang relented and signed a confession in 1956 in exchange for release. The deal struck was that Wang would make a public confession and would affiliate with the TSPM. He did the former, then was so chagrined at what he had done that he retracted his confession and refused to join the TSPM after all. For this he was returned to prison, where he languished for more than 20 years. The Wang Mingdao affair is interesting because it also features a role by K. H. Ting (Ding Guangxun), principal of Nanjing Union Seminary and on the rise in the TSPM as a protégé of Y. T. Wu. Ting led much of the attack on Wang in the pages of *Tianfeng*. After the Cultural Revolution, Ting succeeded Wu as head of the TSPM. Historians differ deeply in evaluations of the significance of Ting's role in the clash between Wang and the TSPM, with Ting being excoriated by some and treated sympathetically by others.[22]

The Fate of Evangelicals in the TSPM: The Case of Chen Chonggui (Marcus Ch'eng)

We last observed Chen in the late 1940s, in the presidency of Chungking (Chongqing) Theological seminary. By this time, after nearly three decades of vicissitudes, Chen had succeeded in achieving a position of considerable autonomy, responsibility, and national stature in Chinese Protestantism. He continued to work with foreign missionaries, but not as a second-class junior associate, as he had been forced to do early in his career. His name was recognized and respected by most Chinese Christians as a traveling evangelist and revival speaker, as the longtime editor of "Evangelism," and as the author of still-popular daily devotional essays.[23] By dint of his talents and hard work, as well as the influence of outside events, Chen was now among those senior Chinese Protestant leaders who for all their lives had hoped to complete the transition from a foreign mission-run church to a church operated by Chinese nationals.

In the late 1940s national politics, especially the civil war between the Nationalists and the communists, intruded into all spheres of life in China. Chen Chonggui was no exception in being faced with some fateful choices as the civil war wound down with the communists as clear victors. Chen chose to return to his seminary presidency in Chongqing rather than to remain in safe haven in the US, as several other Chinese religious and academic leaders did.

During 1950–1951 Chen publicly threw in his lot with the new Communist government and with Y. T. Wu and other "progressive" Christian leaders. There must have been many reasons for this: patriotism, idealism, a desire to protect the Chongqing seminary, perhaps naïvety. At any rate, in the summer of 1950 Chen, always the journalist, began writing extensively for *Tianfeng* magazine in Shanghai. He was highly critical of the missionary record in China, and praised fulsomely the new regime and its policies.[24]

During 1951 Chen consummated his commitment to the new political regime. He attended the crucial April meeting in Beijing which created the TSPM, and he became one of the four vice-chairpersons of the preparatory council of the TSPM. The theologically liberal YMCA leader Y. T. Wu was chairman, of course, and most of the other high level leaders of the TSPM were also liberals. Thus the participation at such a high and visible level of the evangelical Chen Chonggui, as well as that of another evangelical, Jia Yuming, who later also became a vice-chairman, tended to validate the TSPM as a legitimate organization in the eyes of more conservative Chinese Christians. Chen also continued to write for *Tianfeng* magazine, along the lines of the articles he had been contributing since 1950.[25] Chen retired as president of Chongqing Theological Seminary in 1953 and moved to Dalian in the Northeast (Manchuria). Not long after this the seminary was closed and merged with others to form a union seminary. Chen, however, remained visible in national-level events; he was present at the important National Christian Conference of Protestants in 1954, and he remained a vice-chairman of the TSPM preparatory council.[26]

In 1957 Chen was 73 years old. He was in effect retired, and might have expected to live out his days in peace, watching younger church leaders carry on. This was not to be. In March 1957, due to his TSPM vice-chairman's position, Chen attended as a delegate a meeting of the Chinese People's Political Consultative Conference (CPPCC) in Beijing. The CPPCC, made up of prominent non-communist figures, can be counted on for compliant cooperation with the communist regime. Its meetings are usually character-ized by unstinting praise of the government and communist party and undeviating approval of all measures put before it by the regime. This particular meeting, however, was held at the height of the "100 Flowers Movement," in an atmosphere of candid expression of views actively encouraged by Mao Zedong and a few other party leaders.[27] As a result, this meeting of the CPPCC was quite lively; it was the occasion of some unusually frank public criticisms of many different aspects of the rule of the communist party and the government. Religious policy was one issue discussed. At one point Chen Chonggui had the floor and the limelight. He politely but forthrightly decried the harsh and punitive attitude toward religious believers that had often characterized the first years of Communist rule, despite the seemingly generous official national policy of freedom of religious belief in the constitution of 1954. Chen's speech, given on 19 March, was reported in full in the 25 March Beijing *People's Daily*, the foremost national newspaper, and later reprinted in the 13 May issue of *Tianfeng* as well.[28] This was unusually wide national circulation for the remarks of a religious figure.

Unfortunately for Chen, the 100 Flowers Movement was followed within a few weeks by the "Anti-Rightist Campaign" of mid 1957 to 1958, an extended campaign in which most of those individuals who had criticized the government or the Communist Party in the spring of 1957 now became targets of vigorous denunciation and lost their positions, some being sent to labor camps. Party members and non-party members alike fell victim to the purge. Religious leaders who had expressed doubts or open criticism of government policy were among those attacked. Chen Chonggui, because of his remarks at the CPPCC in March, was one of the most prominent targets of denunciation among Protestant leaders during these months. His fate was sealed when Mao Zedong himself blasted Chen as an obvious rightist. The attack on Chen was actually led by Y. T. Wu, Chen's close colleague in the TSPM.[29] The denunciation of Chen was unrelenting. Although perhaps because of his age he escaped the rigors of a labor camp, he lost his position in the TSPM and he became a non-person. He spent the next few years in obscurity, and he died in 1963. Almost thirty years after his death his reputation was officially rehabilitated. This was first marked by the appearance in mid 1990 of a brief biographical sketch in the *Jinling shenxuezhi* (Nanjing Theological Review),[30] soon followed by a substantial commemorative volume put out in 1991 by the national Three-Self Committee and by the 1993 reprint of his daily devotional essays of 1950.

For us, Chen's life and career, which we have followed in some detail, has been both an example of success in the Sino-foreign world of twentieth-century Protestantism, and a cautionary tale reminding all Christians of the tenuousness of faith in a militantly secular society.

By 1958, Protestants entered the dark valley that they would traverse in the next two decades. But before carrying the Protestant story further, we must turn to the saga of China's Catholics after 1949.

Catholics 1949–1957: Resistance

Scenario for a showdown

The Roman Catholic Church in China at the transition to communist rule was very different from that of the Protestants. With about three million followers, 3–4 times the number of Protestants, nevertheless Catholics were more rooted in rural areas, and had fewer urban institutions. For example, Catholics only had three colleges, whereas Protestants had 13. Catholics had only a few modern hospitals; Protestants had many more, including some world-class ones, such as the Peking Union Medical College. There were, however, a few cities with substantial numbers of Catholics. Beijing and Tianjin certainly would be counted among these, but clearly Shanghai was the most important bastion of Catholicism in 1949. There were about 110,000 Catholics in Shanghai, or about 1.8 percent of the city's population of 6 million, a much higher figure than the nationwide percentage of Catholics, about 0.6 percent.[31] Moreover, Shanghai was home to a couple of the most prestigious sites in the Chinese Catholic world: 1) the Marian shrine and church at Sheshan in the Shanghai suburbs, with its enthusiastic (and potentially unruly) annual pilgrimage, which attracted tens of thousands; and 2) the cathedral, library, and other facilities of Xujiahui (Zikawei) in the southwest part of the city, which was a Jesuit stronghold (as it had been since the 1840s, when French Jesuits reasserted control in the whole area of Jiangnan (Jiangsu Province plus southern Anhui and northern Jiangxi, of which Shanghai was the core; see Chapter 3). Jiangnan as a resource and personnel backstop was another source of strength for the Shanghai church; Catholics could quickly get from Suzhou and other Yangzi River valley cities to Shanghai to participate in protests and demonstrations. After 1948 another important entity, the Catholic Central Bureau, an organization for the use of the bishops all over the country, which did publicity, publications and external relations, internal communications and coordination, and political strategizing as well, was established in Shanghai. Finally, we should remember that the Catholic community in Shanghai was an old and well established one dating back to the late Ming dynasty, that is, the seventeenth century. This community still maintained some degree of wealth, status, and social capital, and they were very conscious of their descent from early well-established Catholic families. Thus in many ways Shanghai loomed as the largest challenge to the state and the party in bringing the Catholics under control.

The game begins

There had been friction between communists and Catholics for some time before 1949, much of it centered on the extensive landholdings and landlord operations of the Church, which were often reduced or confiscated by CCP cadres for redistribution during the land reform campaign, which began in the Northeast before the end of 1946. All across north China some lay leaders and priests, including a few foreigners, had been treated harshly, even killed.

It must be said that the persons, institutions, and policies of the Roman Catholic church in China in the late 1940s aggravated to a significant degree the already – present hostility between the Church and the CCP. Pope Pius XII seemed as virulently anticommunist in the late 1940s as his predecessor Pius XI had been in the 1937 papal letter quoted at the beginning of this chapter. In 1946 the Holy See appointed Antonio Riberi to be Papal Nuncio, the Pope's representative in China, possessing extraordinary authority over the various Catholic provinces, vicariates, and dioceses. Originally Riberi was accredited to the Nationalist government, so he was on site when the change of regime took place in 1949. One of Riberi's tasks was to organize and establish the new Catholic Central Bureau, which he did, staffing it with dozens of capable priests, both foreign and Chinese; many of them lived at the Catholic Central Bureau. Riberi was also charged with reviving and mobilizing two kinds of Catholic devotional organizations in the Shanghai church. These were the Legion of Mary, and a variety of Marian sodalities.[32] He did indeed infuse these organizations with vigor, both clergy and laypeople, and they created significant problems for the new government, for example in mobilizing the Catholic youth of the city to turn churches into sites for protest rallies and for heavily attended devotional events which were thinly disguised as piety. Finally, Riberi reinforced and reminded all and sundry of the directive from Rome in 1949 which ordered all Chinese Catholics to refuse cooperation with the communists, under sanction of excommunication. It is hard to imagine a set of actions and policies more likely to arouse the suspicions and the ire of the new communist authorities. It is not surprising that Riberi was thoroughly denounced and unceremoniously expelled from the country in mid 1951.

An interesting feature of this set of (some would say) provocative policies was the continuing primary leadership role of the foreign parts of the Catholic community. Nationwide, the late 1940s was still a time of overwhelming foreign dominance of leadership posts, especially of those in territorial jurisdictions. Catholics had been very slow to indigenize leadership, compared with Protestants. There were several hundred foreign priests in and around Shanghai as of 1949–1950. Many of them were still in leadership positions even when it appears that there were potential Chinese leaders available.[33] Of course this had been the case in Chinese Catholicism for over one hundred years, despite a counter-trend pushed by the Vatican beginning with the consecration of the six Chinese bishops in 1926. At any rate, the foreign prominence in the church was a problem when in 1951 the government turned to the "imperialism issue" with a vengeance in its search for leverage over the church.

One significant exception to the continuing pattern of foreign leadership was the August, 1950, choice of Gong Pinmei to be the new Bishop of Shanghai. Shanghai Catholics were ecstatic at this appointment. Not only was this the first Chinese bishop of Shanghai, but Gong was a native son of the city. This alone was sufficient to arouse the enthusiasm of the community. And further, Gong seems to have been, as far as we can tell, a pious, conscientious, capable, and courageous person even before he later took on the status of hero-martyr. This only enhanced the reverence in which he was later held.

The battle for Shanghai[34]

For the first period of more than a year after the "liberation" of Shanghai in April 1949, Catholics were not aggressively pursued as targets. Their many foreign priests and sisters mainly stayed put; few left China. Churches remained open, priests said mass and performed other sacraments, Catholic schools and medical facilities remained in operation. This involved 60 churches and worship sites, 63 schools, six hospitals, and six thousand rental properties. This all may have made up a significant, although still very small, proportion of the land of the central city.[35] Although Catholic landholdings in the countryside were often an inflammatory issue and incidents of violence occurred, the modernizing role of these largely urban institutions meant that they would be regulated, not destroyed, and even the foreign role tolerated, at least for a time.[36] However, the state did intrude on these parts of the Catholic presence. Heavy taxes were levied on properties, and the curriculum of the schools was substantially modified, removing all elements of religion. But churches were open, where children could still be taught doctrine, and the sodalities had an educational role for young people, as well. It would be inappropriate to call this a "honeymoon period," but at least it was one without an imminently threatening stance on the part of the new government.

As had been the case with Protestants, beginning in the fall of 1950 the spillover of the tensions of the Korean War to Chinese domestic affairs was great. By early 1951 the CCP began to interrogate, detain, and deport foreign Catholic missionaries, of which there were still several hundred in Shanghai. Some who were active in the Catholic Central Bureau or in developing the enthusiasm for the Legion of Mary were expelled and a few jailed, accused not for religious reasons but allegedly for spying and collecting intelligence information. The fact that the Little Brothers of St. John Baptist, under both Father Lebbe and FatherMegan, were involved in intelligence gathering and had relations with both Guomindang and US intelligence services during the Pacific war, facilitated this. For the next several years of the PRC a steady drumbeat of accusations of espionage punctuated the unrelenting, continuous pressure on the remaining missionaries to "confess their crimes" and leave. The communist government did perform an ill-advised miscue by creating a martyr. This was Father Beda Zhang, who was vicar of the cathedral at the Jesuit headquarters in Xujiahui. In late summer 1951, the public security forces took Zhang in for "questioning," in this case really torture, for several weeks. By November 1951 the rigors of this killed him – although he was still barely alive when the guards sent him to hospital. His death after obvious mistreatment, the furtive manner of his hasty burial with the police promising to turn over his body and then changing their minds, and a public gathering the next day, were emotional occasions for unifying and consolidating the resistance of a large number of Shanghai Catholics. The young people of the church, who had loved Father Zhang, were especially upset by his murder, and there was an influx of new recruits to the Legion of Mary. The determination to resist the government hardened.

The Legion of Mary gave the communist regime nightmares. The English term itself has connotations of the military or something militaristic; this alone worried some members of the government. They feared a plot for an uprising by thousands of Legionnaires armed with weapons from Taiwan or the US. Some of this was communist paranoia, some was the default stance of suspicion of popular movements or secretive behaviors. The regime's solution was to crack down hard on the Legion. In 1951–1952 the security apparatus launched a large campaign to ferret out the Legion members, who were ordered to register themselves with local security offices. Normally people would comply with such a directive. But the Shanghai members of the Legion were not willing to cooperate.

The larger context for Beda Zhang's martyrdom in November 1951, therefore, was that 1951 had not been a very good year for the RAB cadres of Shanghai. Having failed to uncover more than a few Legion members and getting them to register, they spent a good deal of time trying to convince even a small number of Catholic priests and lay leaders to join the Catholic equivalent of the Three-Self movement, which eventually was called the (Chinese) Catholic Patriotic Association (CPA).[37] During 1951, in a few locations, notably Sichuan, some priests and lay Catholics created a "manifesto" not unlike that of the Protestants, pledging to eliminate foreign influence in the church. But the results were very different. While the resulting Protestant TSPM had a certain credibility among many Christians, even if not among some evangelicals, the CPA had virtually none. Especially in Shanghai, only a handful of Catholics joined. They were joining the Legion of Mary instead, especially after the death of Beda Zhang. Bishop Gong Pinmei and other Shanghai leaders were invited to meetings with city officials, even some from the mayor's office, and urged to come on board with the CPA. But Bishop Gong and his colleagues consistently refused for years. The problem, of course, was that for Gong to join the CPA in effect denied some of the legitimate authority which the Pope had over the church, especially the election and consecration of new bishops. The Shanghai Catholics held the local government and party authorities at bay in 1951–1952.

Meanwhile, both sides, the Vatican and the Chinese government, kept the conflict going by rolling out their heavy artillery. A January, 1952, encyclical from Pius XII, "Cupimus In primis," praised Chinese Catholics for their loyalty and compared them to the persecuted believers of the early church.[38] Then in October 1954 Pius XII issued another encyclical, *Ad Sinarum Gentes* (To the People of China), which strongly defended the record of foreign missions, and criticized the CPA and the government. He encouraged the faithful to stand firm, and urged those who had erred (joined the CPA) to repent and leave it.[39] The Chinese government claimed this encyclical was very offensive to itself, and decried it as inappropriate interference in China's internal affairs. One cannot but think of the Kangxi emperor's high dudgeon over the Pope daring to tell him what his own subjects must do in the rites controversy of the early eighteenth century. Regardless, within a few months the Chinese authorities confronted the church more rigorously. Bishop Gong was arrested in October, 1955, along with several hundred priests and sisters, and lay people as well. By the end of the year over 1500 Shanghai Catholics were in prison. This was not just a Shanghai phenomenon; at this time Bishop Deng Yiming of Guangzhou, a colleague and friend of Bishop Gong, was also imprisoned.

The decision to jail Bishop Gong was not the preferred strategy of the RAB; that would have been to co-opt him into the CPA. But with Gong unwilling, the RAB went forward anyway, trying to minimize political damage as best they could. In fact the regime's strategy for crushing Catholic resistance in Shanghai proved to be feasible. This strategy was clearly spelled out in some internal documents of the Public Security Bureau and the RAB of the mid 1950s which were found and copied in the Shanghai Municipal Archives. These indicate that the phases of action were: 1) label the foreign missionaries as engaging in imperialist "criminal activities" and expel (or jail) them. Get them out of the way. The missionaries were "always linked with foreign reactionaries"; 2) repeat continually that the government "insists on protecting religious freedom," but those who use religion to harm the nation's and the people's security must be punished. Thus is implanted the seed of splitting the church, with some in the church accused of participating in criminal acts such as espionage; and 3) call for and facilitate "the mass of believers and religious personnel" to "actively participate", that is, to join in the denunciation of designated targets of "struggle."[40]

The way this strategy worked in practice was first to expel the remaining foreigners, tarring them with the brush of imperialism, at the same time making foreign imperialism and its Chinese partners the focus of massive propaganda. The next step was to identify some of those church leaders who had not been cooperative (for example in refusing to join the CPA) and accuse them of criminal activity (plotting with foreigners). Then, while loudly proclaiming the regime's defense of religious freedom, to punish these victims as criminals, whipping up mass enthusiasm in meetings with those attending hearing "evidence" of the "crimes' of the accused. Often the evidence included a "confession" of the accused. One of the results of this strategy was often division of opinion in the church. With the church divided, it was easier for the government to co-opt some Catholics, as part of the church community became confused in the pressure cooker of charges against those arrested. For example, the solidarity of 1951–1952 of those Catholics who had joined the Legion of Mary, many of them less than 20 years of age, was eroded by the arrest of the local Shanghai Catholic hierarchy in 1955 and after, precisely because their arrest was not permitted to be treated as a political issue, which it was, but only as a criminal one. There was sufficient doubt cast on those arrested that people began to comply with the police and register their membership in the Legion of Mary and drop out of its activities. Young members of the Legion of Mary were also pressured by their families to confess and register with the police. By the time of the late 1955 incarceration of Bishop Gong and the others, religious and lay, the regime basically had won the contest with the church. There really was never any doubt that they eventually would win, and bend the Catholics to their will. It was just a matter of when.

Finally, albeit several years later than had originally been planned, a docile group of 241 "patriotic Catholics" gathered in Beijing in mid July, 1957, to launch officially the CPA. Nothing else of note seems to have happened at the meeting. It was held soon after the start of the "Anti-rightist Movement," which reversed the course of the liberal "100 Flowers" period of spring 1957 and took retribution on those who had spoken out in the spring. By the time that the CPA meeting was held, it was clear that dissenting opinions were no longer welcomed by the party; the reverse course had been struck in early June. Many people, Protestants (such as Chen Chonggui) as well as Catholics, had already been criticized or denounced as "rightists," and it was very clear that their fate was going to be an unpleasant one. So at this, their first national gathering, the CPA delegates said almost nothing. A few months after the inaugural meeting of the CPA, in early 1958, the first Catholic bishops were appointed by the RAB without reference to Rome or the Pope. Thus began the "illicit" (though, ironically, also "valid") consecration of bishops in China, which has been a large obstacle in Chinese–Vatican relations ever since. In June 1958, Pope Pius XII issued yet another encyclical, Ad Apostolorum Principis, refusing to recognize consecration of clergy not nominated or sanctioned by the Holy See. This negative note, plus of course continued diplomatic recognition by Rome of the Guomindang regime of Chiang Kai-shek in Taiwan, heralded a frosty atmosphere for decades to come.

Denouement

Bishop Gong Pinmei and 13 of those arrested with him in 1955 were actually not tried in court until 1960.[41] But everything that transpired regarding the church in the late 1950s seems to have been touched by the unfinished status of the Gong affair. The most important diocese in the country went for five years with 14 important members of its hierarchy, including its bishop, imprisoned and unable to perform their jobs, which largely went undone.[42] In other areas, new bishops were being consecrated; from early 1958 until summer 1959, 26 new bishops were (illicitly) consecrated around the country. But nothing was done in Shanghai. Finally in 1960, ready to set up the CPA in Shanghai, the local officials, as they prepared for the trials, made one last attempt to win over Gong. The chief prosecutor came to see Gong in prison, and offered him leadership of the Shanghai church under the CPA and release from jail if he would break relations with the Pope. Gong refused, so on March 16, 1960, in the Shanghai Municipal Court began the trial of Bishop Gong and 13 others, all alleged members of the "Gong Pinmei traitorous counterrevolutionary clique." What is especially interesting here is the authorities' willingness, even after five years, to make Gong the head of the entire Shanghai CPA; they probably both respected him and feared him.

After the two-day trial, the verdicts were never in doubt. The verdicts drew heavily from the text of the indictments; Gong's own "counterrevolutionary" nature was specifically mentioned as evident in Gong's alleged opposition to the Korean War, opposition to land reform, conspiring to procure intelligence for the alleged American spymaster, Bishop James E. Walsh, and opposition to the general socialist line.[43] Gong was the only one of the defendants who received a life sentence; the other 13 received sentences ranging from five to 20 years. There was no appeal, although in 1979, 19 years after trial and 24 years after his first incarceration, Gong wrote an "appeal" of his sentence, which he followed with annual appeals in detail contesting and refuting the specific charges.

The very next day, March 18, Bishop James E. Walsh, an American Maryknoller who was apparently the last missionary remaining in China, was tried and convicted of espionage. Walsh, an old China hand who had returned to China in 1948 to be in charge of the Catholic Central Bureau, had been kept under house arrest for several years, then was taken into custody in late 1958. Finally he was tried and convicted of espionage (including being the recipient of intelligence information from Bishop Gong and his colleagues) and given a 20-year prison sentence in March 1960.[44] It is not known exactly why Bishop Walsh was kept in detention instead of just being exiled from China. He was released in 1970, early in the thaw in Sino-American relations.

From the Great Leap to the Cultural Revolution, 1958–1966

For both Catholics and Protestants, clergy and lay people alike, those who participated in the TSPM or the CPA as well as those who thought these bodies were too subservient to the party and avoided them – that is, for all Christians, the darkest time was the two decades from the late 1950s to the late 1970s.

Catholics and Protestants had taken different routes to the late 1950s, with the Catholic route being more arduous and traumatic. This was because Catholics had, at least in Shanghai, mounted a well-run and spirited resistance which derailed the new regime's timetable for gaining control of what it saw as an important ad dangerous remnant of imperialism. This of course earned the Catholics more severe punishment. The foreign component of the Catholic presence was also greater than that of the Protestants. At the time that foreign Protestants had virtually all been expelled, there were still several dozen to one hundred foreign Catholics in Shanghai. Many of these were in leadership positions. It was 1955 before these were removed and the foreign priests deported or arrested. Protestants, on the other hand, offered virtually no coordinated actions or reactions regarding the ideas and policies of the TSPM, with the exception of Wang Mingdao and a handful of others, who all seemed to operate autonomously (perhaps a lesson was learned here in the 1990s, when evangelical house church leaders formed some networks of linked congregations).

In my view, the most devastating blow to all Christians in the late 1950s was the anti-rightist movement, which punished arbitrarily hundreds of thousands, shut down dissent or even dialogue with the state, and nearly criminalized religious belief itself, despite the state constitution.[45] Then came the Great Leap Forward in 1958, which occasioned, for the sake of a total focus on labor mobilization and production, the closing of over 90 percent of the churches which were still open, especially in the countryside. Pastors and priests were sent into the fields to farm. The political atmosphere of the Great Leap was also so frenzied that it generated a resurgence of radical, anti-religious policies and attitudes. Believers were harassed and mistreated. Then came the famine, the result of Mao's hare-brained economic policies. Life was difficult for all; life was worse, downright terrible, in the labor camps during the famine; many, including many Christians, did not survive. Most of those who did survive into the 1960s remained in the camps for another 15–20 years, until after 1976 and the end of the Cultural Revolution. Prisons and labor camps were one important place where the Gospel spread in these two decades.

Although scholars do not know the exact timetable, I believe that some small, private groups of believers, later called "house churches," began to meet soon after the arrest of Pastor Wang Mingdao and Bishop Gong Pinmei in 1955. Both were well known, and their arrest showed the determination of the government to dominate totally the religious scene. At the height of the Great Leap Forward in 1958–1959, the majority of churches still open were shut; in addition, all the Protestant denominations were unified and a generic template for worship was created for the remaining ones. Worship in the remaining churches was self -conscious and strained, and sermons were anemic in theology. These were all reasons for more groups to go private. At any rate it appears that by the 1960s a steady stream of believers was leaving the TSPM and meeting privately. Public venues were not very appealing when some local governments publicly announced that their city or county intended completely to eradicate religion.

It was in this fashion that occurred the first stages of growth of what most call "house churches," but which I usually call "unregistered churches."[46] It was fairly easy to set these up, because Protestant ordained clergy were not necessary; church elders and other lay persons preached, taught children, carried out evangelism, performed marriages and funerals. Not so for Catholics; an ordained priest needed to be present for a proper mass, and the priest played a crucial role in confession and other sacraments. Nevertheless Catholics also had unregistered churches. Most of the country's diocesan priests remained loyal to the Holy See, and a whole system of arrangements was developed where these priests would meet in some inconspicuous site, often a private home, and perform the mass and other sacraments.[47] As for the masses held in the CPA church buildings, most congregations were quite aware of the political stance of the officiating priest, and when a CPA priest was in charge the church members stayed away in droves. On days with multiple masses and more than one priest officiating, masses said by the CPA priest would have a tiny fraction of the attendance at those said by a Vatican loyalist.

The early 1960s were a time of what appeared to be rather bleak prospects for Christianity in China. The Protestant Second National Conference, held in early1961 (the first had been in 1954), was so innocuous that it barely registered on the news bulletins. The more than three hundred delegates elected 145 to the Three-Self Committee, 49 of those to the standing committee. There was basic continuity in the personnel of the TSPM leaders; Y. T. Wu remained chairman. And although Marcus Ch'eng (Chen Chonggui) was, as we have seen, purged in the anti-rightist movement in 1957, his fundamentalist colleague Jia Yuming was still one of seven vice-chairmen. Bishop K. H. Ting (Ding Guangxun), Principal of Nanjing Jinling Union Theological Seminary, who had been one of Wang Mingdao's chief protagonists and was clearly a protégé of Y. T. Wu, also was made a vice-chair. But it did not seem to matter; the Chinese church appeared to be dying. The number of open churches was shrinking, all the pastors were aging, and

almost no seminary students were being trained in the two union seminaries in
Nanjing and Beijing, respectively. At this point, it seemed that those outside
observers who had believed that Christianity did not fit well in China, and at
any rate could never survive without foreign patronage (including some former
missionaries who felt this way), were right. In the early 1960s there was no sign
that the Chinese church could even survive, let alone renew itself. During the
1960s, as China, with its heightening feud with the USSR and a growing US
presence on its doorstep in Vietnam, became more isolated and shrill, it was
more difficult for outsiders to learn of the situation of Christian acquaintances
in China. When communication did occur the Chinese party often would not
even mention matters of religion and faith, even to old friends. So as of 1965 or
1966, the only conclusion could be that the long-term prospects for Protestants
in China were poor at best.

Catholics again had a different experience from Protestants. They had their
second national CPA conference in 1962, with 256 delegates (the first had
been in 1957, with 241 delegates). The CPA, prodded by the RAB, had by this
time nominated and consecrated several new bishops, all of them "illicit" in
the eyes of Rome, of course. And with no serious contact the two sides settled
even more rigidly into their confrontational stance. Ironically, the early 1960s
were also the period of the Second Vatican Council under the leadership of
John XXIII. Almost every other national church around the world was swept
by the winds of change that came out of Rome in those few years; but not
China. With many priests and bishops still in prison, the survival of the church
mainly depended on the community solidarity which had long characterized
rural Catholicism.[48] Chinese traditional Catholics had always been very
hierarchical and centralized, and remained that way, with the utmost reverence for the Pope. Knowing little or nothing of Vatican II, the Chinese
church for the most part continued rooted in its rural foundations, and had
little to do with the CPA (whose members and even its leaders were also
usually equally ignorant of recent reforms in the world-wide church).

Some Thoughts

As of 1965, China had seen over a decade and a half of exhausting mass
campaigns, huge social as well as economic changes, such as the elimination/
liquidation of the landlord class, the desperately foolhardy attempt to develop
the country overnight in the Great Leap Forward, and the tragic man-made
famine it caused. The events of these years sometimes seem larger than life.
China's Christians went through the same historical experiences that non-
Christians did in these years; that had not happened since 1842 and the
treaties with the West after the Opium War. The essential question about both
Chinese Protestants and Catholics as of 1965 was if they were capable of

embedding their Christianity into their Chinese identity, making it possible to hope for new generations of believers – for Christianity not just to survive a few more decades, until all the old believers died out, but in adapting to Chinese culture transform itself into a "Chinese religion." Neither had done so by 1965 (though some of the independent Protestant movements of the pre-Communist period such as the True Jesus Church, had taken a few steps in that direction).

As a whole, government and party hopes for managing its "Christian problem" between 1949 and 1966 were partly but not totally fulfilled. The foreign role had almost entirely been eliminated and the foreign missionary period in modern Chinese history was over. But China's churches, both Protestant and Catholic, preached a Gospel that still sounded faintly foreign to many non-Christian Chinese. Yet as China plunged ahead into the mindless destruction and social chaos of the Cultural Revolution in 1966, Chinese Christians drank deeply from the same bitter draught of which all Chinese must partake, removing some of the barriers between Christians and non-Christians. As we will see, the Cultural Revolution decade had a profound impact on the place of the church in Chinese society, especially for Protestants.

Notes

1. *Documents of the Three-Self Movement*, Wallace C. Merwin and Francis P. Jones, comps. (New York: National Council of the Churches of Christ in the USA, 1963), p. 18.
2. *Documents of the Three-Self Movement*, Wallace C. Merwin and Francis P. Jones, comps. (New York: National Council of the Churches of Christ in the USA, 1963), pp. 19–20.
3. M.M. Elmer Wurth, ed., *Papal Documents related to the New China* (Maryknoll, NY: Orbis Books, 1985), p. 23.
4. More extended discussion in Daniel H. Bays, "A Tradition of State Dominance," in Carol Hamrin and Jason Kindopp, eds, *God and Caesar in China: Policy Implications of Church-State Tensions* (Washington, DC: Brookings Institution, 2004), pp. 25–39.
5. The essays in Jeremy Brown and Paul G. Pickowicz, eds, *Dilemmas of Victory: The Early Years of the People's Republic of China* (Cambridge, MA: Harvard University Press, 2007).
6. Philip L. Wickeri, "The Chinese Christian Movement on the Eve of Liberation," unpublished, (History of Christianity in China Project, University of Kansas, June 17–23, 1990).
7. Or it is possible that Wu was already a party member. There is as yet no scholarly biography of Wu. A short study is Gao Wangzhi, "Y. T. Wu: A Christian Leader Under Communism," in Daniel H. Bays, ed., *Christianity in China: From the*

Eighteenth Century to the Present (Stanford, CA: Stanford University Press, 1996), pp. 338–352. There is also considerable material on Wu in Philip Wickeri's two major books, *Seeking the Common Ground*, and *Reconstructing Christianity in China*.

8. "The Present-Day Tragedy of Christianity," *Documents of the Three-Self Movement*, Wallace C. Merwin and Francis P. Jones, comps.(New York: National Council of the Churches of Christ in the USA, 1963), pp. 1–5.

9. It also temporarily cost him his job as editor of *Tianfeng*, which he regained the following year.

10. *Documents of the Three-Self Movement*, Wallace C. Merwin and Francis P. Jones, comps.(New York: National Council of the Churches of Christ in the USA, 1963), pp. 14–18.

11. The CPPCC is an organ of the "united front," representing non-party elements of society. This body proclaimed the new PRC on Oct. 1, 1949. Its role was largely assumed by the first National People's Congress in 1954.

12. Philip L. Wickeri, *Seeking the Common Ground: Protestant Christianity, the Three-Self Movement, and China's United Front* (Maryknoll, NY: Orbis Books, 1988) p. 139.

13. The full text is in *Documents of the Three-Self Movement*, Wallace C. Merwin and Francis P. Jones, comps. (New York: National Council of the Churches of Christ in the USA, 1963), pp. 19–20.

14. It is generally believed that as of 1949 there were 700,000 to 800,000 Protestants in China.

15. The other two were Zhao Zichen (Chao Tzu-ch'en) and Cui Xianxiang (Ts'ui Hsien-hsiang).

16. Philip L. Wickeri, *Seeking the Common Ground: Protestant Christianity, the Three-Self Movement, and China's United Front* (Maryknoll, NY: Orbis Books, 1988), pp.134–140, tries to put the denunciations in perspective.

17. *Documents of the Three-Self Movement*, Merwin, Wallace C., and Francis P. Jones, comps. (New York: National Council of the Churches of Christ in the USA, 1963), pp. 22–23.

18. An excellent case study of the fate of Yanjing University is Philip West, *Yenching University and Sino-Western Relations, 1916–1952* (Cambridge, MA: Harvard University Press, 1976), Ch. 7.

19. Later Jia Yuming, another well-known evangelical, also was made a vice-chairman of the committee.

20. *Documents of the Three-Self Movement*, Wallace C. Merwin and Frances P. Jones, comps. (New York: National Council of the Churches of Christ in the USA, 1963), pp. 60–65.

21. This was Wang's famous essay, "We, Because of Faith." Wang was arrested in August 1955, two months after its publication. The full text is in *Documents of the Three-Self Movement*, Wallace C. Merwin, and Francis P. Jones, comps. (New York: National Council of the Churches of Christ in the USA, 1963), pp. 99–114.

22. For excoriation, Thomas Alan Harvey, *Acquainted with Grief: Wang Mingdao's Stand for the Persecuted Church in China* (Grand Rapids, MI: Brazos Press,

2003); for sympathy, Philip L. Wickeri, *Reconstructing Christianity in China: K. H. Ting and the Chinese Church* (Maryknoll, NY: Orbis Books, 2007).

23. In 1950 Chen published a new collection of daily devotional essays, *Moxiang zhu Yesu* (Meditations on the Lord Jesus). Reprinted by the China Christian Council, Shanghai, 1993.

24. For a fine study of Chen's thought, especially regarding communism, see Ying Fuk-tsang, *Zhongguo jiyaozhuyizhe de shita yu kunjing—Chen Chonggui de shenxue sixiang yu shidai* (The praxis and predicament of a Chinese fundamentalist: Chen Chonggui (Marcus Cheng)'s theological thought and his times) (Hong Kong: Alliance Seminary, 2001), pp. 192–231.

25. For example, a January 1952 piece in *Tianfeng* entitled "My political thinking has changed," Wallace P. Merwin and Francis P. Jones, comps. *Documents of the Three-Self Movement* (New York: National Council of the Churches of Christ in the USA, 1963), pp. 55–59. For an analytical discussion of the TSPM in the early 1950s see Philip L. Wickeri, *Seeking the Common Ground: Protestant Christianity, the Three-Self Movement, and China's United Front* (Maryknoll, NY: Orbis Books, 1988), esp. Ch. 5.

26. O. Theodore. Roberg, "Marcus Cheng (c. 1883–1963): Apostle or Apostate? Relations with the Covenant Mission in China" (M.A. thesis, North Park Theological Seminary, Chicago, 1982), pp. 109ff.

27. Roderick MacFarquhar, *The Origins of the Cultural Revolution, I: Contradictions among the People, 1956–1957* (New York: Columbia University Press, 1974).

28. A translation is in *Documents of the Three-Self Movement*, Wallace C. Merwin and Francis P. Jones, comps.(New York: National Council of the Churches of Christ in the USA, 1963), pp. 151–156, also in Donald E. MacInnis, *Religious Policy and Practice in Communist China, A Documentary History* (New York: Macmillan, 1972), pp. 201–207.

29. Ironically Wu himself had indirectly but unmistakably criticized implementation of the government's religious policy at the same 1957 CPPCC meeting at which Chen had spoken. In fact Wu spoke first, which perhaps emboldened Chen in his own remarks. If true, this may mean that Wu scapegoated Chen to draw attention away from himself.

30. No. 12 (July 1990), pp. 53–56. This journal is published by the premier national Protestant seminary, in Nanjing.

31. Calculations: 3 million Catholics, 500 million total population.

32. Sodalities, or "confraternities,' were communal organizations for useful purposes, from piety to charity.

33. Many missionaries were only temporarily in Shanghai because of disruption and fighting in various places around the country in the civil war.

34. The only work by a Western scholar other than Mariani directly relevant is Jean Lefeuvre, *Shanghai: les enfants dans la ville: Vie chretienne a Shanghai et perspectives sur l'Eglise de Chine, 1949–1961* (Tournai, Belgium: Casterman, 1962). Lefeuvre is a French Jesuit.

35. Paul Mariani, "Communist Power and Catholic Resistance: Shanghai, 1949–1960" (Ph.D. dissertation, University of Chicago, 2008), p. 123.

36. For a classic account of late 1940s land reform in a north China village with a substantial Catholic population, William Hinton, *Fanshen: A Documentary of Revolution in a Chinese Village* (New York: Alfred A. Knopf, 1966).

37. For a time the Catholic organization also used the Three Self name, but soon adopted the CPA.

38. Some, for example, Jean-Pierre Charbonnier, *Christians in China A.D. 600 to 2000*, trans. M.N.L. Couvé de Murville, original French edition, Paris, 2002 (San Francisco, CA: Ignatius Press, 2007), pp. 433–434, think that the encyclical was in direct response to the Internuncio Riberi's expulsion the previous summer.

39. A very brief summary of these events is in John Tong, "The Church from 1949 to 1990," in Edmond Tang and Jean-Paul Wiest, eds, *The Catholic Church in Modern China: Perspectives* (Maryknoll, NY: Orbis, 1993), pp. 7–27.

40. Paul Mariani, "Communist Power and Catholic Resistance, Shanghai, 1949–1960" (Ph.D. dissertation, University of Chicago, 2008), p. 238.

41. Fourteen were arrested but one died before trial.

42. Gong was also the bishop of Suzhou.

43. For detail of both indictments and verdicts, Beatrice Leung, *Sino-Vatican Relations: Problems in Conflicting Authority, 1976–1986* (Cambridge: Cambridge University Press, 1992), pp.162–168.

44. Jean-Paul Wiest, *Maryknoll in China: A History, 1918–1955* (Armonk, NY: M. E. Sharpe, 1988).

45. The constitution of the PRC provides freedom of religious belief, but only "normal religious activities" are permitted.

46. I prefer "unregistered" because in later times, after the 1980s, these groups included some with several hundred or more members. The Chinese term, *jiating jiaohui*, may also be translated "family church."

47. One is reminded of the Catholic priests sneaking into China to provide sacraments to the faithful in the decades after the proscription of Christianity in 1724.

48. Richard Madsen, *China's Catholics: Tragedy and Hope in an Emerging Civil Society* (Berkeley, CA: University of California Press, 1998).

The Chinese Church from the End of the Cultural Revolution to the Early Twenty-first Century

Prologue

Easter Sunday, 1985. I had arrived in Shanghai just the evening before, my second trip to Shanghai but the first one traveling alone. Very early I made my way to the "International church" (Guoji libaitang), often still called the "Community church," located in the old French Concession area. Before 1949 it had been the church of the foreign community, mainly British and Americans and Westernized Chinese. I was warmly welcomed and shown to a seat in the balcony with a handful of other foreigners. The prelude was a lovely Bach violin piece. Then we rose to sing the first hymn. I could read the characters in the hymnbook but not the musical notation, so I did not recognize the melody until the music told me it was the translation of the old Anglo-American Evangelical hymn, "He Arose" (the chorus of which is "Up from the grave He arose, with a mighty triumph o'er his foes"). It was familiar enough from my childhood that I could have sung at least the first two verses in English from memory. But here I was joining in the Chinese version, as part of a world-wide Christian celebration. It was very moving. The sermon was uninhibited in discussing the literal resurrection (*fuhuo*) of Christ as well as his coming again in the future. That directness was repeated in the Protestant church in Tianjin the following Sunday when they still had the large Easter poster over the pulpit saying" The Lord is

A New History of Christianity in China, First Edition. Daniel H. Bays.
© 2012 Daniel H. Bays. Published 2012 by Blackwell Publishing Ltd.

risen!" (*Zhu fuhuole!*) The Easter service in Shanghai continued with an anthem by the choir in red and white robes, then there was the Lord's supper, or communion. It was clearly indicated that I was free to join, and so I did. Another special memory.

November 1986, about a year and a half later. Accompanied by Thomas S. Y. Li (Li Shih-yu) of Tianjin, the two of us were standing in the building in Mazhuang village in Tai'an county which had been the chapel, or house of worship, of the Jesus Family (Yesu jiating), the egalitarian Christian community established here in the 1920s. Thomas Li and I had suddenly appeared at the county office of the RAB (Religious Affairs Bureau) in Tai'an city to request permission for a visit to Mazhuang (to have asked in advance would surely have been denied). We were in luck; the RAB head was intrigued, ordered a government car, and personally escorted us to Mazhuang. The RAB chief was clearly pleased with this community (he referred to them several times as "our Christians"); he noted that they were law-abiding and caused him no headaches. When we gathered in the home of the village head to eat the lunch that the RAB chief had called ahead and told them to prepare, all except the RAB head and driver joined in a prayer sung with words from one of the Psalms (several Psalms were written out and pasted on the walls). After lunch, we learned that several older members of today's community still follow customs deriving from the original Jesus Family, such as arising long before dawn to pray and commune with God. They actually consider themselves to be the Jesus Family. A group photo on a wall of the village head's house was captioned "1983 annual meeting of the Jesus Family of Tai'an county."

These two vignettes are suggestive of the variety of Christianities in China in the recent past and down to the present. On the way back to Tai'an in 1986 after the Jesus Family visit we saw on the horizon a large church steeple. The RAB chief said, "Oh, that's a Catholic village; all the people there are Catholics; law-abiding, cooperative; good people." As I look back on these 25-year-old experiences today, I realize that these experiences were mileposts, markers in my own understanding of the evolution of Christianity from a foreign creed to an indigenized and acculturated reality in China today. Moreover, it appears in retrospect that the Cultural Revolution as a national event, seen at the time as an unmitigated disaster for the church, was actually of great assistance to the growth of Christianity in many places in China. I will trace the events of this decade, then return to their impact on Christianity.

Into the Maelstrom, 1966

Mao Zedong's "Great Proletarian Cultural Revolution" that he launched in 1966 was not aimed primarily at Christians or Christianity. It was aimed at removing from power several top leaders of the communist party, his close colleagues for decades. Since these leaders (including Liu Shaoqi and Deng Xiaoping) controlled the Party apparatus, Mao had to seek elsewhere for allies; he found them in the People's Liberation Army (PLA) and the youth of the nation, mainly of college and high school age. The former did his bidding through its commander, Lin Biao, the latter did so out of zeal and eagerness to answer Mao's call. To train the youth and accustom them to challenge, attack, and destroy such lofty targets, Mao first gave them some easy targets to attack. These were called "the four olds," that is, the "ideas, culture, customs, and habits of the exploiting classes." They were urged on by Mao, who personally "blessed" these young people (who were now called Red Guards) in huge rallies in Tian'anmen Square. In their enthusiasm to follow Chairman Mao's commands, the Red Guards ran amok in cities all across the land, hounding people who were vulnerable (for example, those who had ever had any contact at all with foreigners), ransacking their homes, often beating them, sometimes to death. Or they made public spectacles of their victims, torturing and humiliating them, causing yet more thousands of suicides. This early phase of the Cultural Revolution was the one that most affected Chinese Christians. In countless places, Christians were put through such abuse that many did not survive the ordeal.[1]

As Mao and his fellow perpetrators of the Cultural Revolution envisioned it, all truth would spring from "the people" (spoken for by Mao), through "class struggle" (that is, violence). Any ideology other than Mao's interpretation of Marxism-Leninism was heresy. At this point, still early in the Cultural Revolution (fall 1966 to late 1967), all religions were abolished, and all houses of worship were closed. This was the only time in the past sixty years that a nationwide eradication policy for Christianity was attempted (some local governments did so in the late 1950s). By the logic of the situation, with religion outlawed, there was no conceivable use for the TSPM (Three Self Patriotic Movement) or the CPA (Catholic Patriotic Association), or for that matter, the RAB. All three were summarily abolished (as were the national organizations for Buddhism, Daoism, and Islam). The only concession the regime granted would come in the early 1970s, when more foreigners were living in China and the Christians among them needed a place to worship. The government set aside a series of venues, from the former American Bible Society building near Wangfujing to the Gangwashi church in Xicheng, west of the Forbidden City, for the foreigners to use on Sundays only.

From 1967 on, the entire next 10 or 11 years of Christian history in China are still a black hole, the details of which are very scarce. There are almost no documentary sources to consult, no statistics, very few photographs (and those of uncertain provenance). We are left with the anecdotal stories of things that happened to people individually or that they personally witnessed during these years. With the life and death struggle for power going on at the top, few were paying attention to the results of the Cultural Revolution at the bottom of society. The party, government, and other authority structures at the local level all over the country were paralyzed or dismantled by the chaos of the Cultural Revolution. Anarchy ensued in some areas, with groups of Red Guards, radical workers, and others engaged in deadly armed warfare. In other areas, coalitions of army, party, and government representatives maintained a fragile stability. The PLA maintained an uneasy sway over the country as a whole, pending the resurrection of the party and government.

The overall result seems similar to what happened in the Dominican mission of northeast Fujian Province in the Ming-Qing transition of the mid seventeenth century (Chapter 2). The turmoil of the Cultural Revolution in similar fashion gave Christianity an opening, an opportunity to grow. Not only the TSPM and RAB were gone, but in many places so were the public security forces and the police. All churches during these years were by definition house churches, and some proved very adept at adjusting to the new situation. Talented and charismatic leaders emerged among the believers, and proved to be effective evangelists, recruiting many new converts. Despite the almost total lack of empirical evidence, my guess is that Protestants increased their numbers by a factor of five or six during the 12 years from 1966 to 1978, when churches reopened.

Obviously this level of analysis is very crude. Conditions varied around the country, and different factors were undoubtedly in play. The message preached by the evangelists was largely (as far as we can tell) the old pre-1949 salvationist and revivalist message typical of most theologically conservative missionaries such as those of the CIM and of Chinese leaders like John Sung, Watchman Nee, and Wang Mingdao. It was millenarian, looking to the imminent return of Christ, and it was to an extensive degree Pentecostal, that is, highlighting "gifts of the spirit" such as speaking in tongues, prophecies, and miraculous healings. Some of the old sectarian enthusiasm of the True Jesus Church and of Watchman Nee's teachings have provided renewed impetus to grow. In fact many home churches at this time were in effect shaped by True Jesus input or by followers of Nee (who died in a prison camp in 1972). I am not sure we can go much further than these observations about the kind of Protestant developments that took place during the Cultural Revolution, or if the later crossover between Protestants and Chinese folk religion or popular religion was already occurring. Finally: my estimate is five to six million Protestants, and a very rapid growth rate, in the late 1970s.[2]

Thus Protestants emerged from the Cultural Revolution after 1976 in a dynamic mode, spreading rapidly and naturally. Catholics were not so vigorous. As part of a world- wide organization (despite the CPA's claims of independence from Rome), Catholics were not as adaptable and creative as Protestants could be. Catholic numbers had been increasing but only about as

Figure 8.1   Worshippers celebrating Christmas eve. Credit: Lou linwei/Alamy.

fast as general population growth. Catholic families were reproducing themselves in steady but unspectacular growth. There must have been at least five or six million Catholics in the late 1970s, most of them living in rural areas, as they had tended to do for well over a century.[3] The details of their story are even less known than that of the Protestants. But we know that Vatican-loyalist priests continued to administer mass and the sacraments, and rural community solidarity, which responded to outside pressures with a renewal of consolidation and unity, prevailed in most Catholic enclaves. It was probably in the late 1970s that Protestants came to outnumber Catholics for the first time.

Reform and Opening

Christianity re-entered the public arena beginning in 1979 and 1980 riding on the coattails of Deng Xiaoping's package of economic reforms. Under Deng's leadership the country's entire focus was economic growth. To facilitate this aim of growth at all costs, people were given more freedoms from government interference in many aspects of their lives. In addition to de-collectivization of agriculture and a market economy, including private ownership of housing and private vehicles, the state largely removed itself from close monitoring of cultural and social practices, including religion. Therefore religious belief and

Figure 8.2   Shanxi Christians. Credit: Aurora Photos/Alamy.

activities were largely de-criminalized, and believers were urged to work for the modernization of China. From this point on, the CCP has expressed very little interest in what religious people actually believe, only that they not challenge the hegemony of the state. The state and party view believers as an administrative problem, essentially. Among religious issues Christianity was not even the main one. That would be Islam, already of concern to the regime by the early 1980s for its strategic implications for China's heavily Moslem far West. Therefore it was not difficult for this reformist party-state to view with equanimity the renewal of Christian life and activities in the public sphere. Why not let religious believers meet peaceably? How much trouble could a few Christians and other non-Islamic believers be? This also may explain the readiness of the government to re-establish almost intact the old control system of the 1950s, with the TSPM, the CPA, and the RAB all being rebuilt to play their old roles under the direction of the Party's United Front Work Department (UFWD). The decision-makers at the top apparently did not know, or perhaps did not care, that these administrative bodies were viewed as tools of repression by many Chinese Christians, and that the people appointed to staff them were the same ones that had been there in the 1950s, many of whom were reviled by most Christians as traitors to the faith. Among Protestants, for example, Y. T. Wu, head of the TSPM until its earlier demise, was very ill (he died in 1979), and his protégé Bishop K. H. Ting (Ding Guangxun), a vice-chair of the old TSPM and Principal (since 1953) of the

Nanjing Union Theological seminary, was appointed chair of the national Three-Self Committee.[4]

It is interesting to speculate whether the regime had an inkling in advance that it would be fairly unpopular among Christians to re-impose the TSPM/CPA upon them. For both Protestants and Catholics, a supplementary interfacing organization was created for more communication with local church congregations on various matters: issues of ritual, church doctrine, training and stop-gap theological education to address the lamentable shortage of pastors or even minimally trained lay church leadership, especially among Protestants. Such issues of congregational life were to be turned over to the new organization, the China Christian Council (CCC), formed in 1980. One senses a real desire for pastoral and congregational nurturing and spiritual development in the CCC, and perhaps a desire to separate from the direct political role of the TSPM. But who was appointed head of the national CCC? None other than K. H. Ting. So Ting held three crucial posts – four, actually – for over 20 years: chair and CEO of both TSPM and CCC, principal of Nanjing Seminary, and as a long-serving delegate and vice-chair of the National Chinese People's Political Consultative Conference. And despite some differing roles at times, Chinese Christians view them as a single entity – the *liang hui* (twin committees).[5] In a similar way, the Catholic Bishops' Conference was established in 1980, to take on part of the task of direct liaison with the parish congregations. Like the Protestant case of the CCC, the Catholic Bishops' Conference has not succeeded in differentiating itself from its more politicized "twin."[6] At any rate, the state found itself unable to use these two pairs of bodies as it had hoped. This leads to the question of why it bothered to set them up, and why the mistake was compounded by appointing such widely despised individuals as leading cadres in the system. Many of these cadres had earned the enmity of believers in the 1950s by their politicized, "leftist' behavior, yet now here they were back in power again. One can only conclude that the leadership did not rank the management of Christianity among its most important tasks or challenges, at least not in 1980. Indeed, there was a long agenda of other issues. Deng Xiaoping was eager to get on with his reform program, which was already outraging some of the conservative party elders. And he was off to have a smashing visit to the US in 1979, showing China's new desire for trade, communications, and training for Chinese students. There were tasks to take on in the United Nations, where China wished to project the image of a responsible member of the international community; and repairs to be made to that image in the aftermath of China's disastrous 1979 invasion of Vietnam. And then there was the looming confrontation with the UK over the fate of Hong Kong. With all this on his plate, he also confronted daunting domestic tasks, including the decollectivization of agriculture, the jarring transition to a market economy, and the massive revamping of the system of higher education, which was in a sorry state. It is not surprising that the management of religious affairs was not a time-consuming matter for top officials – especially when, after all, Marxists knew that religion was the "opiate of the people" and was doomed to historical obsolescence and extinction.

The 1980s: Protestant Growth, Catholic Recalcitrance

Protestant churches began to reopen during the Christmas season, 1978, and Catholic churches soon thereafter. The pace of reopening of old church buildings, plus the enthusiastic construction of new houses of worship, especially by Protestants, seems not to have been anticipated by the authorities. Eventually, after more than 20 years of church recovery and adding new churches, by the early twenty-first century there were over 20,000 churches registered with the TSPM. When party leaders and high-level organs such as the State Council and the Central Committee realized the dynamism of the Christian scene, one of their responses was a long directive issued by the Central Committee of the CCP on March 31, 1982, "The Basic Viewpoint and Policy on the Religious Question during our Country's Socialist Period."[7] This directive, known as Document 19, was the most detailed description and explanation of government religious policy that had ever been issued; moreover it remains the most authoritative exposition of that policy down to the present. It has not been superseded by any of the documents put out by the government since 1982. Document 19 constituted a fairly realistic statement on the current situation of religion, with guidelines for policy makers appropriate for China's being in a reform period. Although Document 19 maintained a version of the Marxist-Leninist interpretation of religion, it was a non-militant version, with no mention of "opium." It rejects the coerced suppression of religion, and clearly states that religion will continue to exist under socialism for a very long time.[8] It provided a much more secure defense for Christianity than anything previous.

Nevertheless, there were still certain problems with Document 19. It makes a vague distinction between "normal" religious activities and those that are deemed not normal and therefore are subject to suppression. This problem was (and still is today) acute with regard to how one considers the status of the "house churches," that is, the hundreds of thousands of believers' homes where religious activities go on. Document 19 disallows these activities in homes but also sanctions them, urging that they not be harassed by the authorities. Interestingly, although most government and party officials worried that home worship meetings would get out of control, Bishop K. H. Ting consistently has supported the home worship meetings. The situation of these venues has become more complicated recently because many unregistered gatherings are not in anyone's home, but in larger, in effect public, places. Document 19 also pointed the way for the revision of the "religious freedom" clause in the national state constitution several months later in 1982, which gave Christians, in effect, more protections, although the constitution kept the reference to "normal religious activities," with its ominous implications of abnormal and therefore illegal activities.

Having by about 1983 gained a situation of some stability of existence through the framework of Document 19 and the revised state constitution, for the rest of the decade both Protestants and Catholics set about the tasks of "running the church well," including trying to make provision for the spiritual growth of the many new converts. Seminaries and Bible schools were re-established and some new ones created, to address the urgent need for training in a fast-growing movement with strong tendencies to idiosyncratic sectarianism and heterodox ideas and rituals. This was more of an urgent task for Protestants than for Catholics, because of the higher growth rate of the former, especially in rural areas where educated and trained leadership was most scarce. As early as the mid 1980s, in cities like Beijing, Shanghai, Jinan, and Hangzhou, the seminary or Bible school ran short-term classes typically of three or four months' duration, to provide very basic knowledge of the Bible and doctrines of the church to pastors and lay leaders alike. The need for such grounding in the essentials of the faith stemmed from the fact, evident by the mid 1980s, that the doctrines and the rituals of Chinese popular religion, especially those of a sectarian millenarian bent, held a great attraction for new Christians. This should not have been surprising, for there were several examples of this phenomenon earlier in Chinese history, for example in the Dominican mission in Northeast Fujian in the late Ming and early Qing, in the interplay between the White Lotus sect and Christians, and in the Taiping Rebellion of the mid nineteenth century.[9] In the 1980s and since, down to the present, foreign sectarian Christian elements have entered China to proselytize. For example, the followers of Watchman Nee and later of Witness Li, who had developed Nee's ideas in Taiwan and then in North America, in the mid 1980s sent many books, tapes, and people to spread a movement which was declared utterly heterodox by both the TSPM and the state authorities. They were called the "Shouters" (Huhan pai), and in 1983 they were banned, the first group to have the distinction of going on an official list of "evil cults" (*xiejiao*), a list created by the government with the approval of the TSPM.

The explosive spread of Protestantism revealed not only the paucity of human resources to manage the growth, but the demographics of the church as well. There had been almost no pastors or Bible teachers trained for about three decades, so the burden of the pastoral work fell extremely heavily on the old generation trained pre-1949, and many of these were not in the best of health, due to long years of prison or labor camp. Nevertheless, these old clergy, of whom I met several in the 1980s, were delighted to be needed by the churches, whether TSPM-registered or not. More than one stated flatly that he would never retire, and planned to die in the pulpit.

While Protestants had problems of growth in the 1980s, as well as those stemming from the registered/unregistered divide, in my opinion Catholics had yet more serious problems. It was true that the atmosphere of total resistance and hostility to the new government which had been fostered among Chinese Catholics by the Holy See in the 1950s was somewhat abated, though it resurfaced regularly. Although the CPA had not been a stirring success it had established an institutional identity as a national Catholic church, claiming to be part of the church universal but not taking directions from Rome, for example consecrating its own bishops whether the Vatican approved or not. In the post-Cultural Revolution years there occurred several cases of joint agreement on candidates for bishops, and dialogue between the CCP and Rome was intermittent. Setbacks were regular, because of the basic mistrust each still had for the other. China will not consider giving up the "right" to control consecration of bishops and so far the Vatican refuses China's claim. This standoff, more than a half-century old, brings to mind the strenuous objections which the Kangxi emperor made in the early 1700s to Rome for its interference with the integrity of his rule by its directives on ancestral ritual matters.[10]

Internal divisions among Catholics remained large in the 1980s; a substantial number of Catholics, probably a majority, remained in the orbit of the "underground church" or "Vatican loyalists," and boycotted masses said by CPA priests. Their ranks were bolstered by the release from jail of many bishops and priests from the 1950s. Some of these became pro-Vatican activists. They promoted loyalist theological training in makeshift underground seminaries, and developed networks across the country. Bishop Joseph Fan Xueyan of Baoding diocese in Hebei Province upon his release from prison in 1979 devoted himself to building up the loyalist church. Early in the 1980s, without permission from Rome, Bishop Fan began to consecrate new bishops and ordain new priests. Questioned about this radical step of consecrating loyalist bishops with unknown (to the Vatican) credentials, Bishop Fan made a vigorous written defense of his actions, claiming that the exigencies of the situation in China justified such radical action. This document made its way to Rome, where the pope (John Paul) read it and approved it. Thus Bishop Joseph Fan and his colleagues, "loyal" to the Holy Father in Rome, consecrated dozens of bishops and ordained hundreds of priests during the approximately two decades this policy was in effect.[11] It resulted in the creation of a rival bishops' conference which held its meetings underground. And these locally ordained priests, known as "little black priests," many of whom received only the sketchiest of educations and have a very simple and uncomplicated view of the world, have been a constant source of pressure for a stance of total intransigence on even having contact or discussions with the CPA. This "loyalist" element has actually been a hindrance to Vatican negotiators who have had periodic low-key talks with Chinese diplomats in recent years. Moreover, this privatized practice of creating bishops and priests also created networks of relationships between bishops, and many sets of patron–client relationships, which has contributed greatly to the practice of factionalism in the church. It is little wonder that Benedict, in his remarkable pastoral letter of 2007 to the Chinese people on reconciliation in the church, also rescinded the right of local clergy in China any longer to make these important personnel decisions on their own.[12] Unfortunately, after almost twenty years of such actions, the recalcitrance of this ultra-loyalist sector of the Chinese Catholic church may be a problem in finding some compromise formula for a modus vivendi between the CPA and the "underground" Catholics, and more broadly between China and the Vatican.

A Rural Decade: Christianity as Folk Religion

The revival and expansion of Christianity in the 1980s was substantially a rural phenomenon for both Catholics and Protestants. That is, the rural growth rate was in percentage terms higher than the urban growth rate. Part of this pattern may have been due to the greater momentum of rural Christianity coming off the decade of the Cultural Revolution. For Catholics, the rural character of most dioceses simply continued the model of the past. For Protestants, it was in the 1980s that some of the inherent similarities between Protestant radical millenarianism and the eschatological features of traditional Chinese popular religion became visible and interactive. It is important to understand the rural context and dynamics of this phenomenon:

1. The missionaries were long since gone; there remained very few informed voices capable of raising an alarm to the appearance of heterodox Christian doctrines.
2. Rural church congregations had been more thoroughly devastated than urban ones in the 1950s: the land reform campaign of the early 1950s destroyed at least hundreds of thousands of landlord families, a number of whom were Christians. Moreover, because typically all local churches were locked up during land reform, and most of those were never or not until after 1979 reopened, large swathes of rural territory were left entirely churchless. For the rest of the 1950s and early 1960s, some large counties, each with a population of several hundred thousand people, were left without a single open church.

3. The Great Leap Forward. The GLF of 1958–1960 had its most severe effect on the countryside. The man-made famine that killed over 30 million resulted directly from human causes, including (Mao's) conscious policy to squeeze out of the agricultural sector and the longsuffering peasantry resources to build China's national economy.

As a result, for three decades, 1949–1979, China's rural sector was exploited, inefficient, tied to a pre-modern, indeed in many ways medieval or feudal society, and ready for change. In my view, the biggest and most important of Deng Xiaoping's reforms in the 1980s was the decollectivization of agriculture. Introducing the market into the rural economy was a great boon for farmers, making a real difference in rural incomes and prosperity for many. Rural society and life took a turn for the better. Farmers received higher prices for their crops, especially if they lived near a city. Independent entrepreneurs and light industry came to the countryside, and foreign investors as well. Rural incomes soared. There also came evangelists of the Christian gospel, speaking of concepts already familiar to many rural dwellers – the coming eschaton and the new millennial age or "Kingdom of Heaven"; and a savior figure, like the orthodox Buddhist guanyin, or the less orthodox "unborn mother" (*wusheng laomu*), or the pre-Buddhist Queen Mother of the West. All of these were already present on the Chinese sectarian scene and all proved quite compatible with veneration of another female figure, Mary the mother of Jesus. Peasants were also accustomed to petitioning the divine for healing from sickness and disease; and to praying to multiple entities in the spirit world, with a wide choice whether the variety was of gods in the traditional village pantheon or of the dozens of Catholic saints. Christianity was often considered for its efficaciousness, not its truth; for its *guanxi* *w*ith the supernatural, not as a statement of faith for an individual or a congregation. This is indicative of the competitiveness of Christianity with the other players in the religious arena.

A final factor in Protestant growth in the countryside was that quasi-Pentecostalism became the "style" (*zuofeng*) of a clear majority of rural churches. Classical Pentecostalism, and its Chinese version as well, usually includes the following as basic: belief in miracles; divine intervention in people's lives for physical and spiritual healing; and special direct communications with God and Jesus including speaking in tongues, dreams, and visions. All of these characteristics are substantially the same as Pentecostals in the West, but introducing them to urban churches in most urban settings very likely would have brought problems of the police authorities' suspicion, RAB ire, and older believers' opposition to these practices. So these Pentecostal behaviors became very common in rural areas, then only somewhat later spread in the cities, in the 1990s and since.[13]

The extensive growth of the "underground" Protestant church sector in the 1980s derived mostly from the pre-1949 independent churches. An avalanche of information from groups overseas on Christianity – books, pamphlets and tracts, audio tapes, videos – swept through south, southeastern, and east central China in the 1980s. Much of this was from the overseas followers of Watchman Nee and Witness Li, and also materials and missionaries of the True Jesus Church, whose headquarters have been in Taiwan since the 1950s. The foundations of most of the important sectarian movements, including many on the list of today's designated "evil cults," were laid at this time. The first important sectarian group to emerge was the "Shouters," in 1982–1983. The lack of formal theological training, indeed the devaluing of it, meant that "spiritual gifts" and personal charisma created their own ecclesiastical authority, which was passed along in master–disciple relationships. Several of the more extreme groups, fired by an apocalyptic millenarian enthusiasm, went so far as to depict the TSPM churches, the RAB, and the party as the Antichrist of the book of Revelations, so that persecution at their hands was martyrdom, a good thing. There was a spectrum of unregistered Protestant churches in the 1980s, some of which remained within the boundaries of orthodox evangelical Christianity. Two of the networks of unregistered churches, both based in southern Henan province, grew very large; these were the "Weepers" (Kupai), later part of the China Gospel Fellowship, and the Fangcheng Church. Their leaders, Xu Hongze and Zhang Rongliang, respectively, are orthodox Christians, but because of the government's paranoia concerning large networked groups, both Xu and Zhang have been harassed and jailed from time to time[14] Not nearly as large as the Fangcheng church or the China Gospel Fellowship are a number of more radical sectarian groups which were products of the great impact that the millenarian teachings of the "Shouters" had when they entered China in the 1980s. Several of these groups are still active in China today, and have a total of a few million followers. I will give only a summary description of some of these:[15]

- The Established King sect (Beiliwang). Wu Yangming (1945–1995), after a few years in jail as a Shouters evangelist, claimed that he himself was the "established king" and concocted a mystical shroud for his personal sexual gratifications, which led to his execution in 1995.
- The Lord God sect (Zhushenjiao), an offshoot of the Beiliwang, also deified its leaders, and kept tight organizational control.
- The Narrow Gate in the Wilderness (Kuangye zhaimen). Also called the Disciples sect (Mentuhui), it was founded as a byproduct of the Shouters by Ji Sanbao (1940–1997), a farmer in the poor inland province of Shaanxi. When the Shouters came under fire in 1983, Ji set up his own operation centered on himself, appointed 12 disciples, claimed being directly commissioned by God as savior, repeatedly predicted the imminent end of the

world, and created a remarkably well organized movement. Like almost all sects, it had extremely tight internal organization. It became a target of suppression in the early 1990s, when it had several hundred thousand adherents in several provinces. Despite the death of its founder, in the 2000s it has still had a following of a few hundred thousand.

- The Three Grades of Servants (Sanban Puren). A humble poor farmer, like many other of the sect founders, in his youth Xu Shuangfu (1946–2006) was heavily influenced by evangelists with Jesus Family ties, and in the 1970s Xu himself became a wandering evangelist. In the 1980s he joined an anti-TSPM group influenced by the Shouters, then started setting dates for the end of the world. In the 1990s he developed his own highly secretive organization, the Three Grades of Servants, with himself as the "great servant" and keeping the other "servants" of lower grade on a tight leash, inflicting physical punishment such as lashes on the disobedient. In the apparent urge to control all aspects of the lives of his followers, Xu may have been showing the influence of ideas derived from the old Jesus Family of the pre-communist era. Three Grades of Servants continued to grow into the twenty-first century, with a claim of over one million followers.

- The Lightning out of the East (Dongfang Shandian). This is yet another of the sects with its roots in the Shouters. In the early 1990s Zhao Weishan (1956?–) reorganized several former Shouters into the dynamic and extremely creative network called Lightning out of the East. This became a major presence on the sectarian scene, partly because of the violence it produced. A woman surnamed Deng was one of the early leaders, who then became the "female Christ," who was divine and had already fulfilled the Second Coming. She made startling prophecies, creatively using the mystical lexicon of the "Little Flock" and the Shouters to press the idea of the urgently imminent millenarian end of time. It also appears that there was a considerable gender appeal from a movement with several female leaders. The "female Christ's" pronouncements were considered more authoritative than the Bible, and energized converts for aggressive evangelizing. The startling growth of Lightning from the East was partly at the expense of other sects. It first drew converts from the Shouters and then from Three Grades of Servants, using sophisticated infiltration, deception, kidnapping, blackmail, and even murder. After 2000 Three Grades of Servants retaliated, ferreting out Lightning operatives and defectors and "disciplining" them by means of, for example, strangulation, drowning, stabbing, and burying alive. Three Grades founder Xu was captured and executed in 2006; Lightning leader Zhao fled to political asylum in the US in 2000, where he set up an international headquarters. The alleged death of the female Christ, Deng, in 2005, did not seem to dampen the eschatological exuberance of the movement.[16]

Although all of these sects are anathema to the religious and political authorities, their very existence gives fascinating insights into one of the largest examples in Christian history anywhere of creative cross-cultural adaptation. Important aspects of Chinese traditional popular religion seem to be clearly visible in the cultural agglomeration which characterizes sectarian Chinese rural Christianity. Moreover, no one can be sure that such radical sectarian movements will not be at least as important in future as they have been in the last three decades. As Professor Lian Xi has speculated, "they offer intimations of the future of popular Christianity."[17]

Not all of the sectarian independent churches of the post-Mao period evolved into "evil cults". In fact two of the most important movements from pre-1949, which had been denounced and dismantled in the 1950s and their leaders imprisoned, were the True Jesus Church and Watchman Nee's "Little Flock." These were both partially rehabilitated and removed from the list of illegal organizations in the early 1980s. Their adherents were welcome at TSPM churches, especially in Hunan, Zhejiang, and Fujian Provinces, where the numbers of their followers were so great by the mid 1990s that they have been accorded a measure of autonomy within the orbit of the registered church. The only other church able to gain a measure of recognition of its own identity has been the Seventh day Adventists, whose Saturday worship (like that of the True Jesus Church) sets them apart anyway. These three, however, are within the TSPM structure, and are not considered cults or sects. This situation compromises somewhat the TSPM claim of being a "post-denominational" church, although it is a good tradeoff for the latter, which can also thereby show its flexibility and "reasonableness."

Roman Catholicism as Chinese folk religion

Implicit in the work of several of the scholars who have studied Catholics in China is the fact that beyond issues of doctrine, ecclesiastical questions, the question of the role or the pope, or other issues of church–state relations, lies the reality of the rural communities that still form the bulk of the church in China. The sociologist Richard Madsen proposed about ten years ago that we actually treat Catholicism as a rural folk religion, stating flatly, "Catholicism in China, especially in the rural areas where the vast majority of Chinese Catholics live, is as much folk religion as world religion."[18] Rural folk Catholics seem very similar to the folk Buddhist sects of the late imperial period of dynastic history (late Ming–early Qing). That folk Buddhism, steeped in the supernatural, visions, and miracles, was quiescent in normal times; the sect members were usually integrated into the entire community, doing the same family rituals and observances. However, the sect's millenarian face could emerge in times of crisis.

Figure 8.3   People attending church, Shanghai. Credit: TAO Images Limited/Alamy.

Figure 8.4   Pages of printed Bibles at bindery, Amity Press, Nanjing. Credit: M. Scott Brauer/Alamy.

One result might well be starting or joining an open rebellion against the state, albeit a rebellion couched in the apocalyptic religious language of the sect. Therefore the state could never fail to monitor the sects; from the state's point of view, it was absolutely imperative to keep them under supervision and control. The driving force of centuries of visceral suspicion and fear of sectarian movements was made clearly manifest when the Chinese government launched its large and fierce campaign of suppression against the Falun gong in 1999.[19]

Like the White Lotus sect and other late imperial sects, Catholics have largely been incorporated into the "fabric of village and family culture" in the countryside.[20] They celebrate the same traditional festivals as their neighbors, interweaving their Catholic feast days with the rhythm of traditional observances. Observers seem to agree that the only significant difference from their fellow villagers is in ritual behavior, especially funeral ritual. Of course, in some areas where many villages are entirely Catholic, or nearly so, the Catholic community can by consensus among themselves work out the mixture of catholic and traditional village practice.[21] But despite the effective combining of rural Chinese and Catholic identities, the tension between Catholics and the state remains. This is partly due to the intractable long-standing issues on a high political level between Beijing and the Vatican. But no matter how those issues are settled, it may not have much of an effect on the folk Catholicism that has been developing for centuries. Just as the state has a historical memory of suspicion of folk Catholics as heterodox and an instinct to monitor them, the Catholics in turn inherit a penchant for freewheeling adaptations which makes the Chinese government and the church hierarchy alike somewhat uneasy.

Urban Christianity: "Cultural Christians," and the Opium War Revisited

Sometime between the late 1980s and the late 1990s, Christian growth slowed in the countryside and grew stronger in China's cities. The rural weighting of both the Protestant and Catholic church toward the country-side had meant that the converts, and their pastors and leaders who emerged from their ranks, were on the whole neither well-educated nor wealthy.[22] Most of the urban congregations in several cities which I visited in the 1980s were (to generalize egregiously) middle or lower middle class, with few members as well appointed sartorially as a typical cadre. Within the past decade and a half the makeup of many urban churches has changed dramatically. Many well-paid professionals, white-collar workers, and teachers can now be found in urban churches, both TSPM-registered and unregistered churches. After the acceleration from rapid to pell-mell economic development and expansion created by Deng Xiaoping in 1992, a massive restructuring of the economy began. First, investment poured even faster into the coastal cities of the Southeast coast and Shandong Province. Urban jobs were plentiful, setting off the migration of probably more than 100 million people from interior rural places to coastal urban places. The economic boom was paralleled by an urban church boom. Many of the migrants were already Christians, and many others became Christians in their new surroundings. Several urban congregations in cities along the southeast coast in Zhejiang and Fujian Provinces have become quite prosperous. Some have active members who are businessmen or entrepreneurs.[23] They fund a variety of programs of material welfare or evangelization efforts directed at the migrants. At any rate, urban churches all over China have become more attuned to social contributions that the churches can make, both in their own cities and beyond; witness the outpouring of concern and the generosity of response by the Christian communities to the Sichuan earthquake of spring 2009.

Not only have the "typical" Protestant congregations changed, but the role of intellectuals in the churches and in the Christian movement more broadly has changed. Intellectuals traditionally have been leery of the vagaries of popular religion, and in the twentieth century were largely anti-Christian in instinct, partly for nationalistic reasons. For them to take Christianity seriously as objective study or normative belief is a big change from the past. The past of course provided the ideological underpinning for the dismissal of religion in the lexicon of Marxism-Leninism, which calls religion an opiate of the people and presumes that it will die out as human society progresses. The only question was whether religion, while doomed, had a long-term or short-term life expectancy. From the 1950s on, there was some discussion among intellectuals and party ideological watchdogs on questions such as the difference between the terms "religion" and "superstition."[24] But it was only in the 1980S that some intellectuals challenged the old "opiate of the people" shibboleth and argued that religion should be seen as a permanent part of society, and indeed that it can make significant ongoing contributions to Chinese society and culture. These propositions were debated during the 1980s, and the discussion constituted what some have called the "second Opium War."[25]

By the 1990s, critics of the opiate idea had prevailed sufficiently for some intellectuals to engage in serious study and evaluation of what Christianity, both Protestant and Catholic, but primarily the former, might mean for China as a model for public ethics. Some sought clues to solving China's seemingly endemic problems of corruption and low standards of public ethics. Some were (and remain) fascinated by the role Christianity has played, or seems to have played, in Western history. They often associate Christianity with the rise of a "public sphere" or "civil society" in early modern Europe. Others subscribe to the Weberian linkage between the Protestant Reformation and the rise of capitalism. They are looking for "lessons" from Western "Christian" history. These scholars, who did not come from the churches or the seminaries, but from several of China's elite secular universities, have been called "culture Christians" or "cultural Christians" by some observers of the intellectual scene. It seems apparent that this term should be used carefully, to designate those scholars interested in the study of Christianity, either for China's benefit, their own personal faith, or both. [26] Probably most of these are not believers. However, some so-called cultural Christians have in fact become believers. Of those, some attend worship services, mainly in non-registered churches; some do not attend any church, but occasionally gather with friends. One of the reasons why few of them go to registered churches, besides the obvious chance of future harm if a large anti-Christian campaign were to come along, is that the intellectual level of the registered churches is quite low. Universities, not the seminaries, are where the work on Christianity, including theology, is being done. Some leaders in this theological reflection openly discuss the creation of a "Sino-Christian theology." Church representatives and seminary faculty members are seldom invited to academic conferences on Christianity, of which there have been at least two dozen in the past twenty years. One interesting byproduct of the activities of these "culture Christians" is that China now has more than twenty university-based centers, or institutes, focused on the study of Christianity, or more generically, religion (but what is meant is usually Christianity). History and Philosophy are the most frequently used departments for housing these centers and institutes.[27]

Some "culture Christians" are convinced that the right course for Chinese Protestants is to work for the establishment of a comprehensive "religious law" by the National People's Congress. This would supplant Document 19, now over a quarter century old, as well as superseding other sets of guidelines which have appeared in the 1990s and the 2000s. It would have the status of "real" law, as opposed to so many of the regulations and administrative guidelines which now constitute a hodge-podge of rules. It is clear that those promoting the "religious law" idea are also hoping to contribute to a more general movement towards the "rule of law," with the party and the state accepting some legal restraints on its habitual arbitrariness of action. A few small conferences bringing together foreign legal scholars and cadres from the RAB have been held in recent years, and the government officials have been exposed to scholarly reports on the state of the unregistered churches. They have heard these reports strongly recommending the decriminalization of a simple failure of a church to register with the TSPM. Some cadres have indicated they agree. It is my guess that there may be some movement toward a religious law fairly soon.

Figure 8.5　Church dwarfed by skyscrapers, Shanghai. Credit: Robert Harding Picture Library Ltd/Alamy.

China in the Arena of World Christianity

Both Catholics and Protestants seem to have forged a sustainable presence in China, with both making accommodations with traditional Chinese popular religion and cultural patterns. It has been more than a half-century since the consolidation of Communist rule in China, the expulsion of all the missionaries, and subjection of the church to the demands of the new order. By the late 1950s prospects for the church appeared to be rather dim, and many former missionaries despaired that surely the Chinese Christians left in China would not be up to the demands required to survive.[28] In the West, scholarly studies of missionaries lagged and those still published became more critical of missions as part of the apparatus of Western imperialism.[29] Finally, most who considered the matter concluded that on the whole this issue was of little consequence because Christianity had been a failed venture in China. Of course, reality has been different. The church has not only survived, but, especially among Protestants, it has prospered. The events of the past two to three decades have constituted one of the most dramatic episodes in all of world-wide Christian history. Despite continuing problems of church–state relations for both Catholics and Protestants, one senses that tensions are in the process of winding down, though it may take another decade for that to develop fully. Catholics have the toughest issues to solve; the Chinese church is virtually unique in the world-wide Roman Catholic church in having an entity such as the CPA. It will not be easy to merge the two parallel Catholic hierarchies in existence today, and to work out terms of agreement on who appoints bishops, in name and in fact. Protestants, especially those leading the unregistered churches, are faced with the need for more effective doctrinal monitoring to try to prevent the rise of radical cults, which will be difficult because of the decentralized nature of Protestantism. The fertile production of cults, however, can be expected to continue; they are a natural product of the interface between the more exuberant forms of Protestantism and Chinese popular religious traditions. As well, unregistered churches also need to make more transparent the foreign contacts that they have, some of which involve significant amounts of resources. This should ease government concerns about the likelihood of their becoming anti-state. I look for fitful progress in all of these areas in the next decade.

It should also be said that it is very much in order for those foreign elements that do indeed maintain clandestine relationships in China and smuggle Bibles and other literature to their Chinese contacts, to cease these activities or else to re-negotiate them in good faith among all parties involved. Americans have been among the most active in publicizing and championing the "persecuted church" in China.[30] There are particular historical reasons why this is so. For more than a century, Americans have had special, even romantic notions about China becoming a "Christian nation," one modeling itself after the US.[31] China was the largest mission field in the world, and in the first half of the twentieth century it was also the field to which more Americans felt God's call than to any other, supplanting the British by the early 1900s. When China fell under CCP control in 1949, there arose American disappointment and anger at how China had been, as it were, hijacked from friendship with the US and the blessings of Christianity. Out of this disquiet, and using it effectively, came a group of apologists and cheerleaders for Chiang Kai-shek, including public officials, bureaucrats, journalists, businessmen, and others who maintained a vigilant loyalty to Chiang partly because he was a Christian. Referred to by all as the "China lobby," they constituted one of the most important interest groups in American politics during two decades. They had total success in enforcing a rigid stance of implacable opposition to even minimal US contact with "Red China." Not a single American politician or elected official dared defy the China lobby. This situation held firm for more than twenty years, until President Nixon's 1972 trip to Beijing.[32] Thus there was a tradition of agitated discourse with no lack of exaggeration and alarmist rhetoric in the American public discussion of China, especially concerning memories of the hopes for a Christian China. From the late 1970s, as news of surviving Christians trickled out of China, Hong Kong became an echo chamber for rumors about the reviving church in China, and also for news on continuing cases of persecution of Christians. A large number of Hong Kong organizations were created to observe, report on, and also to engage in liaison with Christians in China for evangelical purposes. One example of the latter is surreptitiously taking large quantities of Bibles into China. Catholics as well as Protestants established such organizations. The TSPM-related Amity Foundation, China's first Christian NGO, set up an office in Hong Kong as well. All of the issues and tensions among the TSPM and the CPA, the Chinese state, the unregistered churches, and diverse agencies of interested Western churches and parachurch organizations have been rehearsed and played out over the past 30 years in Hong Kong. This cottage industry of China church-watching delivers news and speculation concerning Christianity in China. This feeds the information machine of several groups in the US, mainly conservative evangelical groups. The message transmitted here to the public is usually that the unregistered churches are "persecuted," and the TSPM is hopelessly compromised, working hand in glove with the RAB. Further, while the house churches are exemplary and noble in their martyrdom, the TSPM and the government are evil, intending to destroy the "real churches." Moreover, it is often claimed to be necessary for foreign Christians to continue to smuggle Bibles into China for various reasons, none of which (in my opinion) is convincing.[33] Virtually no organization asking North Americans to give money for Bibles for China (several do so) mentions that the TSPM-related Amity Press in a suburb of Nanjing has printed over fifty million Bibles in the past several years, and now after an expansion it has the capacity for more than five million every year. (I will say no more about these contemporary issues, except that I personally hope that some of the worst offenders in circulating questionable claims and half-truths, especially in connection with fundraising, will rethink their strategy.)

As the twenty-first century proceeds, I think we can expect to see continued Christian growth, though perhaps not as fast as in the last three decades. I do not believe that China is in process of becoming a "Christian nation," as at least one important observer, David Aikman, has suggested, that is, with up to 30 percent of the population in some way Christian.[34] That would be more than the figure for South Korea, and in my view unlikely. Likewise I doubt that Christianity will make a significant difference in China's geopolitical strategic position in the world, or that China may become an ally of the US due to their common Christian identity.[35] Chinese Christianity will probably make a mark on the world, but not in the kingdom of nation-states.

Christianity, especially Protestantism, has grown very rapidly during the past few decades in many parts of the non-Western world, especially in Latin America, Africa, and parts of Asia. China has been part of this phenomenon, which has transformed the face and the identity of Christianity globally. From being "Christendom," the religion mainly of the North and West, Christianity has become a religion of the East and South. This historical sea change took place over decades, steadily but almost unremarked, except for a handful of scholars led by Andrew Walls and Lamin Sanneh, and including Dana Robert and Philip Jenkins, among others.[36] Chinese Christianity is already one of the, if not the single, most interesting and important examples of inculturation of the essential doctrines and rituals of "world Christianity" into an originally non-Christian cultural setting. As Andrew Walls has said, we are in new and uncharted seas. All around us are the debris and the artifacts of the "post-Christian West," and taking shape on the horizon is "post-Western Christianity." I would guess that it is here, in the kingdom of post-Western Christianity, that China may contribute something out of the treasure trove of her own rich Christian history.

Notes

1. The best single-volume work on the Cultural Revolution is Roderick MacFarquhar and Michael Schoenhals, *Mao's Last Revolution* (Cambridge, MA: Harvard University Press, 2006).
2. My own conviction is that no one knows "how many" Christians there are, or were at any given point in the last 30 years. There are no real estimates, just guesses.
3. Richard Madsen, *China's Catholics: Tragedy and Hope in an Emerging Civil Society* (Berkeley: University of California Press, 1998).
4. Ting was supposedly bishop of the Anglican church for Zhejiang, consecrated by an unorthodox means in 1955.
5. For example, the CCC manages all visits abroad by Chinese church delegations, and reciprocal hosting of foreigners.
6. In addition to the bishops' conference, a third body was created for Catholics, the (Chinese Christian) Church Administrative Commission. I am not sure what it actually does.

7. Donald MacInnis, *Religion in China Today* (Maryknoll, NY: Orbis Books, 1989), pp. 8–26, has a complete translation.

8. Philip L Wickeri, *Reconstructing Christianity in China: K. H. Ting and the Chinese Church* (Maryknoll, NY: Orbis Books, 2007), pp. 211–212.

9. This is one of the main themes of Eugenio Menegon, *Ancestors, Virgins, and Friars: Christianity as a Local Religion in Late Imperial China* (Cambridge, MA: Harvard University Asia Center, 2009); Thomas H. Reilly, *The Taiping Heavenly Kingdom: Rebellion and the Blasphemy of Empire* (Seattle, WA: University of Washington Press, 2004).

10. See Ch. 2.

11. Bishop Fan himself was rearrested by the authorities, sent back to prison, then at age 85, on the eve of being released once again, he was savagely beaten to death in prison.

12. Ideas on Catholics from Edmond Tang and Jean-Paul Wiest, eds, *The Catholic Church in Modern China*; and Kim-Kwong Chan, *Towards a Contextual Ecclesiology: The Catholic Church in the People's Republic of China (1979–1983): its life and theological implication* (Hong Kong: Phototech System Ltd., 1987).

13. The term "quasi-Pentecostal" reflects my reluctance simply to equate phenomena which appear to be the same but which have a different "feel" in the Chinese context. E.g., tongues, words of knowledge/prophecies.

14. For a sympathetic discussion of Xu and Zhang, and of other house church leaders, David Aikman, *Jesus in Beijing: How Christianity is Transforming China and Changing the Global Balance of Power,* rev. and exp. (Washington, DC: Henry Regnery, 2006).

15. For detail on these groups, see Lian Xi, *Redeemed by Fire: Popular Chinese Christianity in the Twentieth Century* (New Haven, CT: Yale University Press, 2010), pp. 215–232.

16. Besides Lian Xi's excellent treatment of Lightning from the East, there is a fine recent article on the movement. Emily C. Dunn, "'Cult,' Church, and the CCP: Introducing Eastern Lightning," *Modern China* 35.1 (January 2009):96–119.

17. Lian Xi, *Redeemed by Fire: Popular Chinese Christianity in the Twentieth Century* (New Haven, CT: Yale University Press, 2010), p. 222.

18. Richard Madsen, "Beyond Orthodoxy: Catholicism as Chinese Folk Religion," Stephen Uhalley and Xiaoxin Wu, eds, *China and Christianity* (Santa Barbara, CA: Eastgate, 2001), pp. 233–250.

19. Among dozens of sources, see David Ownby, *Falun Gong and the Future of China* (Oxford: Oxford University Press, 2008).

20. Richard Madsen, "Beyond Orthodoxy: Catholicism as Chinese Folk Religion," in *China and Christianity: Burdened Past, Hopeful Future,* ed. Stephen Uhalley and Xiaoxin Wu (Santa Barbara, CA: Eastgate, 2001), p. 246.

21. Eriberto Lozada, *God Aboveground: Catholic Church, Socialist State, and Transnational Processes in a Chinese Village* (Stanford, CA: Stanford University Press, 2001). A fine case study of a heavily Catholic Hakka area of eastern Guangdong Province.

22. This of course is an overly broad assertion. There were well-established Christian families of several generations in many areas, including literati families.

23. Nanlai Cao, *Constructing China's Jerusalem: Christians, Power, and Place in Contemporary Wenzhou* (Stanford University Press, 2010), is an extremely well done ethnography of Wenzhou's Christian upper-middle class.

24. For a translation of seven documents from the early years of the PRC on the nature of religion, Donald E. MacInnis, *Religious Policy and Practice in Communist China* (New York: Macmillan, 1972), pp. 35–95.

25. Several documents in Donald E. MacInnis, *Religion in China Today: Policy and Practice* (Maryknoll, NY: Orbis Books, 1989).

26. A thoughtful discussion of what the term really means is Chinese Academy of Social Sciences Institute for the Study of World Religions Director Zhuo Xinping, "Discussion on 'Cultural Christians' in China." In *China and Christianity*, ed. Stephen Uhalley and Xiaoxin Wu, pp. 283–300 (Armonk, NY: M. E. Sharpe, 2001).

27. In 2009, the Ministry of Education banned the creation of any more such centers and institutes.

28. One of the few who was able to give a self-critical assessment of the missionary movement's mistakes was David Macdonald Paton, *Christian Missions and the Judgment of God*, 2nd ed. (Grand Rapids MI: Wm. B. Eerdmans, 1969). First published in 1953.

29. For an interesting critique of the critique, Ryan Dunch, "Beyond Cultural Imperialism: Cultural Theory, Christian Missions, and Global Modernity," *History and Theory* 41 (October 2002):301–325.

30. I discuss this in some detail in Daniel H. Bays, "American Public Discourse on the Church in China,"*The China Review* 9.2 (Fall 2009): 1–16.

31. Richard Madsen, *China and the American Dream*, a *Moral Inquiry* (Berkeley, CA: University of California Press, 1995.

32. A major part of the China Lobby was The Committee of One Million.

33. Other myths about Chinese churches include: children under 18 may not attend church, sermons have to be vetted in advance, attendees have to register, the second coming of Christ or the book of Revelations may not be mentioned, and so forth.

34. David Aikman, *Jesus in Beijing: How Christianity is Transforming China and changing the Global Balance of Power*, rev. and exp. (Washington, DC: Henry Regnery, 2006). The first edition was 2003. On many other counts, however, this is a very worthwhile book, by an excellent reporter.

35. David Aikman, *Jesus in Beijing: How Christianity is Transforming China and changing the Global Balance of Power*, rev. and exp. (Washington, DC: Henry Regnery, 2006).

36. Andrew Walls, *The Missionary Movement in Christian History: Studies in the Transmission of Faith* (Maryknoll, NY: Orbis, 1996); Lamin Sanneh, *Translating the Message: The Missionary Impact on Culture* (Maryknoll, NY: Orbis, 1989); Philip Jenkins, *The Next Christendom: the Coming of Global Christianity* (Oxford: Oxford: Oxford University Press, 2002); Dana Robert, *Christian Mission: How Christianity Became a World Religion* (Oxford: Wiley-Blackwell, 2009).

Appendix: The Russian Orthodox Church and Ecclesiastical Mission in China

Late Seventeenth to Mid Nineteenth Century

The Russian religious interest in China, at least until the twentieth century, seems to have been always subordinate to strategic political and diplomatic interests, as well as commercial and scientific ones.[1] The Ecclesiastical Mission had a dual structure, being subordinate to both the secular authority of the Foreign Ministry and the spiritual authority of the Holy Synod of the Church. Russian church emissaries and clerics resident in China did very little evangelization, and before the mid nineteenth century maintained an unobtrusive presence in Beijing even during the decades of proscription of Christianity by the Chinese emperors.

The two expanding empires, the Russian and the Qing, came into more and more contact during the eighteenth century. Eventually this involved pragmatic diplomacy on the part of both. The first official delegation of the Russian government to China was in 1676, but it failed to reach agreement on border issues. In the 1680s Siberian cossacks, including some Orthodox clerics, built up a settlement at Albazin, on the Amur River. The Kangxi emperor, insisting that Albazin was Chinese territory, attacked the small Russian garrison there with over 10,000 troops and many cannon. The cossacks retreated to Siberia, except for about 30 who joined the Manchu military forces. The geopolitical situation on the Chinese-Inner Asian frontier soon shifted, however, and pragmatic security concerns led Kangxi to deal with Russia on the bass of equality. This resulted in the Treaty of Nerchinsk in 1689, which settled the border and provided for ongoing contact. This included a biannual Russian trade caravan to Beijing, which soon became closely associated with the Russian ecclesiastical mission. This "mission" was at first just the provision of divine services for the Albazinians in Beijing. In the late 1690s Peter the Great took an interest in the Russian presence in Beijing and its potential for advancing Russian interests, and decided to send a priest

A New History of Christianity in China, First Edition. Daniel H. Bays.
© 2012 Daniel H. Bays. Published 2012 by Blackwell Publishing Ltd.

with the rank of archimandrite to China.[2] He also prompted the training of clerics and priests as missionaries, and in 1700 ordered the Metropolite of Kiev to send a priest with two or three monks to Beijing to learn Chinese.[3] Peter could see clearly that the Chinese would always have a certain advantage in negotiation because of the Chinese side providing the interpreters (the Jesuits in the emperor's employ at the Qing court) whenever negotiations took place. A series of steps in the years after 1700, including a Russian-Chinese agreement of 1713, brought the first archimandrites to Beijing, to give pastoral care to the Albazinians and the visiting Russian merchants.

This mixture of political, commercial, and ecclesiastical issues was largely settled by the Sino-Russian Treaty of Kiakhta in 1727. This agreement clarified further the Sino-Siberian border, provided for regulations for commercial relations, and legalized the Russian Mission in Beijing. It provided that a Russian archimandrite would reside at the house given to the Russians by the Chinese; he would be at the same time the head of the Russian Orthodox ecclesiastical mission and the Russian ambassador to the Qing court. The treaty also authorized two or three more Russian priests as helpers and five or six laymen to learn Chinese and Manchu. A school was also provided for in the 1727 treaty for language teaching on the compound of the Mission, and a new church was built on the compound as well. The Mission's staff was to change approximately every ten years.

With the 1727 treaty having defined the parameters of official relations, this framework remained in place all the way to 1860, when it was partially replaced by the multilateral treaty system.[4] Despite the Chinese in the 1760s barring the Russian trade caravans from traveling all the way to Beijing, making them do their trading at the border, nevertheless Russia was the only Western country to have permission to reside in Beijing.[5] This naturally only deepened the chagrin and impatience of the other European and American traders and missionaries as they chafed under the restrictions of the "Canton system" of external relations before 1840.

There were eight missions, that is eight different archimandrites, appointed in succession as head of the mission between the 1720s and the early nineteenth century. Several more followed in the decades to the end of the Qing. Altogether before 1860 about 155 Russians –priests, other clerics, and lay people – had in some capacity served in the ecclesiastical mission. Their historical image is not distinguished. According to one respected historian, "eighteenth-century [Russian] missions are known for their idleness, drunkenness, and debauchery."[6] Most of them did study Chinese and/or Manchu during their time in Beijing, however, and some became interpreters and translators for the Russian Ministry of Foreign Affairs. The Russian academic tradition of Sinology, which was quite respectable, also derived from the experiences and training that these individuals gained in the mission in Beijing.[7]

One thing the Russian mission did not do during this time frame, however, was to spread the Gospel or evangelize among the Chinese and Manchus all around them. The Russians carried on essentially no missionary activities among these. Not surprisingly, the result was that of the typical number of at most two or three dozen members of the Orthodox community, no more than a handful, five or fewer, were Chinese.[8] Thus Russian Orthodoxy played a very minor religious role in the decades to 1860, though its strategic political and diplomatic role was very important. Historical circumstances did not until the early twentieth century test the drawing power of Orthodoxy, with its spectacle of worship including pomp and ceremony, incense and music, to the Han Chinese commoners.

Circa 1860–2000

The Russian Orthodox Ecclesiastical Mission to China had been a dual institution since its creation before 1700. The pattern of a combined Russian ecclesiastical and diplomatic mission in Beijing ended about 1860, with the appointment of the first Russian diplomatic plenipotentiary.[9] The Mission was no longer subordinate to the Russian state, but only to the Holy Synod. The secular members of the Ecclesiastical Mission departed, most to join the Asian Department of the Ministry of Foreign Affairs. With fewer duties, the Mission lost some of its allocated personnel and budget, as well. At the same time, some members of the royal family and the government wanted to accelerate dramatically the activity of the Mission in something it had never done – make religious converts to Orthodoxy among Han Chinese and Manchus. There was still a strategic purpose even here: some Russian officials were convinced that the French and the British intended to transform China into a Catholic and Protestant country and that Russia must forestall this by an aggressive campaign to establish an Orthodox bastion. The Mission duly tried, without much enthusiasm, to evangelize effectively; for example, they began to translate parts of the Bible and some pieces of Orthodox literature. Schools and medical services for Chinese were established; even a choir was begun for the main church in Beijing. But for the most part the results were minimal. There was no surge of baptisms. The number of converts did rise steadily, however.[10] In the late 1890s, the human resources of the Mission included the head of the Mission, two hieromonks, one priest, and one deacon.[11] Two Chinese candidates for the priesthood were also being trained. The parish, including Beijing and Tianjin, had 120 Russians and over 450 Chinese; in 1898 14 people were baptized.

Enjoying this slow but encouraging increase in the number of Chinese converts, the Mission suffered a nearly fatal blow during the Boxer Uprising in the summer of 1900. The Orthodox community in Beijing and environs numbered only about 450 to begin with, and fully 222 were massacred by Boxers the night of June 10–11.Strangely, the violence was visited only on the Chinese. Several priest candidates were killed, as were some of the Albazi-nians (Chinese of Russian descent); no Russian clergy were harmed. This was a terrible blow to the small Orthodox group, now only half its former size. To intensify the pain, some critics in the government's Ministry of Foreign Affairs back in St. Petersburg took advantage of the situation to attempt to put an end to the Mission altogether. Even those at the top of the church hierarchy cabled the Beijing archimandrite suggesting strongly that the Mission be relocated, either to Siberia near the Chinese border or to Port Arthur (the port city and naval base at the southern tip of the Liaodong peninsula, thoroughly controlled by Russia at this time). But the head of the Beijing mission, Archimandrite Innokentij (Ivan Appolonovich Fugurovskij, 1863–1931), was determined to save it; he disregarded his orders and temporarily moved what remained of the mission to Shanghai. The Russian government called the archimandrite back to St. Petersburg in June 1901, prepared to give him an unambiguous order which he could not evade, to shut down the mission once and for all. But the powerful Metropolitan of St. Petersburg intervened (probably at Innokentij's behest), and the mission was saved. In fact, the mission's budget was doubled, and Innokentij was consecrated to be a bishop in June 1902. When he returned to China he brought with him more than thirty clerics and monks, far more religious personnel than the mission had ever enjoyed.

I have earlier, in Chapter 5, portrayed the first two decades of the twentieth century as a "Golden Age" for missions in China. It was that for the Russian Orthodox mission, as well. New mission stations were established in several places in central and even southern China, not just in the familiar northeast. Orthodox missionaries began to behave like those of other denominations – preaching, baptizing, managing schools. Despite the tense and even hostile relationship with Russian diplomats in Beijing, the years until 1917 were very successful, at least in terms of basic statistics. Between 1900 and 1913, 1340 Chinese were baptized. In 1916 alone 706 received baptism, with the total Orthodox community now more than 6200 souls.[12] The Mission had 32 mission stations, 19 churches, and 20 schools. At this time, on the eve of the Bolshevik Revolution, there were over 30 Russians and more than 40 Chinese working in the Mission. These indices of growth were quite respectable, even remarkable, considering the devastation at the hands of the Boxers in 1900, and the attempts early in the century to withdraw or eliminate the Mission. This was the apex of the Orthodox attempt to forge a ministry to Chinese.

The events of 1917 in European Russia, that is, the Bolshevik Revolution, plunged the Mission back into the treacherous shoals of domestic politics, and forced the Mission to return to its historical role of serving Russians who were in China, not Chinese. By 1919 there was no more outreach to Chinese and all the mission stations had been closed. There were plenty of works of charity and relief of suffering to do among the several hundred thousand Russian refugees from the revolution and the ensuing civil war. There was also the contentious issue of who "owned" the Mission's property in Beijing. Around the world, everywhere the Orthodox church split asunder in choosing loyalties to the old regime or the new Soviet government. An Orthodox synod-in-exile (Synod Abroad) came into existence, drawing the loyalties of many in the hierarchy. Among the latter was Bishop Innokentij, still head of the Mission, as he had been since the 1890s.[13] He remained loyal to the anti-Communist Synod Abroad during the 1920s, for example successfully rebuffing attempts by the Soviet embassy in Beijing to take control of the Mission's old properties. The Holy Synod in turn elevated him to the rank of Metropolitan in 1928. Innokentij died in 1931.

Meanwhile, there surfaced a fissure among the Russian and Chinese clergy over the issue of Chinese versus foreign control. The church did not have very many Chinese priests, but the oldest of them, Sergij Chang Fu, contested the appointment of a Russian to replace Innokentij in 1931. When the new appointee died in 1933, Sergij Chang Fu continued his claim to be the legitimate successor to Metropolitan Innokentij, taking his claims to the Chinese government of Chiang Kai-shek. Chiang's Guomindang government actually did formally appoint Sergij as head of mission, but the ensuing uproar and "fierce resistance" of the Russian clergy made this impossible to implement.[14] Thus the Russian Orthodox Church did not yet take any steps toward making a significant part of its hierarchy in China Chinese. The Russian refugees in China, by the 1930s were mainly in the parishes of Harbin (Manchuria), Beijing, and Shanghai, where they vastly outnumbered the Chinese Orthodox, which made it difficult to put Chinese leadership at the top. Real indigenization, rather a facsimile thereof, would wait until the 1950s.

Bishop of Shanghai Viktor Svyatin was chosen by the Synod Abroad as head of the Twentieth Mission, from 1933 until the closing of the Mission in 1956. Bishop (Archbishop after 1947) Victor and the church and mission survived the Japanese occupation of the late 1930s and 1940s, continued hostility between pro- and anti-Soviet factions among the Russians, and the transition to the new government in China after 1949. Viktor had successfully made reconciliation with the church back in the Soviet Union, and had come out on top in a complicated power struggle in the late 1940s. In 1949 Viktor made ambitious plans for the resumption of many former activities of the Russian Mission, and some new ones, including several new seminaries, extensive evangelization, and other schemes, most of which involved Russian leadership. But the Patriarch of the church in Moscow (Viktor had reconciled with the Moscow church and the Soviet Union some time before) instead ordered Viktor to accelerate the pace of transition in the church from mission to Chinese church, and to complete the job in ten years, that is, by 1959. Already in late 1950 Viktor ordained five new Chinese priests and four deacons. He also opened a catechists' school in Beijing. However, the early 1950s was not a propitious time for expansion of Christian activities. Besides having the Korean War on the doorstep of both China and the Soviet Union, there was a massive exodus of tens of thousands of Russian parishioners returning to the Soviet Union. By 1954 all across China Orthodox churches (73) were virtually empty. This resulted in the July, 1954, decision of the Holy Synod of the Moscow Patriarchate to put an end to the Russian Ecclesiastical Mission.

Archbishop Viktor was undoubtedly very disappointed with this outcome. He had reconciled with the Soviet and the church authorities in Moscow apparently in hopes of both of them approving some sort of continuation of the Mission, at least some institution that would permit an ongoing Russian role. That was not to be. Moreover, he finally had no choice in the end but to surrender on the issue of the Mission's extensive property holdings in Beijing and other sites; he agreed, as the Soviet government had long insisted, to turn the property over to the Chinese and Soviet governments. The bulk of it went to the former; the latter received the site of the "Northern Yard" (*beiguan*), a piece of land originally given to the earliest Russian mission by the Kangxi emperor. Here they built a new Soviet embassy. With most of the paperwork of property transfers finished, in 1957 the Moscow Patriarchate formally granted autonomy, full independence, to the "Chinese (Autonomous) Orthodox Church" (Zhonghua Dongzhengjiao Hui). Here again, as in the case of the decision to end the Mission, the decision was made in Moscow.

The newly named church, a transmogrified Russian institution staffed mainly by Chinese, immediately ran into rough going. Not only the Chinese Orthodox, but all Chinese and especially Protestants and Catholics as well, had to endure the traumas of the anti-rightist movement and the Great Leap Forward in the late 1950s, and the Cultural Revolution after 1966. Symbolically, the Russian ambassador to Beijing, as soon as he obtained possession of the old compound of the mission in 1957, demolished all of the old buildings of the Mission, burned all the books in its library, and disinterred the remains of the Romanov family and the 222 Boxer martyrs, sending them to the old Russian cemetery at the Anding gate. There they remained; they are now presumably at the bottom of the lake in the amusement park which was built when the St. Seraphim church in the Russian cemetery was torn down in 1986.

Today all traces of the Orthodox presence in Beijing are gone. The last church was torn down in 1991, and the last living Orthodox priest in China died in Beijing in 2003. In Shanghai, two church buildings have survived; one contains a bank and a restaurant, the other is a warehouse. There may be more than a handful of believers, it appears. A Chinese estimate of 1984 is of 8000 persons. An estimate of the late 1990s claims 3000 in the northeast three provinces, 3000 in Xinjiang, 30 in Shanghai, and 300 Albazinians in Beijing.[15] But there are no priests, and no places of worship. It appears that the Chinese Autonomous Orthodox Church (its full name) is suffering the fate once predicted for Protestants and Catholics, that is, extinction. And yet, the revival of Christianity in Russia, including the Orthodox church there, together with the opening of Russia's borders, may have increased chances of new baptisms among the hundreds of thousands of Chinese residing in or visiting Russia.

Notes

1. This has been treated by Standaert in "Russian Orthodox Church," in *Handbook of Christianity in China, Volume I: 635–1800*, ed. Nicolas Standaert (Leiden: Brill, 2001), pp. 367–375.
2. An archimandrite, in the Orthodox hierarchy, is more or less the equivalent of a bishop.
3. A metropolite or metropolitan is the approximate equivalent of an archbishop, generally of a fairly large urban area.
4. After 1860, the Russians had the advantages of its old treaties of Nerchinsk and Kiakhta, as well as the new ones.
5. This was a period of general tightening up of China's management of its external relations. At the other end of the country from the Sino-Mongolian frontier used by the Russians, along the southeast coast where a number of coastal cities had previously been sites of European seaborne trade, in 1760 the emperor closed all other ports but Canton to foreign trade. This was the beginning of the "Canton system," which required the traders and missionaries alike to shuttle between Macau and Canton.
6. Joseph Fletcher, "Sino-Russian Relations, 1800–1862," *The Cambridge History of China*, Vol. 10, *Late Ch'ing, 1800–1911*, Part I, ed. John K. Fairbank (Cambridge: Cambridge University Press, 1978), p. 524.
7. For the early history of the Mission, Eric Widmer, *The Russian Ecclesiastical Mission in Peking in the eighteenth century* (Cambridge, MA: East Asian Research Center, Harvard University, 1976).
8. The majority of the Orthodox even into the nineteenth century continued to be the Albazinians, that is, the descendants of the original Albazinians of the 1680s.
9. This has been treated by Alexander Lomanov, "Russian Orthodox Church," *Handbook of Christianity in China, Volume 2: 1800–Present*, ed. R. G. Tiedemann (Leiden: Brill, 2010), pp. 193–211, 553–563, 826–835.
10. As I indicated above, if Catholic missionaries were correct in their assessment that rural folk were very partial to Catholic ceremony and even spectacle such as saints' processions on feast days, the Orthodox, with their even grander pomp and spectacle, should have been successful if they had addressed themselves to that audience.
11. In the Orthodox churches, a hieromonk is a monk who is also ordained as a priest.

12. This was more than many small European and American missions could claim.

13. Symbolic of the loyalty of the Beijing orthodox to the old regime in Russia was the April 1920 delivery to the Mission of the dead bodies of several members of the Romanov family who had been executed by the Bolsheviks in July 1918. They were first buried in the Russian cemetery near the Anding gate, then in 1938, when Japan invaded, the coffins were brought to the Mission property and buried in the Church of All Holy Martyrs, close to the spot where had been buried the more than the 200 Chinese Orthodox victims of the Boxer Uprising.

14. This quotation is from Alexander Lomanov, "Russian Orthodox Church," *Handbook of Christianity in China, VolumeTwo: 1800–Present,* ed. R. G. Tiedemann (Leiden: Brill, 2010), p. 826.

15. Alexander Lomanov, "Russian Orthodox Church," *Handbook of Christianity in China, Volume 2: 1800–Present,* ed. R. G. Tiedemann (Leiden: Brill, 2010), p. 834.

Bibliography

Adeney, David H. *China: Christian Students Face the Revolution.* Downers Grove, IL: InterVarsity Press, 1973.

Adeney, David H. *China: The Church's Long March.* Ventura, CA: Regal Books, 1985.

Aikman, David. *Jesus in Beijing: How Christianity is Transforming China and Changing the Global Balance of Power.* Revised and expanded. Washington, DC: Henry Regnery, 2006.

Anderson, G., R. Coote, N. Horner, and J. Phillips, eds, *Mission Legacies: Biographical Studies of Leaders of the Modern Missionary Movement.* Maryknoll, NY: Orbis Books, 1994.

Armitage, Carolyn. *Reaching for the Goal: The Life Story of David Adeney.* Wheaton, IL: Harold Shaw, 1993.

Austin, Alvyn. *China's Millions: The China Inland Mission and Late Qing Society, 1832–1905.* Grand Rapids, MI: Wm. B. Eerdmans, 2007.

Ballard, J.G. *Empire of the Sun.* London: Grafton, 1985.

Barnett, Suzanne Wilson, and John King Fairbank, eds, *Christianity in China: Early Protestant Missionary Writings.* Cambridge, MA: Committee on American-East Asian Relations, Dept. of History, Harvard University, 1985.

de Bary, William Theodore, and Irene Bloom,comps. *Sources of Chinese Tradition: Vol. I: From Earliest Times to 1600.* New York: Columbia University Press, 2000.

Bays, Daniel H."American Public Discourse on the Church in China." *The China Review* 9.2 (Fall 2009): 1–16.

Bays, Daniel H. "Chang Chih-tung After the '100 Days': 1898–1900 as a Transitional Period for Reform Constituencies." In *Reform in Nineteenth-Century China,* ed. Paul A. Cohen and John E. Schrecker, pp. 317–325. Cambridge, MA: Harvard University, East Asian Research Center, 1976.

Bays, Daniel H. *China Enters the Twentieth Century: Chang Chih-tung and the Issues of a New Age, 1895–1909.* Ann Arbor, MI: University of Michigan Press, 1978.

Bays, Daniel H. "A Chinese Christian 'Public Sphere'?: Socioeconomic Mobility and the Formation of Urban Middle Class Protestant Communities in the Early Twentieth Century." In *Constructing China: The Interaction of Culture and Economics,* ed. Kenneth Lieberthal, Shuen-fu Lin, and Ernest P. Young,

A New History of Christianity in China, First Edition. Daniel H. Bays.
© 2012 Daniel H. Bays. Published 2012 by Blackwell Publishing Ltd.

pp. 101–117. Ann Arbor, MI: Center for Chinese Studies, University of Michigan, 1997.

Bays, Daniel H. "Christian Revival in China, 1900–1937." In *Modern Christian Revivals*, ed. Edith L. Blumhofer and Randall Balmer, pp. 161–179. Urbana, IL: University of Illinois Press, 1993.

Bays, Daniel H. ed. *Christianity in China: From the Eighteenth Century to the Present.* Stanford, CA: Stanford University Press, 1996.

Bays, Daniel H. "The Growth of Independent Christianity in China, 1900–1937." In *Christianity in China: From the Eighteenth Century to the Present*, ed. Daniel H. Bays, pp. 307–316. Stanford, CA: Stanford University Press, 1996.

Bays, Daniel H. "*Ihetuan zongjiao tiyan yu 20 shiji 20 niandai Shandong Jidujiao 'Yesu Jiating' de bijiao*" (Comparison of the religious experience of the Boxers with the Christian Jesus Family in 1920s Shandong). In *Ihotuan yundong yu jindai Zhongguo shehui guoji xueshu yantaohui lunwenji* (Papers of the international academic symposium on the Boxer movement and modern Chinese society), ed. Chinese Society for Boxer Studies, pp. 521–525. Jinan: Jilu shushe, 1992.

Bays, Daniel H. "Indigenous Protestant Churches in China, 1900–1937" In *Indigenous Responses to Western Christianity*, ed. Steven Kaplan, pp. 124–143. New York: New York University Press, 1995.

Bays, Daniel H. "The Protestant Missionary Establishment and the Pentecostal Movement." In *Pentecostal Currents in American Protestantism*, ed. Edith Blumhofer, Russell Spittler, and Grant Wacker, pp. 50–67. Urbana, IL: University of Illinois Press, 1999.

Bays, Daniel H. "The Soong Family and the Chinese Protestant Christian Community." In *Madame Chiang Kaishek and her China*, ed. Samuel C. Chu, pp. 22–32. Norwalk, CT: Eastbridge, 2005.

Bays, Daniel H. "A Tradition of State Dominance." In *God and Caesar in China: Policy Implications of Church-State Tensions*, ed. Carol Hamrin and Jason Kindopp, pp. 25–39. Washington, DC: Brookings Institution, 2004.

Bays, Daniel H., and Grant Wacker, eds *The Foreign Missionary Enterprise at Home.* Tuscaloosa: University of Alabama Press, 2003.

Bays, Daniel H., and Ellen Widmer, eds, *China's Christian Colleges: Cross-Cultural Connections, 1900–1950.* Stanford, CA: Stanford University Press, 2009.

Bennett, Adrian A. *John Fryer: The Introduction of Western Science and Technology into Nineteenth-Century China.* Cambridge, MA: East Asian Research Center, Harvard University, 1967.

Bennett, Adrian A. *Missionary Journalist in China: Young J. Allen and His Magazines.* Athens: University of Georgia Press, 1983.

Bohr, Paul Richard. *Famine in China and the Missionary: Timothy Richard as Relief Administrator and Advocate of National Reform, 1876–1884.* Cambridge, MA: East Asian Research Center, Harvard University, 1972.

Bohr, Paul Richard. "Liang Fa's Quest for Moral Power." In *Christianity in China: Early Protestant Missionary Writings*, ed. Suzanne Wilson Barnett and John King Fairbank, pp. 35–46. Cambridge, MA: Council on East Asian Studies, 1985.

Bondfield, G. H., ed. *China Missions Year Book.* Shanghai: Christian Literature Society of China, 1913.

Breslin, Thomas A. *China, American Catholicism, and the Missionary.* University Park: Pennsylvania State University Press, 1980.

Brockey, Liam Matthew. *Journey to the East: The Jesuit Mission to China, 1579–1724.* Cambridge, MA: Harvard University Press, 2007.

Brook, Timothy. *Collaboration: Japanese Agents and Local Elites in Wartime China.* Cambridge, MA: Harvard University Press, 2005.

Brook, Timothy. "Toward Independence: Christianity in China under the Japanese Occupation." In *Christianity in China: From the Eighteenth Century to the Present,* ed. Daniel H. Bays, pp. 317–337. Stanford, CA: Stanford University Press, 1996.

Brown, Jeremy, and Paul G. Pickowicz, eds. *Dilemmas of Victory: The Early Years of the People's Republic of China.* Cambridge, MA: Harvard University Press, 2007.

Brown, William A. "The Missionary and China's Rural Problems: The Protestant Rural Movement in China (1920–1937)." In *American Missionaries in China: Papers from Harvard Seminars,* ed. Kwang-Ching Liu, pp. 217–248. Cambridge, MA: Harvard East Asian Research Center, Harvard University, 1966.

Bundy, David. "Missiological Reflections on Nestorian Christianity in China during the Tang Dynasty." In *Religion in the Pacific Era,* ed. Frank K. Flynn and Tyler Hendricks, pp. 14–30. New York: Paragon House, 1985.

Cao, Nanlai. *Constructing China's Jerusalem: Christians, Power, and Place in Contemporary Wenzhou.* Stanford, CA: Stanford University Press, 2010.

Carlberg, Gustav. *China in Revival.* Rock Island, IL: Augustana Book Concern, 1936.

Carlson, Ellsworth C. *The Foochow Missionaries, 1847–1880.* Cambridge, MA: East Asian Research Center, Harvard University, 1974.

Chan, Kim-Kwong. *Towards a Contextual Ecclesiology: The Catholic Church in the People's Republic of China (1979–1983): Its Life and Theological Implication.* Hong Kong: Phototech System Ltd., 1987.

Chao, Jonathan T'ien-en. "The Chinese Indigenous Church Movement, 1919–1927: A Protestant Response to the Anti-Christian Movements in Modern China," Ph.D. Dissertation, University of Pennsylvania, 1986.

Charbonnier, Jean-Pierre. *Christians in China A.D. 600 to 2000.* Translated by M.N.L. Couve de Murville. Original French edition, Paris, 2002. San Francisco, CA: Ignatius Press, 2007.

Chen Rongzhan. "Notes on Dr. Song's Preaching." In *One Day in China: May 21, 1936,* ed. and trans. Sherman Cochran *et al.,* pp. 186–188. New Haven, CT: Yale University Press, 1983.

Ch'eng, Marcus(Chen Chonggui). *After Forty Years.* London: n.p., 1947.

Ch'eng, Marcus(Chen Chonggui). *Echoes from China: The Story of My Life and Lectures.* Chicago: Covenant Book Concern, 1921.

Ch'eng, Marcus(Chen Chonggui). *Moxiang zhu Yesu* (Meditations on the Lord Jesus). Shanghai: China Christian Council, reprinted 1993.

Cheng, Pei-kai, and Michael Lestz, with Jonathan D. Spence. *The Search for Modern China: A Documentary Collection.* New York: W.W. Norton, 1999.

China Centenary Missionary Conference Records: Report of the Great Conference Held at Shanghai, April 5th to May 8th, 1907. New York: American Tract Society, 1907.

Cliff, Norman. *Courtyard of the Happy Way.* Evesham, UK: Arthur James, 1977.

Cohen, Paul A. *Between Tradition and Modernity: Wang T'ao and Reform in Late Ch'ing China*. Cambridge, MA: Harvard University Press, 1974.

Cohen, Paul A. "Christian Missions and Their Impact Until 1900." In *The Cambridge History of China*, Vol. 10, *Late Qing, 1800–1911, Part I*, ed. John K. Fairbank, pp. 545–590. Cambridge, UK: Cambridge University Press, 1978.

Cohen, Paul A. *China and Christianity: The Missionary Movement and the Growth of Chinese Antiforeignism, 1860–1870*. Cambridge, MA: Harvard University Press, 1963.

Cohen, Paul A. *History in Three Keys: The Boxers as Event, Experience, and Myth*. New York: Columbia University Press, 1997.

Crawford, Mary. *The Shantung Revival*. Shanghai: China Baptist Publication Society, 1933.

Cronin, Vincent. *The Wise Man from the West*. London: Rupert Hart-Davis, 1955.

Crouch, Archie R. *Rising through the Dust: The Story of the Christian Church in China*. New York: Friendship Press, 1947.

Culpepper, C. L. *The Shantung Revival*. Dallas: Baptist General Convention of Texas, 1968.

Cummins, James S. *A Question of Rites: Father Domingo Navarette and the Jesuits in China*. Aldershire, UK: Scholar, 1993.

Dillon, Nara. "New democracy and the demise of private charity in Shanghai." In *Dilemmas of Victory: The Early Years of the People's Republic of China*, ed. Jeremy Brown and Paul Pickowicz. Cambridge, MA: Harvard University Press, 2007.

Drake, Fred W. "Protestant Geography in China: E. C. Bridgman's Portrayal of the West." In *Christianity in China: Early Protestant Missionary Writings*, ed. Suzanne Wilson Barnett and John King Fairbank, pp. 89–106. Cambridge, MA: Council on East Asian Studies, 1985.

Dunch, Ryan. "Beyond Cultural Imperialism: Cultural Theory, Christian Missions, and Global Modernity." *History and Theory* 41 (October 2002): pp. 301–325.

Dunch, Ryan. *Fuzhou Protestants and the Making of a Modern China, 1857–1927*. New Haven, CT: Yale University, 2001.

Dunn, Emily C. "'Cult,' Church, and the CCP: Introducing Eastern Lightning." *Modern China* 35.1 (January 2009): pp. 96–119.

Dunne, George H., S.J. *Generation of Giants: The Story of the Jesuits in China in the Last Decades of the Ming Dynasty*. Notre Dame, IN: University of Notre Dame Press, 1962.

Eastman, Lloyd E. *The Abortive Revolution: China under Nationalist Rule, 1927–1937*. Cambridge, MA: Harvard University Press, 1971.

Entenmann, Robert. "Catholics and Society in Eighteenth-Century Sichuan." In *Christianity in China: From the Eighteenth Century to the Present*, ed. Daniel H. Bays, pp. 8–23. Stanford, CA: Stanford University Press, 1996.

Entenmann, Robert. "Chinese Catholic Clergy and Catechists in Eighteenth Century Szechuan." *Actes du Vie colloque international de sinology, Chantilly 1989* (Variétés Sinologiques, 78). Taibei: Ricci Institute, 1995: pp. 389–410.

Entenmann, Robert. "Christian Virgins in Eighteenth Century Sichuan." In *Christianity in China: From the Eighteenth Century to the Present*, ed. Daniel H. Bays, pp. 180–193. Stanford, CA: Stanford University Press, 1996.

Esherick, Joseph. *The Origins of the Boxer Uprising*. Berkeley: University of California Press, 1987.

Fairbank, John King. *The Great Chinese Revolution, 1800–1985*. New York: Harper and Row, 1986.

Fairbank, John King,with Merle Goldman. *China: A New History*. Enlarged edition. Cambridge, MA: Harvard University Press, 1998.

Fay, Peter Ward. *The Opium War, 1840–1842*. Chapel Hill: University of North Carolina Press, 1975.

Fletcher, Joseph. "Sino-Russian Relations, 1800–1862." In *The Cambridge History of China*, Vol. 10, *Late Ch'ing, 1800–1911*, Part I, ed. John K. Fairbank. Cambridge: Cambridge University Press, 1978.

Gao, Wangzhi. "Y. T. Wu: A Christian Leader Under Communism." In *Christianity in China: From the Eighteenth Century to the Present*, ed. Daniel H. Bays, pp. 338–352. Stanford, CA: Stanford University Press, 1996.

Garrett, Shirley. *Social Reformers in Urban China: The Chinese Y.M.C.A. 1895–1926*. Cambridge, MA: Harvard University Press, 1979.

Gernet, Jacques. *China and the Christian Impact*. Translated by Janet Lloyd. Cambridge, UK: Cambridge University Press, 1985.

Gilkey, Langdon. *Shantung Compound*. New York: Harper & Row, 1966.

Girardot, Norman J. *The Victorian Translation of China: James Legge's Oriental Pilgrimage*. Berkeley: University of California Press, 2002.

Goforth, Jonathan. *By My Spirit*. London: Marshall, Morgan, and Scott, n.d.

Goforth, Jonathan. *When the Spirit's Fire Swept Korea*. Grand Rapids, MI: Zondervan, 1943.

Goforth, Rosalind. *Goforth of China*. Grand Rapids, MI: Zondervan, 1937.

Gulick, Edward V. *Peter Parker and the Opening of China*. Cambridge, MA: Harvard University Press, 1973.

Hamrin, Carol Lee, with Stacey Bieler. *Salt and Light: Lives of Faith that Shaped Modern China*, 2 vols. Eugene, OR: Pickwick Publications, 2008, 2010.

Hancock, Christopher. *Robert Morrison and the Birth of Chinese Protestantism*. London: T&T Clark, 2008.

Harvey, Thomas Alan. *Acquainted with Grief: Wang Mingdao's Stand for the Persecuted Church in China*. Grand Rapids, MI: Brazos Press, 2002.

Hattaway, Paul. *Back to Jerusalem*. Carlisle, UK: Piquant, 2003.

Hayhoe, Ruth, and Lu Yongling, eds, *Ma Xiangbo and the Mind of Modern China*. Armonk, NY: M. E. Sharpe, 1996.

Hefner, Robert W. *Conversion to Christianity: Historical and Anthropological Perspectives*. Berkeley: University of California Press, 1993.

Hevia, James L. *English Lessons: The Pedagogy of Imperialism in Nineteenth-Century China*. Durham, NC: Duke University Press, 2003.

Hinton, William. *Fanshen: A Documentary of Revolution in a Chinese Village*. New York: Alfred A. Knopf, 1966.

Honig, Emily. "Christianity, Feminism, and Communism: The life and times of Deng Yuzhi." In *Christianity in China*, ed. Daniel H. Bays, pp. 243–262. Stanford, CA: Stanford University Press, 2009.

Honig, Emily. *Sisters and Strangers: Women in the Shanghai Cotton Mills, 1919–1949*. Stanford, CA: Stanford University Press, 1986.

Huang, Xiaojuan. "Christian Communities and Alternative Devotions in China, 1780–1860." Ph.D. dissertation, Princeton University, 2006.

Hutchison, William R. *Errand to the World: American Protestant Thought and Foreign Missions*. Chicago: University of Chicago Press, 1987.

Hyatt, Irwin T. Jr., "Protestant Missions in China, 1877–1890: The Institutionalization of Good Works." In *American Missionaries in China: Papers from Harvard Seminars*, ed. Kwang-Ching Liu, pp. 93–128. Cambridge, MA: East Asian Research Center, Harvard University. 1966.

"Indigenous Revival in Shantung." *Chinese Recorder* (1934): 768–72.

Israel, John. *Lianda: A Chinese University in War and Revolution*. Stanford, CA: Stanford University Press, 1998.

Jenkins, Philip. *The Next Christendom: The Coming of Global Christianity*. Oxford: Oxford University Press, 2002.

Keller, Charles. "Nationalism and Chinese Christians: The Religious Freedom Campaign and Movement for Independent Chinese Churches, 1911–1917." *Republican China* 12.2 (April 1992): 30–51.

King, Marjorie. *China's American Daughter, Ida Pruitt (1888–1985)*. Hong Kong: The Chinese University Press, 2006.

Kinnear, Angus. *The Story of Watchman Nee: Against the Tide*. Wheaton, IL: Tyndale House, 1973.

Kohn, Livia. "Embodiment and Transcendence in Medieval Taoism." In *The Chinese Face of Jesus Christ*. Vol. 1, ed. Roman Malek, SVD. Monumenta Serica Monograph Series, no. 50. Sankt Augustin: Germany, 2002.

Kuhn, Philip A. *Soulstealers: The Chinese Sorcery Scare of 1768*. Cambridge, MA: Harvard University Press, 1990.

Laamann, Lars. *Christian Heretics in Late Imperial China: Christian Inculturation and State Control, 1720–1850*. London: Routledge, 2006.

Latourette, Kenneth Scott. *A History of Christian Missions in China*. London: SPCK, 1929.

Lautz, Terrill E. "The SVM and Transformation of the Protestant Mission to China." In *China's Christian Colleges: Cross-Cultural Connections, 1900–1950*, ed. Daniel H. Bays and Ellen Widmer, pp. 3–21. Stanford, CA: Stanford University Press, 2009.

Lefeuvre, Jean. *Shanghai: les enfants dans la ville: Vie chretienne a Shanghai et perspectives sur l'Eglise de Chine, 1949–1961*. Tournai, Belgium: Casterman, 1962.

Leung, Beatrice. *Sino-Vatican Relations: Problems in Conflicting Authority 1976–1986*. Cambridge, UK: Cambridge University Press, 1992.

Levenson, Joseph R. *Confucian China and Its Modern Fate, Vol. 2, The Problem of Monarchical Decay*. Berkeley: University of California Press, 1964.

Lian Xi. *The Conversion of Missionaries: Liberalism in American Protestant Missions in China, 1907–1932*. University Park, PA: Penn State Press, 1997.

Lian Xi. *Redeemed by Fire: Popular Chinese Christianity in the Twentieth Century*. New Haven, CT: Yale University Press, 2010.

Lian Xi. "The Search for Chinese Christianity in the Republican Period (1912–1949)." *Modern Asian Studies*, 38.4 (2004).

Liang, Fa. "Good Words to Exhort the Age" (*Quanshi liangyan*). In *The Search for Modern China: A Documentary Collection*. Pei-kai Cheng and Michael Lestz, pp. 132–136. New York: W.W. Norton, 1999.

Ling, Samuel. "The Christian May Fourth Movement." Th.D dissertation, Westminster Seminary, Philadelphia, 1980.

Litzinger, Charles A. "Rural Religion and Village Organization in North China: The Catholic Challenge in the Late Nineteenth Century." In *Christianity in China: From the Eighteenth Century to the Present*, ed. Daniel H. Bays, 41–52. Stanford, CA: Stanford University Press, 1996.

Liu Jiafeng. "Same Bed, Different Dreams: The American Postwar Plan for China's Christian Colleges, 1943–1946." In *China's Christian Colleges: Cross–Cultural Connections, 1900–1950*, ed. Daniel H. Bays and Ellen Widmer, pp. 218–240. Stanford, CA: Stanford University Press, 2009.

Lomanov, Alexander. "Russian Orthodox Church." In *Handbook of Christianity in China, Vol. 2: 1800–Present*, ed. R. G. Tiedemann. Leiden: Brill, 2010.

Lozada, Eriberto. *God Aboveground: Catholic Church, Socialist State, and Transnational Processes in a Chinese Village*. Stanford, CA: Stanford University Press, 2001.

Lutz, Jessie Gregory. *China and the Christian Colleges, 1850–1950*. Ithaca, NY: Cornell University Press, 1971.

Lutz, Jessie Gregory. *Chinese Politics and Christian Missions: The Anti-Christian Movements of 1920–1928*. Notre Dame, IN: Cross-Cultural Publications, 1988.

Lutz, Jessie Gregory. *Opening China: Karl F. A. Gutzlaff and Sino-Western Relations, 1827–1852*. Grand Rapids, MI: Wm. B. Eerdmans, 2008.

Lutz, Jessie Gregory. ed. *Christian Missions in China: Evangelists of What?* Lexington, MA: D.C. Heath, 1965.

Lutz, Jessie Gregory. ed. *Pioneer Christian Women: Gender, Christianity, and Social Mobility*. Bethlehem, PA: Lehigh University Press, 2010.

Lutz, Jessie Gregory, and Rolland Ray Lutz, *Hakka Chinese Confront Protestant Christianity, 1850–1900*. Armonk, NY: M.E. Sharpe, 1998.

Lyall, Leslie T. *Three of China's Mighty Men*. London: Overseas Missionary Fellowship, 1973.

Ly, Andre(Andreas Ly or Li Ande). *Journal d'Andre Ly, pretre chinois, missionaire et notaire apostolique, 1747–1763*, ed. Adrien Launay. Paris: Alphonse Picard et fils, 1906.

MacFarquhar, Roderick. *The Origins of the Cultural Revolution, I: Contradictions among the People, 1956–1957*. New York: Columbia University Press, 1974.

MacFarquhar, Roderick, and Michael Schoenhals. *Mao's Last Revolution*. Cambridge, MA: Harvard University Press, 2006.

MacGillivray, D. *A Century of Protestant Missions in China (1807–1907), being the Centenary Conference Historical Volume*. Shanghai: American Presbyterian Mission Press, 1907.

MacGillivray, D. *China Centenary Missionary Conference Records: Report of the Great Conference*. New York: American Tract Society, 1907.

MacInnis, Donald E. *Religion in China Today: Policy and Practice*. Maryknoll, NY: Orbis Books, 1989.

MacInnis, Donald E. *Religious Policy and Practice in Communist China, A Documentary History*. New York: Macmillan, 1972.

Madsen, Richard. "Beyond Orthodoxy: Catholicism as Chinese Folk Religion." In *China and Christianity: Burdened Past, Hopeful Future*, ed. Stephen Uhalley and Xiaoxin Wu, pp. 233–250. Santa Barbara, CA: Eastgate, 2001.

Madsen, Richard. *China and the American Dream: A Moral Inquiry*. Berkeley: University of California Press, 1995.

Madsen, Richard. *China's Catholics: Tragedy and Hope in an Emerging Civil Society*. Berkeley: University of California Press, 1998.

Mariani, Paul. "Communist Power and Catholic Resistance: Shanghai, 1949–1960" (Ph.D. dissertation, University of Chicago, 2007).

Mariani, Paul. *The Secret History of Bishop Kung Pinmei, The Jesuits, and Catholic Militants in Communist Shanghai, 1949–1960*. Harvard: University Press, 2011.

Menegon, Eugenio. *Ancestors, Virgins, and Friars: Christianity as a Local Religion in Late Imperial China*. Cambridge, MA: Harvard University Asia Center, 2009.

Merwin, Wallace C. *Adventure in Unity: The Church of Christ in China*. Grand Rapids, MI: Wm. B. Eerdmans, 1974.

Merwin, Wallace C., and Francis P. Jones, comps. *Documents of the Three-Self Movement*. New York: National Council of the Churches of Christ in the USA, 1963.

Michell, David. *A Boy's War*. Littleton, CO: OMF Books, 1988.

Minamiki, George. *The Chinese rites Controversy: From Its Beginning to Modern Times*. Chicago: Loyola University Press, 1985.

Moffett, Samuel Hugh. *A History of Christianity in Asia, Vol. I: Beginnings to 1500*. Maryknoll, NY: Orbis, 1998.

Moffet, Samuel Hugh. *A History of Christianity in Asia, Vol. II: 1500–1900*. Maryknoll, NY: Orbis, 2005.

Monsen, Marie. *The Awakening: Revival in China, A Work of the Holy Spirit*, translated by Joy Guiness. London: China Inland Mission, 1961.

Mungello, David E. *The Forgotten Christians of Hangzhou*. Honolulu: University of Hawaii Press, 1994.

Mungello, David E. "The Return of the Jesuits to China in 1841 and the Chinese Christian Backlash." *Sino-Western Cultural Relations Journal* XXVII (2005): 9–46.

Mungello, David E. *The Spirit and the Flesh in Shandong, 1650–1785*. Lanham, MD: Rowman and Littlefield, 2001.

Mungello, David E., ed. *The Chinese Rites Controversy: Its History and Meaning*. Nettetal: Steyler Verlag, 1994.

Ownby, David. *Falun Gong and the Future of China*. Oxford: Oxford University Press, 2008.

Palmer, Martin. *The Jesus Sutras: Rediscovering the Lost Scrolls of Taoist Christianity*. New York: Ballantine, 2001.

Parker, Michael. *Kingdom of Character: The Student Volunteer Movement for Foreign Missions, 1886–1926*. Lanham, MD: University Press of America, 1998.

Paton, David Macdonald. *Christian Missions and the Judgment of God*, 2nd edition. Grand Rapids, MI: Wm. B. Eerdmans, 1969.

Patterson, James Alan. "The Loss of a Protestant Missionary Consensus: Foreign Missions and the Fundamentalist-Modernist Conflict." In *Earthen Vessels: American Evangelicals and Foreign Missions, 1880–1980*, ed. Joel A. Carpenter and Wilbert R. Shenk, pp. 73–91. Grand Rapids, MI: Wm. B. Eerdmans, 1990.

Perrier, Pierre, and Xavier Walter. *Thomas Fonde L'Eglise en Chine (65–68 Ap. J-C)*. Paris: Editions du Jubilé, 2008.

Price, Frank Wilson. *The Rural Church in China*. New York: Agricultural Missions, 1948.

Rabe, Valentin H. *The Home Base of American China Missions, 1880–1920*. Cambridge, MA: Council on East Asian Studies, 1978.

Rambo, Lewis R. *Understanding Religious Conversion*. New Haven, CT: Yale University Press, 1993.

Rankin, Mary Backus. *Elite Activism and Political Transformation in China: Zhejiang Province, 1865–1911*. Stanford, CA: Stanford University Press, 1986.

Records of the General Conference of the Protestant Missionaries in China, Held at Shanghai, May 7–20, 1890. Shanghai: American Presbyterian Mission Press, 1890.

Records of the General Conference of the Protestant Missionaries in China, Held at Shanghai, May 10–24, 1877. Shanghai: American Presbyterian Mission Press, 1878.

Reed, James. *The Missionary Mind and American East Asia Policy, 1911–1915*. Cambridge, MA: Council on East Asian Studies, 1983.

Reilly, Thomas A. *The Taiping Heavenly Kingdom: Rebellion and the Blasphemy of Empire*. Seattle: University of Washington Press, 2004.

Reynolds, Douglas. *China, 1898–1912: The Xinzheng Revolution and Japan*. Cambridge, MA: Council on East Asian Studies, 1993.

Ricci, Matteo. *Fonti Ricciane*, ed. Pasquale M. d'Elia, S.J. *Storia dell' Introduzione del Christianesimo in Cina*. 3 vols. Rome, 1942–1949.

Roberg, O. Theodore. "Marcus Cheng (c. 1883–1963): Apostle or Apostate? Relations with the Covenant Mission in China." M.A. thesis, North Park Theological Seminary, Chicago, 1982.

Robert, Dana. *Christian Mission: How Christianity became a World Religion*. London: Wiley-Blackwell, 2009.

Sanneh, Lamin. *Translating the Message: The Missionary Impact on Culture*. Maryknoll, NY: Orbis, 1989.

Seagrave, Sterling. *The Soong Dynasty*. New York: Harper and Row, 1985.

Service, Grace. *Golden Inches: The China Memoir of Grace Service*, ed. John Service. Berkeley: University of California Press, 1989.

Shemo, Connie. "Shi Meiyu, an 'Army of Women' in Medicine." In *Salt and Light: Lives of Faith that Shaped Modern China*, Vol. 1, Carol Lee Hamrin with Stacey Bieler, 50–63. Eugene, OR: Pickwick Publications, 2008.

Showalter, Nathan D. *The End of a Crusade: The Student Volunteer Movement for Foreign Missions and the Great War*. Lanham, MD: Scarecrow Press, 1998.

Smith, Arthur H. *Chinese Characteristics*, reprint of 1894 edition with new introduction by Lydia H. Liu. Norwalk, CT: Eastbridge, 2003.

Smith, Carl T. *Chinese Christians: Elites, Middlemen, and the Church in Hong Kong*. Hong Kong: Oxford University Press, 1985.

Soothill, W.E., and Lewis Hodous, comps. *A Dictionary of Chinese Buddhist Terms.* London: Kegan Paul, 1937.

Spence, Jonathan D. *God's Chinese Son: The Taiping Heavenly Kingdom of Hong Xiuquan.* New York: W.W. Norton, 1996.

Spence, Jonathan D. *The Memory Palace of Matteo Ricci.* New York: Viking, 1984.

Spence, Jonathan D. *To Change China: Western Advisers in China 1620–1960.* New York: Penguin, 1980.

Standaert, Nicolas, ed. *Handbook of Christianity in China, Vol. 1: 635–1800.* Leiden: Brill, 2001.

Stanley, Brian. *The World Missionary Conference Edinburgh 1910.* Grand Rapids, MI: Wm. B. Eerdmans, 2009.

Stauffer, Milton T., ed. *The Christian Occupation of China: A general Survey of the Numerical Strength and Geographical Distribution of the Christian Forces in China Made by the Special Committee on Survey and Occupation, China Continuation Committee, 1918–1921.* Shanghai: China Continuation Committee, 1922.

Sweeten, Alan Richard. "Catholic Converts in Jiangxi Province: Conflict and Accommodation, 1860–1900." In *Christianity in China: From the Eighteenth Century to the Present,* ed. Daniel H. Bays, pp. 24–40. Stanford, CA: Stanford University Press, 1996.

Tang, Edmond, and Jean-Paul Wiest, eds, *The Catholic Church in Modern China: Perspectives.* Maryknoll, NY: Orbis, 1993.

Tao Feiya. "Pentecostalism and Christian Utopia in China: Jing Dianying and the Jesus Family Movement, 1921–1952." In *Interpreting Contemporary Christianity: Global Processes and Local Identities,* ed. Ogbu U. Kalu, pp. 238–252. Grand Rapids, MI: Wm. B. Eerdmans, 2008.

Tao Feiya. *Zhongguo de Jidujiao wutobang: Yesu Jiating, 1921–1952* (A Chinese Christian Utopia: The Jesus Family, 1921–1952). Hong Kong: Chinese University Press, 2004.

Tao Feiya, and Liu Tianlu. *Jiaohui yu jindai Shandong shehui* (Protestantism and Modern Shandong society). Jinan, China: Shandong Daxue chubanshe, 1995.

Tawney, R. H. *Land and Labor in China.* New York: Harcourt, Brace and Co., 1932.

Taylor, Mrs. Howard. *The Triumph of John and Betty Stam.* London: China Inland Mission, 1935.

Thomson, James C. Jr. *While China Faced West: American Reformers in Nationalist China 1928–1937.* Cambridge, MA: Harvard University Press, 1969.

Thompson, Roger R. "Twilight of the Gods in the Chinese Countryside: Christians, Confucians, and the Modernizing State, 1861–1911." In *Christianity in China: From the Eighteenth Century to the Present,* ed. Daniel H. Bays, pp. 53–72. Stanford, CA: Stanford University Press, 1996.

Tiedemann, R.G. "Indigenous Agency, Religious Protectorates, and Chinese Interests: The Expansion of Christianity in Nineteenth-Century China." In *Converting Colonialism: Visions and Realities in Mission History, 1706–1914,* ed. Dana L. Robert, pp. 206–241. Grand Rapids, MI: Wm. B. Eerdmans, 2008.

Tiedemann, R.G., ed. *Handbook of Chrisitanity in China, Vol. 2: 1800–Present.* Leiden: Brill, 2010.

Tong, John. "The Church from 1949 to 1990." In *The Catholic Church in Modern China: Perspectives*, ed. Edmond Tang and Jean-Paul Wiest, pp. 7–27. Maryknoll, NY: Orbis, 1993.

Tsou Mingteh. "Christian Missionary as Confucian Intellectual: Gilbert Reid (1857–1927) and the Reform Movement in the Late Qing." In *Christianity in China: From the Eighteenth Century to the Present*, ed. Daniel H. Bays, pp. 73–90. Stanford, CA: Stanford University Press, 1996.

Twain, Mark. "To My Missionary Critics," *North American Review* 172 (1901): 520–534.

Twain, Mark. "To the Person Sitting in Darkness." *North American Review* 172 (1901): 161–176.

Wacker, Grant. "The Waning of the Missionary Impulse: The Case of Pearl S. Buck." In *The Foreign Missionary Enterprise at Home*, ed. Daniel H. Bays and Grant Wacker, pp. 191–205. Tuscaloosa: University of Alabama Press, 2003.

Waley, Arthur. *The Opium War Through Chinese Eyes*. New York: George Allen & Unwin, 1958.

Walls, Andrew. "From Christendom to World Christianity." In *The Cross-Cultural Process in Christian History*, ed. Andrew Walls. Maryknoll, NY: Orbis, 2001.

Walls, Andrew. *The Missionary Movement in Christian History: Studies in the Transmission of Faith*, pp. 49–71. Maryknoll, NY: Orbis, 1996.

Walls, Andrew. "The Nineteenth-Century Missionary as Scholar." In *The Missionary Movement in Christian History: Studies in the Transmission of Faith*, ed. Andrew Walls, pp. 187–198. Maryknoll, NY: Orbis, 1996.

Wang, Dong. *China's Unequal Treaties, Narrating National History*. Lanham, MD: Lexington Books, 2005.

Wang Mingdao. *Wushi nianlai* (These Fifty Years). Hong Kong: Bellman House, 1950.

Webster, Rev. James. *Times of Blessing in Manchuria*, 4th edition. Shanghai: Methodist Publishing House, 1909.

West, Philip. *Yenching University and Sino-Western Relations, 1916–1952*. Cambridge, MA: Harvard University Press, 1976.

Wickeri, Philip L. "The Chinese Christian Movement on the Eve of Liberation," unpublished, History of Christianity in China Project, University of Kansas, June 17–23, 1990.

Wickeri, Philip L. *Reconstructing Christianity in China: K. H. Ting and the Chinese Church*. Maryknoll, NY: Orbis Books, 2007.

Wickeri, Philip L. *Seeking the Common Ground: Protestant Christianity, the Three-Self Movement, and China's United Front*. Maryknoll, NY: Orbis Books, 1988.

Widmer, Eric. *The Russian Ecclesiastical Mission in Peking in the Eighteenth Century*. Cambridge, MA: East Asian Research Center, Harvard University, 1976.

Wiest, Jean-Paul. *Maryknoll in China: A History, 1918–1955*. Armonk, NY: M. E. Sharpe, 1988.

Williams, S. Wells. *The Middle Kingdom*, 2 vols. New York: Putnam, 1848, rev. edition. 1883.

Witek, John W., S.J., "The Emergence of a Christian Community in Beijing During the Late Ming and Early Qing Period." In *Encounters and Dialogues: Changing*

Perspectives on Chinese-Western Exchanges from the Sixteenth to Eighteenth Centuries, ed. Xiaoxin Wu, pp. 93–116. Sankt Augustin, Germany: Nettetal, 2005.

Wong, John H.,"*Tao-Logo:* Jesus, Lao Tzu, Philo, and John Compared." In *The Chinese Face of Jesus Christ.* Vol. 1, ed. Roman Malek, SVD. Monumenta Serica Monograph Series, no. 50. Sankt Augustin: Germany, 2002.

Wong Ming-Dao. *A Stone Made Smooth.* Southampton, UK: Mayflower Christian Books, 1981.

Wu, Silas H. *Dora Yu and Christian Revival in 20ᵗʰ-Century China.* Boston: Pishon River Publications, 2002.

Wurth, Elmer, M.M., ed. *Papal Documents Related to the New China.* Maryknoll, NY: Orbis, 1985.

Yao, Kevin Xiyi. *The Fundamentalist Movement among Protestant Missionaries in China, 1920–1937.* Lanham, MD: University Press of America, 2003.

Yao, Kevin Xiyi. "The North China Theological Seminary: Evangelical Theological Education in China in the Early 1900s." In *Interpreting Contemporary Christianity: Global Processes and Local Identities,* ed. Ogbu U. Kalu, pp. 187–206. Grand Rapids, MI: Wm. B. Eerdmans, 2008.

Ying Fuk-tsang. *Zhongguo jiyao zhuyizhe de shijian yu kunjing: Chen Chonggui de shenxue sixiang yu shidai* (The praxis and predicament of a Chinese fundamentalist: Chen Chonggui [Marcus Ch'eng], his theological thought and his times). Hong Kong: Alliance Press, 2001.

Yip, Ka-che. *Religion, Nationalism, and Chinese Students: The Anti-Christian Movement of 1922–1927.* Bellingham: Western Washington University, 1980.

Young, Ernest P. "The Politics of Evangelism at the End of the Qing: Nanchang, 1906." In *Christianity in China: From the Eighteenth Century to the Present,* ed. Daniel H. Bays, pp. 91–114. Stanford, CA: Stanford University Press, 1996.

Yu, Maochun. *OSS in China: Prelude to Cold War.* New Haven, CT: Yale University Press, 1996.

Zetzsche, Jost Oliver. *The Bible in China: The History of the Union Version or the Culmination of Protestant Missionary Bible Translation in China.* Sankt Augustin, Germany: Institut Monumenta Serica, 1999.

Zha Shijie. *Zhongguo Jidujiao renwu xiaozhuan* (Biographies of Leading Chinese Christians). Taipei: Chinese Evangelical Seminary Press, 1983.

Zhuo Xinping. "Discussion on 'Cultural Christians' in China." In *China and Christianity,* ed. Stephen Uhalley and Xiaoxin Wu, pp. 283–300. Armonk, NY: M. E. Sharpe, 2001.

Index

A New History of Christianity in China, First Edition. Daniel H. Bays.
© 2012 Daniel H. Bays. Published 2012 by Blackwell Publishing Ltd.

CPSIA information can be obtained
at www.ICGtesting.com
Printed in the USA
LVHW050247211218
601119LV00023B/80